The

PRINCE *of*
PREACHERS

GREAT CHRISTIAN BOOKS
LINDENHURST, NEW YORK

The
PRINCE of
PREACHERS

A Biography of
CHARLES HADDON
SPURGEON

William Y. Fullerton

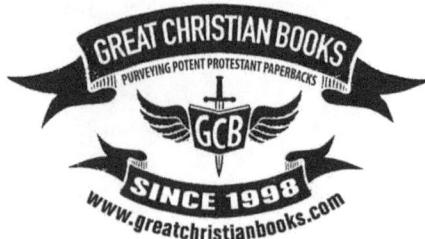

Great Christian Books

is an imprint of Rotolo Media
160 37th Street Lindenhurst, New York 11757,

ISBN 978-1-61010-042-7

Fullerton, William Young, 1857–1932,
The Prince of Preachers-A Biography of Charles Haddon Spurgeon /
by William Y. Fullerton
p. cm.
A "A Great Christian Book" book
GREAT CHRISTIAN BOOKS an imprint of Rotolo Media
ISBN 978-1-61010-042-7
Recommended Dewey Decimal Classifications: 920, 922, 922.2, 251.092
Suggested Subject Headings:
1. Religion—Christianity literature—Biographical
2. Christianity—Non-Fiction—Biography
I. Title

Book and cover design are by Michael Rotolo, www.michaelrotolo.com. This book is typeset in the Minion typeface by Adobe Inc. and is quality-manufactured on acid-free paper stock. To discuss the publication of your Christian manuscript or out-of-print book, please contact us.

Manufactured in the United States of America

"What the hand is to the lute,
What the breath is to the flute,
What is fragrance to the smell,
What the spring is to the well,
What the flower is to the bee,
That is Jesus Christ to me.

"What's the mother to the child,
What the guide in pathless wild,
What is oil to troubled wave,
What is ransom to the slave,
What is water to the sea,
That is Jesus Christ to me."
Arranged by C. H. SPURGEON.

CONTENTS

CHAPTER I

THE SPURGEON COUNTRY

The county of Essex—Godly ancestry—Horatio Nelson— The spoiling of the name—Parentage—The grandfather— Memories of Stambourne—Spurgeon as a boy—At school— Newmarket—Surrey—Mentone.

CHAPTER II

THE SEARCH FOR GOD

Five years' quest—His mother's influence—Wesley's mother— The terrors of the Jaw—Scepticism—Essay on "Antichrist Unmasked"—The search becomes intense—The memorable morning—"I thought I could dance all the way home "

CHAPTER III

THE APPRENTICE PREACHER

Preaching as a boy—Richard Knill's prophecy—The cook at Newmarket—Baptism—Tract distribution—Sunday School addresses—His first speech—At Cambridge—His first sermon—The Church at Waterbeach—Incidents—His first convert—"The sauciest dog that ever barked in a pulpit"—His first hymn—The word of the Lord.

CHAPTER IV

THE VOICE IN THE CITY (THE JOHN KNOX CHAPTER)

The unexpected invitation—The first Sunday in London—London as it then was—Farewell to Cambridge—His first home—The Baptists of London—The verdict of Sheridan Knowles—A fit instrument for God's use—The irresistible impulse—Cholera in London.

CHAPTER V

THE PROPHET OF THE PEOPLE (THE GEORGE WHITEFIELD CHAPTER)

Trained in the desert—New Park Street crowded—His audacity—Exeter Hall—Caricatures—Criticism and slander—The enlarged chapel—Hackney Downs—John Anderson—Conceit— Estimates of the young preacher—The Royal Surrey Gardens Music Hall—The panic—The renewed ministry—Dr. Campbell—Principal Tulloch—Preaching at the Crystal Palace— *The Times*—Three years' ministry.

CHAPTER VI

THE ROMANTIC YEARS (THE JOHN CALVIN CHAPTER)

The fourteen early years—The Agricultural Hall services—Incessant labour—Scotland—Ireland—Paris—The first holiday—Geneva—John Calvin's preaching—Spurgeon's Calvinism—Crowds in all parts of the country—Some Scotch incidents— American invitations—Lectures—-John Bright—Ovation on London Bridge—"Over the water to Charlie."

CHAPTER VII

THE GREAT TABERNACLE

The Romance within the Romance—Choice of site—The design of the building—The opening—The great thirty years—A Sunday morning service—A Sunday evening service—Report of a sermon—One of the sights of London—Comparisons—The silver wedding—The jubilee—Dr. James A Spurgeon—Dr A T Pierson—Thomas Spurgeon.

CHAPTER VIII

AN INTIMATE INTERLUDE

Courtship—Marriage—Twin sons—The new home—John Ruslan's visits—Sir James Y. Simpson—An opal ring and a bullfinch—Westwood—Titles of books—Mrs Spurgeon's Book Fund—Sunday evening services—Burglary—Holidays in Scotland—The habit of prayer—Soliloquies at the Lord's Table—Two nights in prayer—His wide outlook.

CHAPTER IX

A WORD PORTRAIT

At Cambridge—The philosophy of clothes—Early descriptions —<u>Hist</u> personality—Various opinions—The face—The eye—The voice—Pulpit action—Timidity—His diction—His memory— His freedom—A Puritan—Finding texts—Proud rather than vain—Was he a scholar?—Was he a gentleman?—Examples—Rebuking with gentleness—Firmness —Humility with dignity—Generosity—Rhapsody.

CHAPTER X

SPURGEON'S "SERMONS" (TIIE HUGH LATIMER CHAPTER)

Published for sixty-three years—Sir William Robertson Nicoll—Hugh Latimer—The Pulpit Library—*The New Park Street Pulpit*—World-wide acceptance—Some notable utterances— Preaching in his sleep—Instances of blessings—More incidents.

CHAPTER XI

"SPURGEON'S COLLEGE"

The name—Its simple origin—Number of students—The building of the College—Friday afternoon lectures—The College Series of books—Spurgeon's sayings—The Tabernacle and the College—The Pastor's College Conferences.

CHAPTER XII

"SPURGEON'S ORPHANAGE"

Mrs. Hillyard's proposal—Choosing the site—Opening of the early buildings—Rev V J Charlesworth—The Girls' Wing—The President's visits—Mr Charles Spurgeon—Spurgeon's greatest sermon—Memorial by George Tinworth.

CHAPTER XIII

A CHAPTER OF INCIDENTS

His power of recognition—When the light failed—Random shots—Flank attacks—God hears the ravens—Baptism—Mentone stones—Painless dentistry—Dr Clifford—Redhead —Three madmen—Visitors and visiting—Dean Stanley—Charles Spurgeon—Letters to children—Music—Mortifying the "old man"—Repartees—Lord Rosebery—Crying child—"Jesus died for me."

PREFACE

THE contemporary sketches of the life of Spurgeon are an interesting conglomerate of significant facts, but they scarcely give an adequate picture of the man as he lived and laboured with such prodigious energy. It seemed desirable, therefore, that before those who knew him and shared in his ministry had passed away, some one who had the privilege of his friendship should say the things about him that still needed to be said, and place the familiar things in truer perspective than was possible at the time.

That pleasant burden has been placed upon me, and in fulfilment of the charge I have allowed to drop out of sight a multitude of particulars which were only interesting at the moment, not chronicling events as in an epoch, but presenting the personality as in an epic, although I can only summon common prose in the doing of it.

Sir Sidney Lee, in his Leslie Stephen lecture on the "Principles of Biography," says excellently that "the aim of biography is, in general terms, to hand down to a future age the history of individual men and women, to transmit enduringly their character and exploits. Character and exploits are for biographical purposes inseparable. Character which does not translate itself into exploit is for the biographer a mere phantasm. But character and exploit jointly contribute biographic personality. Biography aims at satisfying the commemorative instinct by exercise of its power to transmit personality."

This biography is only historic, in its earlier chapters; beyond these it seeks to focus the light on different aspects of the man, rather than to diffuse it in a narrative of the years and their happenings. This plan has its drawbacks, but I hope that the advantages may be appreciated, and if any seek the details of the time they will find them available elsewhere.

Very heartily I express my indebtedness to Mr. William Higgs for placing at my disposal his remarkable collection of contemporary records, and to the Rev. Charles Spurgeon and Mrs. Thomas Spurgeon for their generous co-operation.

To introduce Spurgeon to a generation that never knew him, and to keep alive his memory in a century he never knew, is honour enough for any man: a supreme privilege to a man who knew and honoured and loved him, and owes to him more than he can ever express or repay.

CHAPTER I

THE SPURGEON COUNTRY

1465-1769

June 19, 1834—*January* 31, 1892

THE whole of East Anglia may claim the Spurgeon family, but Essex holds the primacy as the Spurgeon country, and the parishes round about Stambourne still bear that name. With its great hemisphere of sky, Essex, like Nazareth of the olden days, lies near the stream of the world's traffic, but is shut off from it. And Spurgeon, in his touch with the life of his time, his aloofness from it, and his open vision of the wide heavens, resembles his native country.

"There is a gap in the suburbs of London. The suburbs of London stretch west and south, and even west by north, but to the north-eastward there are no suburbs; instead there is Essex. Essex is not a suburban county; it is a characteristic and individualised country which wins the heart. Between dear Essex and the centre of things lie two great barriers, the East End of London, and Epping Forest. Before a train could get to any villadom with a cargo of season-ticket holders, it would have to circle around the rescued woodland and travel for twenty unprofitable miles; and so once you are away from the main Great Eastern lines, Essex still lives in the peace of the eighteenth century, and London, the modern Babylon is, like the stars, just a light in the nocturnal sky."[1]

As far back as 1465 we find the names of two Spurgeons as witnesses to a legal document; in 1575 Thomas Spurgeon was tenant of the Manor of Dynes, Great Maplestead, where even today there is a holding known as Spurgeon's; at Much Dunmow, Felsted, Blacknotlye, Eastwood, Thundersley, and South Beanflet there were also Spurgeons at the end of the sixteenth century.

In the seventeenth century one Job Spurgeon, who was C. H. Spurgeon's great-grandfather's great-grandfather, had a distress levied on him for attending a Nonconformist meeting, and six years later was fined for the same offence. As he refused to pay the fine, he and three others were required

---

[1] *Mr. Britling Sees it Through*, by H. G. Wells, p. 6.

to give sureties for their good behaviour or go to prison. To prison they went, and in a winter remarkable for its cold, three of them lay upon straw for fifteen weeks, but Job Spurgeon, "being so weak that he was unable to lie down, sat upon a chair the most of the time."[1] Upon which C. H. Spurgeon remarked with some pride, "I had far rather be descended from one who suffered for the faith, than bear the blood of all the emperors in my veins."

The direct line of the preacher's ancestry can be traced through the Spurgeons of Halstead for eleven or twelve generations. In 1551 a Richard Spurgeon held land in the district; in 1718 Clement Spurgeon took sittings in the Independent Chapel: two years later the same Clement Spurgeon and his wife conveyed to the trustees, for £15, the piece of ground on which the meeting-house was built, and in his will he disposed of considerable property. His brother, John Spurgeon, an apothecary, bequeathed £100 to be invested towards the repairs of the Meeting House, and his son, Samuel Spurgeon, was minister of the church that worshipped in it. An interesting entry in the Church Book, one of several of a similar nature, may be cited: "April 9th, 1736. To cash paid ye Rev. Mr. Spergin for preaching one whole Lord's Day 15s." Another son was the grandfather of that James Spurgeon, minister of Stambourne, who was grandfather to Charles Haddon Spurgeon.[2]

By far the most notable item in the old records is in the Parish Register of Burnham Thorpe. Under date March 18, 1769, the certificate of marriage of Elizabeth Spurgeon has the name spelt by the Rector in that form in the second line, and on the seventh line signed by the lady herself as Elizabeth Spurgin. One of the witnesses, a lad of ten years of age, signed as "Horace Nelson," but his first name was afterwards altered, in his father's writing, to "Horatio," no less a person than the great admiral that was to be, and here the lines of two notable men cross, and Trafalgar Square has something to say to Newington Butts.[3]

There are at least nineteen known variants of the family name. Two have already been noted. As early as 1273 we find a William Sprigin in Norfolk; in 1576 Robert Spurgynne was Vicar of Fouldon; in 1712 John Spurgeon Mayor of Yarmouth. Other forms are Spirjon, Spurrgon, Spurggin, Spurrgin, Spourgion, Spugin, Spurgyn, Spurgen, Spurginn, Spourgian, Spurgion, Spurgine, Spurgien, Spurggon. The name is almost as baffling as that of Shakespeare.[4]

It is more than probable that the first Spurgeons in England were Norsemen. The name may be considered as a diminutive of "Sporr," the old

[1] *Autobiography* vol. 1. p. 8.
[2] *The Spurgeon Family*, by W. Miller Higgs, pp. 8, 21, 30, 2.
[3] *Ibid.*
[4] *Ibid.*

Norse word for sparrow, not an inapt suggestion for the heraldry of the family, whether we think of homeliness or of multitude.

The current opinion that the family is of Dutch origin has no evidence to support it. It is probably founded on a misconception of a statement by the preacher of the clan when he said: "I remember speaking to a Christian brother who seemed right happy to tell me that he sprang from a family which came from Holland during the persecution of the Duke of Alva, and I felt a brotherhood with him in claiming a like descent *from Protestant forefathers.*" At the same time it may be conjectured that as so many Dutch refugees settled in East Anglia, it is highly probable that there was an appreciable mixture of Dutch blood in the family. Spurgeon was of conventional Dutch build, and there is a portrait of him and a portrait of Paul Kruger which very closely resemble each other!

Throughout the generations, though few of the Spurgeons seem to have been great in the eyes of the world, there was evidently a tradition of piety handed down from sire to son. Though grace does not run in the blood, there is a disposition towards grace that appears to be hereditary. The children of saints, like the children of consumptive parents, have a tendency in the direction of their parents' chief qualities, but no inevitable destiny in that direction. Spurgeon himself, exponent of God's sovereignty as he was, never thought lightly of his ancestry. "There is a sweet fitness," he said, "in the passing of holy loyalty from grandsire to father, and from father to son." His most ardent desire for his own sons, happily fulfilled, was that they might be in the godly succession, and take up the work of God when it should drop from his hands.

In a quaint little cottage at Kelvedon, in Essex, still standing almost unchanged since that day, C. H. Spurgeon was born on June 19, 1834, ten days after William Carey had died in India. He had no memories of the place, for when he was but ten months old the family removed to Colchester. Few of the people of the village associate the house with the event; when Thomas Spurgeon visited it some years ago he only found one old man who knew of it, and he remarked that he thought Spurgeon's side should buy it. In answer to further inquiry it turned out that he had the very proper notion that the Nonconformists should make the cottage a memorial of the great preacher. [1]

His mother, whose maiden name was Eliza Jarvis, was born at Otton Belchamp on May 3, 1815, so that she was little more than nineteen years of age at the time of her son's birth; his father, born at Clare in Suffolk on July 15, 1810, being about twenty-four.

Of his mother, her second son, James Archer, said that she was "the starting-point of all greatness and goodness that any of us by the grace of

---

[1] *Thomas Spurgeon: a Biography,* p. 269.

God have enjoyed,"[1] and her elder son always held her in reverence. The father was engaged in business during the week, and for sixteen years ministered on Sundays to the Independent congregation at Tollesbury, removing from Colchester to Braintree, afterwards to Cranbrook, then to London to take charge of the church in Fetter Lane. Thence he migrated to the church at Upper Street, Islington, and after a long life died at Croydon on June 14, 1902, his wife having preceded him in 1888.

Our thoughts now travel to Stambourne, its manse, and its minister, and especially to the boy who, towards the end of the year 1835, was taken there, when he was about eighteen months old, to remain with his grandfather for six years. The old legend that he was sent away from home to his grandparents because he was one of seventeen children is a romance. There were, indeed, seventeen children born to his parents, nine of whom died in infancy, but as he was the eldest and his father was not endowed with the prophetic gift, that could scarcely have been the reason for his removal. The fact that the eldest of his six sisters was born in January 1836 may have had more to do with it, and similar reasons no doubt accounted for his prolonged stay at Stambourne. His brother was born on June 8, 1837. In these days of eugenics, when we are told that it is the fifth or sixth child of large families that attains distinction, it may be borne in mind that Spurgeon was the first.

For fifty-four years James Spurgeon, the grandfather, was minister of the people who worshipped in the Meeting House at Stambourne. He was a man of wide sympathies and was on excellent terms with the Rector of the parish. He had great preaching gifts, and wherever he went he was able to call men to Christ. "I heard your grandfather, and I would run my shoes off my feet to hear a Spurgeon," was once said to the grandson in his early preaching days. The grandfather had a dry humour of his own, too; on one occasion, when he was asked how much he weighed, he answered: "Well, that all depends on how you take me: if weighed in the balances I am afraid I shall be found wanting, but in the pulpit they tell me I am heavy enough." His influence on the lad committed to his care was abiding. Grandmother Spurgeon was "a dear, good, kind soul," and no doubt took her share of the training, but it was chiefly Aunt Ann, one of the eight children, the only one who remained unmarried, who mothered him, and for her he ever cherished a warm affection.

A characteristic story of his grandfather conveys a better idea of his attachment to the Gospel, and his unconventional methods in declaring it, than pages of description, and suggests that his grandson had caught his spirit. C. H. Spurgeon, in the after years, was announced to preach at Haverhill in Suffolk, and—an exceptional incident—he was late in arriving.

---

[1] *James Archer Spurgeon,* by G. H. Pike, pp. 20, 23.

So his grandfather began the service, and as the expected preacher was absent, he proceeded with the sermon. The text was "By grace ye are saved." He had got some way into the discourse when some unrest at the door made him aware that his distinguished grandson was in the chapel. "Here comes my grandson," he exclaimed, "he can preach the Gospel better than I can, but you cannot preach a better Gospel, can you, Charles?" Still pressing up the aisle, his grandson replied, "You can preach better than I can. Pray go on." Of course his grandfather refused, but he told him the text, explained that he had already shown the people the source and fountain-head of salvation— "grace"—and was now speaking of the channel of it, "through faith." The younger preacher took up the theme, and advanced to the next, point—"but not of yourselves"—and was setting forth the weakness and inability of human nature, when his grandfather interrupted, and said, "I know most about that." So for five minutes he discoursed, and then his grandson continued again, having his grandfather's whispered commendation "Good! Good!" as he warmed to his subject, until at some special point the old man ejaculated, "Tell them that again, Charles." Ever after, when Charles recalled the text, there came to him with recurring force the words, "Tell them that again." The incident was almost reproduced at a later date in the Tabernacle when he shared the sermon with me, and we both preached on the text, "Him that cometh to me, I will in no wise cast out"—the same Gospel from grandfather to biographer!

Towards the end of his life Spurgeon's mind reverted more and more to those early days: he had an instinct that his life was drawing to a close, and his last book was *Memories of Stambourne.* To choose the views for the volume he went down to the neighbourhood on June 8, 1891, the morning after he had preached what proved to be his last sermon in the Tabernacle. His friends pleaded with him to refrain from the journey, but nothing would hinder him—there was something in his heart that turned him back upon his past. The illness which was to prove fatal seized him while he was away from home, and on the Friday he hurried back, to be laid aside completely for three months.

The memories of those early years include the Manse with its brick hall-floor sprinkled with sand, the sand being kept in a cupboard under the stairs; its windows in part plastered up to escape the window tax; its attic, to which the lad surreptitiously climbed one day and discovered the treasures of darkness—books, books, books. Here he made his first acquaintance with the Puritan writers, though as a boy he was chiefly interested in their bindings; here, too, he fount a copy of *The Pilgrim's Progress* and read it, becoming so enamoured of it that he re-read it during his life at least a hundred times.

Occasionally he used to disappear and was searched for in vain. Not till many years after did he reveal his hiding-places. One was beneath the horsing-block in front of the Meeting House, amongst the leaves of the lime-trees which were thrown there and made a pleasant resting-place; the other was in an altar-like erection over a tomb where one of the slabs of stone at the side moved easily, so that the boy could enter, pull it back again into its place, and shut himself off from all the world. Many a time he heard them call him, heard their feet running in search of him, but he answered not. "Where he went to, his guardian angels knew, but none on earth could tell." "Dreaming of days to come befell me every now and then as a child, and to be quite alone was my boyish heaven."

He records that his climax of delight was to see the huntsmen with their red coats as they chased the fox, and at that time he stoutly declared that he was going to be a huntsman.

"I remember well, in my early days," he says, "seeing upon my grandmother's mantelshelf an apple contained in a phial. This was a great wonder to me, and I tried to investigate it. My question was, 'How came the apple to get inside so small a bottle?' The apple was quite as big round as the phial; by what means was it placed within it? Though it was treason to touch the treasures on the mantelpiece, I took down the bottle and convinced my youthful mind that the apple never passed through its neck; and by means of an attempt to unscrew the bottom, I became equally certain that the apple did not enter from below. I held to the notion that by some occult means the bottle had been made in two pieces, and afterwards united in so careful a manner that no trace of the join remained. I was hardly satisfied with the theory, but as no philosopher was at hand to suggest any other hypothesis, I let the matter rest. One day the next summer, I chanced to see upon a bough another phial, the first cousin of my old friend, within which was growing a little apple which had been passed through the neck of the bottle while it was extremely small. 'Nature well known, no prodigies remain.' The grand secret was out." This became his classic illustration of the necessity of getting young people into the house of God, and into the kingdom of Christ while they are small, that they may grow there.

No doubt the boy was precocious. At his grandfather's house, before he left, he was allowed to read the Scriptures at family worship. Once when the reading was in the Apocalypse he came to the expression "the bottomless pit," and he paused and asked the meaning of it. "Pooh, pooh, child," said his grandfather, "go on." The next morning he read the same chapter, asked the same question, and received the same answer, and so continued, until at length his grandfather capitulated, and inquired what puzzled the child. "If the pit has no bottom, where would all those people fall who dropped out at the lower end?—a question which rather startled the propriety of the worshippers, and had to be answered at another time. His horror when the explanation was given, and he was told that there was no depth to which a soul can sink that has not a deeper depth beyond, made an impression on his heart never to be effaced.

It is easy to see, in retrospect, that those early Stambourne years gave colour and bent to his whole life. It was well that he had no formal schooling (save only such elementary instruction as he could glean from old Mrs. Burleigh of the village) until he had looked out on life from the comparative solitude of the place. He had a mind that did not need to be forced, and the simplicity of his early surroundings remained with him to the end. He describes the people of those days as "mainly real Essex; they talked of places down in 'the Shires' as if they were in foreign parts: and young fellows who went down into 'the Hundreds' were explorers of a respectable order of hardihood." Years after, when he was returning from a continental holiday and heard that there had been an earthquake in Essex, he declared that he was glad that something had shaken the people at last.

When the time came to leave his grandfather, it was the sorrow of his early life. They wept together, and the grandfather sought to comfort him by telling him that when he looked up to the moon that night at Colchester, he was to remember that it was the same moon his grandfather was looking at from Stambourne. For years the boy never looked at the moon thereafter without thinking of his grandfather. There was genius in the thought.

Subsequent holidays were often spent at Stambourne. On one occasion his grandmother promised him a penny for every hymn of Isaac Watts that he could perfectly repeat to her. So quickly did he learn them that she reduced the price to a halfpenny, and still it seemed that she might be ruined by the calls on her purse. But then came a diversion, for his grandfather, finding the place overrun with rats, promised the boy a shilling a dozen for all that he could kill, so he gave up hymn-learning for rat catching, which seemed to pay better. But I have heard him declare in later days that the hymns paid the best, for he was able to use them in his sermons to advantage.

When he went home to Colchester, he found three children there, two sisters and a brother, and naturally he became their hero. Like many another boy, he wrote poems, and edited a magazine. One copy of it remains, in which its readers are reminded of a prayer meeting, and encouraged to attend it by the thought that blessings come through prayer. At first he attended a school kept by a Mrs. Cook, but having mastered all that she could teach him he was transferred, in a little while, to a more advanced establishment conducted by Mr. Henry Lewis. Here, when he was between ten and eleven years of age, he gained the First Class English prize, White's *Natural History of Selborne,* a book which he treasured all his days.

It was in this school that he suddenly seemed to fail in his studies, going steadily down to the bottom of the class. The teacher was at first nonplussed, until it occurred to him that the top place was away from the fire and opposite a draughty door, he therefore reversed the position of the scholars, and very speedily young Spurgeon worked his way up again.

When about fourteen the two brothers were sent to All Saints' Agricultural College (now St. Augustine's) at Maidstone, where an uncle of his was one of the tutors. Here also he quickly mastered his studies. On one occasion he had a discussion with a clerical examiner on the subject of Baptism, and as a result, though he came from a Congregational family and was a student in an Anglican college, he determined that if grace should ever work a change in him he would be baptised. At another time he pointed out an arithmetical mistake of his uncle's, and as a result of this was told that he had better take his books and study under an old oak-tree growing beside the banks of the Medway. His mathematical facility at this time was so pronounced that he was allowed to calculate the tables which are still in use in one of the Life Insurance Societies of London. As I write I have on my desk the copy of *The Christian Year* in calf, presented to him at this school at Christmas 1848, "for proficiency in religious knowledge, mathematics, the languages, and the applied sciences."

"How my father ever contrived to give us the training that he did, puzzles me," said his brother James. "I know that he burdened himself to pay for the best education Nonconformity could command. If it was not better—I do not think it could have been—it was because no better was available."[1]

The Spurgeon country must include Cambridgeshire, for Newmarket, Cambridge and Waterbeach now come into the story. When Mr. E. S. Leeding died at Norwood in 1890, Mr. Spurgeon penned the following note: "Mr. Leeding was usher in the school of Mr. Henry Lewis of Colchester in 1845, and I was one of the boys under his care. He was a teacher who really taught his pupils, and by his diligent skill I gained the foundation upon which I built in the after years. He left Colchester to open a school in Cambridge, and I to go, first to Maidstone and then to Newmarket, for some two years. Then we came together again; for I joined him at Cambridge to assist in his school, and in return to be helped in my studies. He has left it on record that he did not think that there was need for me to go to any of the Dissenting colleges, since I had mastered most of the subject studies therein; and his impression that I might, while with him, have readily passed through the University, if the pulpit had not come in the way."

---

[1] *James Archer Spurgeon,* by G. H. Pike, pp. 20, 23.

Cambridgeshire seemed at first but like a cold stepmother to the lad who had migrated from Essex, but, when he was called to leave it, he left a great part of his heart behind. We may guess how the iron entered his soul in the early days by some references he made, in a moment of confidence, years afterwards. Recalling the time when he taught in the school, "not big enough to be a master, and not small enough to be a boy," he quoted Goldsmith as saying that a man had better be hanged than have such work to do, and declared that if the choice were given to him, though he might hesitate at first, in the end he would choose the alternative of hanging. "I had no college education," he continued. "I do not say this by way of boasting, far from it. I would have learned more if I had had the opportunity, but, that not being the case, I made the very best of the opportunities I had."[1]

When, at forty years of age, he lectured on "Young Men," he said in all seriousness that he was an old one. "I might have been a young man at twelve, but at sixteen I was a sober, respectable Baptist parson, sitting in the Chair and ruling and governing the Church. At that period of my life, when I ought perhaps to have been in the playground, developing my legs and sinews, which no doubt would have kept me from the gout now, I spent my time at my books, studying and working hard, sticking to it, very much to the pleasure of my schoolmaster."[2] All that in Cambridgeshire.

But to the Spurgeon country Surrey must be annexed, the county where he won his great pulpit triumphs, about which he resolved early in his ministry—"God sparing my life, I will not rest till this dark county of Surrey be filled with places of worship," whose lanes and villages were known to him in the after years as to few beside. "England to me for a country," John Ploughman wrote, "Surrey for a county, and for a village give me—no, I shan't tell you, or you will be hunting John Ploughman up. There is a glorious view from the top of Leith Hill in our dear old Surrey, and Hindhead and Martha's Chapel and Boxhill are not to be sneezed at." On Wednesdays, which were his Sabbaths, he would generally seek out some of the county byways, visit some of its churches or historic sites, and drive along the courses of its rivers, the Wey, the Mole and the Wandle, for the last of which he had, like Ruskin, a peculiar affection.

"Twenty years ago there was no lovelier piece of lowland scenery in South England, nor any more pathetic in the world, by its expression of sweet human character and life, than that immediately bordering on the sources of the Wandle, and including the low moors of Addington, and the villages of Beddington and Carshalton, with all their pools and streams. No clearer or diviner waters ever sang with sweet, constant lips of the Hand that 'giveth

---

[1] *Autobiography*, Vol. III. p. 43.
[2] *South London Press*, Nov. 28, 1874.

rain from heaven'; no pastures ever lightened in springtime with more passionate blossoming: no sweeter homes ever hallowed the heart of the passers-by with their pride of peaceful gladness—fain hidden—yet full-confessed."[1]

Of course he travelled throughout Great Britain, he visited Ireland, Holland, Switzerland, Heligoland, Germany, France, but mostly he was a stay-at-home. There is, however, at Mentone one little bit of sunshine land, between the Alps Maritimes and the tideless sea, which, made fragrant and beautiful by its olive orchards, its orange groves, and its flower gardens, and memorable by his repeated visits, might almost be called his second home. There he passed, as he would have wished, from his day's work, so well done, to that other land which is also Spurgeon-country.

---

[1] *The Crown of Wild Olive*, by John Ruskin, pp. 1, 2.

C. H. SPURGEON'S BIRTHPLACE

From a watercolor by Thomas Spurgeon

CHAPTER II

THE SEARCH FOR GOD

January 1845—*January* 6, 1850

THE boy Spurgeon continued in quest of Christ for five years—from the time when he was between ten and eleven years old until he was between fifteen and sixteen. Into those years there was crowded a world of experience which enabled him in his subsequent ministry to probe the secrets of many hearts. He learnt more of the things that matter in those years than most men learn in a lifetime.

That one so young, so sheltered, trained from his babyhood in the ways of God, could have felt so much and have had such exercises of soul may seem impossible, his own account of his darkness and despair may appear exaggerated; but those who are versed in the ways of God will understand. "To make a man a saint," says Pascal, "grace is absolutely necessary, and whoever doubts it, does not know what a saint is or what a man is." Spurgeon early learnt to know both. He arrived at some knowledge of his own heart and some knowledge of God's heart. By his very wanderings he was assured that grace was seeking him all the while.

"I must confess," he says, "that I never would have been saved if I could have helped it. As long as ever I could, I rebelled, and revolted, and struggled against God. When He would have me pray, I would not pray, and when He would have me listen to the sound of the ministry, I would not. And when I heard, and the tear rolled down my check, I wiped it away and defied Him to melt my soul. But long before I began with Christ, He began with me."

> "To all swift things for swiftness did I sue;
>   Cling to the whistling mane of every wind.
>   But whether they swept, smoothly fleet,
> The long savannahs of the blue;
>   Or whether, thunder-driven,
>   They clanged His chariot 'thwart a heaven
> Plashy with flying lightnings round the spurn o' their feet:
>   Fear wist not to evade, as Love wist to pursue." [1]

It was to his mother he owed his first awakening. Her prayers, no less than her exhortations, aroused him to concern of soul. His father has told that once on the way to a preaching engagement his heart smote him that he was caring for other people and neglecting his own family. So he turned back

---

[1] *The Bound of Heaven*, by Francis Thompson.

home. On his arrival he was surprised to find no one in the lower rooms, but on ascending the stairs he heard the voice of prayer. Quietly listening outside the door, he discovered that his wife was pleading for her children, and specially interceding for Charles, her firstborn and strong-willed son. That son repeats the story as it was told him by his father, and adds, "My father felt that he might safely go about his Master's business while the dear wife was caring so well for the spiritual interests of the boys and girls at home, so he did not disturb her, but proceeded at once to fulfil his preaching engagement."[1]

Ambrose might well tell Monica to comfort her heart about Augustine, that it was impossible for the child if such tears as hers to be lost. In this sphere the relieving mother counts most. Ziegenbalg was sent to Tinnevelly by his mother's prayers; they were not answered even when she lay dying, but as she pointed to the corner of the room where she had so often knelt, her last cry to God was, "Father, remember what I said to Thee there." And God remembered. The story of Ziegenbalg stirred the heart of the mothers of the Wesley, and she began in earnest to seek the salvation of her children. To her absent husband, Susannah Wesley wrote: "I am a woman, but I am also the mistress of a large family. And though the superior charge of the souls contained in it lies upon you, yet in your long absence I cannot but look upon every soul you leave under my charge as a talent committed to me under a trust. I am not a man nor a minister, yet as a mother and a mistress I felt I ought to do more than I had yet done. I resolved to begin with my own children; in which I observe the following method:—I take such a proportion of time as I can spare every night to discourse with each child apart. On Monday I talk with Molly, on Tuesday with Hetty, Wednesday with Nancy, Thursday with Jacky, Friday with Patty, Saturday with Charles."[2] What wonder that John and Charles Wesley, the two boys of the home, emerged as God's heralds from such influence, or, from similar influence, Charles and James Spurgeon, the two sons of another home!

Every Sunday evening their mother was accustomed to gather the children round the table, and as they read she would explain the Scripture, verse by verse, to them. Then she prayed, and her son declares that some of the words of her prayers her children can never forget. Once she said, "Now, Lord, if my children go on in their sins, it will not be from ignorance they perish, and my soul must bear swift witness against them at the day of judgment if they lay not hold of Christ." That was not at all in the modern vein, but it was the arrow that reached the boy's soul. "The thought of a mother bearing swift witness against me, pierced my conscience, and stirred

---

[1] *Autobiography*, Vol. I. p. 09.
[2] *Wesley's Journal*, Vol. I. p. 386-7. Everyman's Library Edition.

my heart." There was enough in him to cause his mother anxiety. His father recalled that his wife once said to him, speaking of their eldest son, "What a mercy that boy was converted when he was young."

In the first sermon he published in London, he says, "There was a boy once—a very sinful child—who hearkened not to the counsel of his parents; but his mother prayed for him, and now he stands to preach to this congregation every Sabbath. And when his mother thinks of her first-born preaching the Gospel, she reaps a glorious harvest that makes her a glad woman."

His father, too, shared in the training. When the boy returned home from his grandfather's house, he greatly scandalised the congregation on Sunday by singing the last line of each verse twice. His father took him to task, but he said that his grandfather did it, and he would do it too. So his father told him that if he did it again he would give him a whipping that he would remember as long as he lived. Sunday came, and again the boy sang the last lines twice. It must have been amusing, for he had no singing voice. After the service his father asked him if he remembered what he had said. The boy remembered. Father and son then walked into the wood, passing a wheat-field on the way, the father trying to win his son to repentance. There they knelt and prayed together, and both were greatly moved. Turning back to the wheat-field, the father plucked a stalk of wheat, and told Charles to hold out his hand. The wheat-stalk was laid gently across it. "I told you I would give you a whipping you would never forget. You will never forget that," said his father. The gentle sternness of the punishment broke him down, and won him over, and he never forgot it.

It must not be supposed that the lad became morbid during those years. He lived two lives, one keen, natural, bookish, observant; the other absorbed, fearful, doubting, insurgent. If he had spoken of his trouble there were those round him who could, perhaps, have helped him out of it; but he battled alone, hiding his thoughts from them all, save once when he spoke to his grandfather of his fear of being a lost soul, and was somewhat comforted for a while. He would not believe because others believed; he must have an assurance of his own; he would not rest until he knew.

He bears witness that by restraining grace, and through the influence of his father and grandfather, he was kept from many outward sins, in which others indulged, and that at times he thought he was quite a respectable lad. "But all of a sudden I met Moses," he quaintly observes. "Then there came to my startled conscience the remembrance of the universality of law. I thought of what was said of the old Roman empire, under the rule of Cæsar: if a man once broke the law of Rome, the whole world was one vast prison to him, for he could never get out of the reach of the Imperial power. So did it come to be in my aroused conscience."

"Let none despise the stirrings of the Spirit in the hearts of the young," he says in another place; "let not boyish anxieties and juvenile repentances be lightly regarded. I, at least, can bear my personal testimony to the fact that grace operates on some minds at a period almost too early for recollection. When but young in years I felt much sorrow for sin. Day and night God's hand was heavy on me. If I slept at night I dreamed of the bottomless pit, and when I awoke I seemed to feel the misery I had dreamed. Up to God's house I went; my song was but a sigh. To my chamber I retired, and there, with tears and groans, I offered up my prayer without a hope and without a refuge, for God's law was flogging me with its ten-thonged whip, and then rubbing me with brine afterwards, so that I did shake and quiver with pain and anguish.

"It was my sad lot to feel the greatness of my sin without a discovery of the greatness of God's mercy. I had to walk through this world with more than a world upon my shoulders, and I wonder to this day how it was that my hand was kept from rending my own body in pieces through the awful agony which I felt when I discovered the greatness of my transgression. I used to say, 'If God does not send me to hell, He ought to do it.' I sat in judgment upon myself and pronounced the sentence that I felt would be just. I could not have gone to Heaven with my sin unpardoned, even if I had the offer to do it, for I justified God in my own conscience, while I condemned myself."

In the midst of this "law-work," to use a phrase well understood by our fathers, he used to read the first thing when he woke in the morning from Alleine's *Alarm to Sinners,* or Baxter's *Call to the Unconverted,* or Doddridge's *Rise and Progress of Religion in the Soul,* or James's *Anxious Inquirer,* but about them all he says, "It was like sitting at the foot of Sinai." He read the Bible through, but found that its threatenings seemed to be printed in capitals and its promises in small type. With perverse ingenuity, as with others in the like case, he twisted everything to his own hurt, applied the cheering words to others, the woeful words to himself.

"Oh, the many times I have wished that the preacher would tell me something to *do* to be saved! Gladly would I have done it, if it had been possible. If he had said, 'Take off your shoes and stockings and run to John o' Groats,' I would not even have gone home first, but would have started off that very night if I might win salvation. How often have I thought that if he had said, 'Bare your back to the scourge and take fifty lashes,' I would have said, 'Here I am; come along with your whip, and beat as hard as you please, so long as I can obtain peace and rest, and get rid of my sin.' Yet the simplest of all matters— believing in Christ crucified, accepting His finished salvation, being nothing and letting Him be everything, doing nothing, but trusting to what He has done—I could not get a hold of it."

It is not every one who has a deep experience that can describe it; in the extracts that follow no doubt allowance must be made for the preacher's rhetoric. But there is Reality behind the words, a sense of the Actual that followed him all his life.

Without wonder we find him, when he had attained to peace, saying, "I love to bless God for every terror that ever scared me by night, and for every foreboding fear that alarmed me by day. It has made me happier ever since, for now, if there be a trouble weighing upon my soul, I thank God that it is not such a burden as that which bowed me to the very earth, and made me creep along the ground, like a beast, by reason of heavy distress and affliction." And again, "Full often have I found it good when I have talked with a young convert in deep distress about his sin, to tell him something more of his anxious plight than he knew how to express, and he has wondered where I found it, though he would not have wondered if he had known where I had been, and how much deeper in the mire than he. When he has talked about some terrible thought that he has had, with regard to the impossibility of his own salvation, I have said, 'Why! I have thought that a thousand times, and yet have overcome it by the help of God's Spirit.'"

Let us try, then, to follow him as he seeks to follow himself during those dark years: "Once I, like Mazeppa, lashed to the wild horses of my lust, and bound hand and foot, incapable of resistance, was galloping on with hell's wolves behind me, howling for my body and my soul as their just and lawful prey."

But deeper yet in apprehension of the eternal, this: "When I was in the hands of the Holy Spirit, under conviction of sin, I had a clear and sharp sense of the justice of God. Sin, whatever it might be to other people, became to me an intolerable burden. It was not so much that I feared hell as that I feared sin; and all the while I had upon my mind a deep concern for the honour of God's name, and the integrity of His moral government. I felt that it would not satisfy my conscience if I could be forgiven unjustly." No shallow theology here.

He came to close grips, too, with the power of evil. "Ah! I recollect a dark hour with myself," he says, "when I, who do not remember to have even heard a blasphemy in my youth, much less to have uttered one, found rushing through my mind an almost infinite number of curses and blasphemies against the Most High God. I specially recall a narrow and crooked lane in a country town, along which I was walking one day, while I was seeking the Saviour. On a sudden, it seemed as if the floodgates of hell had been opened: my head became a very pandemonium, ten thousand evil spirits seemed to be holding carnival within my brain, and I held my mouth lest I should give utterance to the words of blasphemy that were poured into my ears. Things I had never heard or thought of before came rushing impetuously into my mind, and I could scarcely withstand their influence. It was the devil throwing me down and tearing me. These things sorely beset me; for half an hour together the most fearful imprecations would dash through my brain. Oh, how I groaned and cried before God! That temptation passed away; but ere many days it was renewed again, and when I was in prayer, or when I was reading the Bible these blasphemous thoughts would pour in upon me more than at any other time."

There came a time when he even persuaded himself that he was an atheist. It was, of course, a passing phase, but it was real while it lasted. In one of his finest early passages, when he was preaching in London, he describes his brief apostasy. In passing we may take this extract as a sample of the rush of his youthful oratory, somewhat flamboyant, it is true, but absolutely compelling. No wonder he gained the ear of the people.

"I have never been thoroughly an unbeliever but once, and that was not before I knew the need of a Saviour, but after it. It was just when I wanted Christ and panted after Him, that, on a sudden, the thought crossed my mind—which I abhorred, but could not conquer—that there was no God, no Christ, no heaven, no hell; that all my prayers were but a farce, and that I might as well have whistled to the winds or spoken to the howling waves. Ah! I remember how my ship drifted through the sea of fire, loosened from the anchor of my faith which I had received from my fathers. I no longer moored myself hard by the coasts of Revelation; I said to reason, 'Be thou my captain'; I said to my own brain, 'Be thou my rudder'; and I started on my mad voyage. Thank God it is all over now; but I will tell you its history. It was one hurried sailing over the tempestuous ocean of free thought. I went on, and as I went, the skies began to darken; but to make up for the deficiency, the waters were gleaming with coruscations of brilliancy. I saw sparks flying upwards that pleased me, and I felt, 'If this be free thought, it is a happy thing.' My thoughts seemed gems, and I scattered stars with both my hands; but anon, instead of these coruscations of glory, I saw grim fiends, fierce and horrible, start up from the waters; and as they dashed on, they gnashed their teeth, and grinned upon me; they seized the prow of my ship, and dragged me on, while I, in part, gloried in the rapidity of my motion, but yet shuddered at the terrific rate with which I passed the old landmarks of my faith. I went to the very verge of the dreary realms of unbelief. I went to the very bottom of the sea of infidelity. As I hurried forward at an awful speed, I began to doubt if there was a world. I doubted everything, until at last the devil defeated himself by making me doubt my own existence. I thought I was an idea floating in the nothingness of vacuity; then, startled with the thought, and feeling that I was substantial flesh and blood after all, I saw that God was, and Christ, and Heaven was, and Hell was, and that all these things were absolute truths. The very extravagance of the doubt proved its absurdity, and then came a Voice which said, 'And can this doubt be true?' Then I awoke from the death-dreams, which, God knows, might have damned my soul and ruined my body if I had not awoke. When I arose faith took the helm; from that moment I doubted not. Faith steered me back; faith cried 'Away! Away!' I cast my anchor on Calvary, I lifted my eye to God, and here I am alive, and out of hell. Therefore I speak what I do know. I have sailed the perilous voyage: I have come safe to land. Ask me to be an infidel! No. I have tried it; it was sweet at first, but bitter afterwards. Now, lashed to God's Gospel more firmly than ever, standing as on a rock of adamant, I defy the arguments of hell to move me, for 'I know whom I have believed, and I am persuaded that He is able to keep that which I have committed unto Him.'"

But not at once did he arrive at such assurance. His intellect seems first to have come to poise, for a month or two before the memorable day when he found God in Christ as a living experience, he wrote an essay entitled *Antichrist and her Brood; or Popery Unmasked,* the manuscript of which has been carefully bound and preserved. It has two hundred and ninety-five pages, and is a distinct achievement for a lad of fifteen years. It was a kind of holiday amusement, and although it did not secure the prize in the competition for which it was entered, two years afterwards a sum of money reached him, in recognition of his effort, from Mr. Arthur Morley of Nottingham, who had initiated the contest.

By that time he was an avowed Christian, and it is more than interesting to see how he used the unexpected gift that came to him. He says in a letter to his father from Cambridge on December 31, 1851: "When I wrote my essay on my knees in the little room upstairs, I solemnly vowed to give two tithes of anything I might gain by it to the Lord's cause." Then he mentions that as to the remainder, he wants to send it "as a little present to you and dear Mother." "I know a lad in Christ," he said long subsequently, "who adopted the principle of giving a tenth to God. When he won a money prize for an essay on a religious subject, he felt that he could not give less than one-fifth of it. He had never after that been able to deny himself the pleasure of having a fifth to give."

But the lad was not in Christ yet, although it is significant that in his essay he quotes on the thirtyeighth page the very text that wrought his deliverance—"Look unto Me, and be ye saved, all the ends of the earth so little does the letter of Scripture avail without the Spirit of God.

The search for God now became intense. "Our own experience," he says, "recalls to us the period when we panted for the Lord, even for Him, our only want. Vain to us were the mere ordinances—vain as bottles scorched by the simoom, and drained of their waters. Vain were ceremonies—vain as empty wells to the thirsty Arab. Vain were the delights of the flesh—bitter as the waters of Marah, which even the parched lips of Israel refused to drink. Vain were the directions of the legal preacher—useless as the howling of the wind to the benighted wanderer. Vain, worse than vain, were our refuges of lies, which fell about our ears like Dagon's temple on the heads of the worshippers. One only hope we had, one refuge for our misery. Save where the Ark floated, North, South, East and West, was one broad expanse of troubled waters. Save where that star burned, the sky was one field of unmitigated darkness. Jesus. *Jesus.* JESUS! He alone, He without another, had become the solitary hiding-place against the storm.

"I cried to God with groanings—I say it without exaggeration—groanings that cannot be uttered! and oh, how I sought, in my poor dark way, to overcome first one sin and then another, and so to do better, in God's strength, against the enemies that assailed me, and not, thank God, altogether without success, though still the battle had been lost unless He had come who is the Overcomer of Sin, and the Deliverer of His people, and had put the hosts to flight."

Then came the memorable 6th day of January 1850. He rose before the sun, to pray and to read one of his bedside books. But he found no rest. As he says himself, God was ploughing his soul, ten black horses in His team—the ten commandments— and cross-ploughing it with the message of the Gospel, for when he heard it, no comfort came to his soul. Already he had been the round of the chapels, but in vain, and "had it not been for the goodness of God in sending a snowstorm one Sunday morning," he might have still wandered in darkness and despair. The storm prevented him reaching the place of worship whither he was bound, and instead he turned into the Primitive Methodist Chapel, Artillery Street, Colchester.

It was not the place of his choice, but it was the place that God had chosen; not the morning of his hope, but the morning of God's deliverance; not the preacher appointed for the day, who was probably snowed up, but the messenger entrusted with the key that led into the light the lad who for five weary years had been groping in the shadows.

There were a dozen or fifteen persons in the chapel—no more, and the preacher was an unlettered man. The minister is unknown, though no doubt he knows now how great a deed he did that day.

The text was "Look unto Me and be ye saved, all the ends of the earth," but the preacher did not pronounce the words rightly. Yet there was a gleam of hope in them to the seeker in the side pew. As Spurgeon recalled it, and he had a remarkable verbal memory, the sermon ran on this fashion—

"My dear friends, this is a simple text indeed. It says, Look. Now lookin' don't take a deal of pains. It ain't liftin' your foot or your finger. It is just 'Look.' Well, a man needn't go to College to learn to look. You may be the biggest fool and yet you can look. A man needn't be worth a thousand a year to be able to look. Any one can look: even a child can look. But then the text says 'Look unto Me.' Ay!" said he in broad Essex, "many on ye are lookin' to yourselves, but it's no use lookin' there. You'll never find any comfort in yourselves. Some look to God the Father. No, look to Him by-and-by. Jesus Christ says, 'Look unto *Me.*' Some on ye say, 'We must wait for the Spirit's workin'.' You have no business with that just now. Look to *Christ.* The text says, 'Look unto *Me.*'"

Whether he had reached the end of his tether, having spun out about ten minutes, or whether he was lifted out of himself, and spoke words given to him at that moment, he fixed his eyes on the stranger, easily distinguished amid the little company, and said, "Young man, you look very miserable." It was a blow struck right home, and although the young man had never had such a personal word from the pulpit before, he was too much in earnest to resent it. He continued, "You always will be miserable—miserable in life and miserable in death if you don't obey my text; but if you obey now, this moment you will be saved." Then lifting up his hands, he shouted, as only a Primitive Methodist of the epoch could, "Young man, look to Jesus Christ! Look! Look! Look! You have nothin' to do but to look and live."

What more he said young Spurgeon never knew, for in a moment he saw the way of Salvation, and was possessed by the thought of the freeness and simplicity of it. "I had been waiting to do fifty things," he said; "but when I heard the word Look, I could have almost looked my eyes away. I could have risen that instant, and sung with the most enthusiastic of them of the precious blood of Christ, and the simple faith that looks alone to Him.

"I thought I could dance all the way home. I could understand what John Bunyan meant when he declared he wanted to tell the crows on the ploughed land all about his conversion. He was too full to hold. He must tell somebody." In the light of the passion that constrained him to witness for Christ in the coming years, it is almost surprising that then and there he did not break out in testimony to the mighty change that had been wrought in him. There was no doubt about it. "As Richard Knill said, 'At such a time of the day, clang went every harp in heaven, for Richard Knill was born again'; it was even so with me." He felt that if beside the door of the place as he went out there had been a pile of blazing faggots, he could have stood upon them without chains, glad to give his flesh and blood and bones to be ashes, if only that might have testified his love to Jesus.

"Between half-past ten, when I entered that chapel, and half-past twelve, when I returned home, what a change had taken place in me!"[1]

He thought at first that he had never heard the Gospel before, that the preachers he had listened to had not preached it, but he came to see the

---

[1] *Autobiography*, Vol. I. Chaps. IX, X and XI.

difference between the effectual calling of God and the general proclamation of the Gospel. As to Ezekiel, the word of the Lord came to him expressly[1] that morning, and he was nevermore separated from his Saviour.

> " I looked to Him, He looked on me,
> And we were one for ever."

A tablet was erected in the chapel in 1897 over the spot where Spurgeon sat, and the pulpit from which the sermon was preached was subsequently removed to the Stockwell Orphanage.

It is interesting that in the East window of the parish church at Kelvedon, the village of his birth, there is, under the figure of the Saviour on the Cross, the text, "Look unto Me and be ye saved."

---

[1] Ezek. i. 3.

THE COTTAGE AT TEVERSHAM WHERE THE FIRST SERMON WAS PREACHED

From a watercolor by Thomas Spurgeon

CHAPTER III

THE APPRENTICE PREACHER

1844–1853

SPURGEON was destined to be a preacher, and he began early. Like many other boys, he held mimic services with his brother and sisters in the Colchester home. He was often found on the hay-rick or in the manger praying or reading aloud. One of the family remembered how frequently he would quote the verse—

> "Now will I tell to sinners round,
> What a dear Saviour I have found."

"I'll point"—and here he would raise his index finger and point upwards. (Evidently a favourite gesture, for one of his early photographs has the finger pointing to the skies.) Then he would finish the stanza—

> "I'll point to Thy redeeming blood
> And say, 'Behold the way to God.'"

But earlier still, when he was but six years of age, he gave evidence of his vocation. It is his Aunt Ann that tells the story. During his first visit to Stambourne he heard his grandfather lamenting, time and again, over the inconsistent life of one of his flock, and one day he suddenly declared his intention to kill old Roads, the man in question; and in spite of the warning his grandfather gave him as to the awful fate of murderers, he persisted in his resolve. "I'll not do anything bad," he declared, "but I'll kill him." Shortly afterwards he astonished them by asserting that he had done the deed. In answer to all questions he declared that he had done no wrong, but that he had been about the Lord's work, that he had killed old Roads, who would never trouble his grandfather any more.

The mystery was solved by the appearance of old Roads himself, who shortly afterwards called at the Manse, and told how he had been sitting in the public-house, with his paper and mug of beer, when the boy entered, and pointing to him said, "What doest thou here, Elijah, sitting with the ungodly, and you a member of the Church, and breaking your pastor's heart? I'm ashamed of you. I wouldn't break my pastor's heart, I'm sure." The sermon in its brevity and simplicity and directness might also be put alongside that other which, ten years afterwards, led the young preacher himself to surrender his life to Christ, as this one led old Roads. During the four years that followed, the old man lived an exemplary life; he could not read, but he knew that the words of life were in the Bible, and with pathetic love for the Book, he counted the very leaves of it.

The greatest impulse the boy Spurgeon received in the direction of the pulpit came from Richard Knill, who visited his grandfather's house on missionary deputation when the boy, ten years of age, was also a guest.

This Richard Knill was a man all aglow for Christ. The story of his own decision to serve the Lord is worth recalling. When he told his mother of his desire to go to India, she flamed forth on him and declared that she would never consent, that he should have waited until she and his father were beneath the clods of the valley before thinking of such a thing. But she presently came to another mind, and not only consented, but urged him to go, glad that she had an Isaac to put on the altar. On the day of his departure she took off her wedding-ring and said, "This is the dearest thing I possess. It was given to me by your dear father, as a pledge of his love, on our wedding-day. I have worn it more than forty years, and now, in the expectation that I shall never see you again in this world, I give it to you. Your father gave it to me as a pledge of his love, and in his presence I give it to you as a token of our united love to you."[1] He was invalided home, and afterwards spent some years in St. Petersburg, subsequently settling in England. His portrait is in the vestry of Queen Street Congregational Chapel, Chester, of which he was the minister, and beneath it he has written his message for all who come after him. "Brethren, the heathen are perishing. Shall we let them perish? God forbid." His mother's ring pledged him to Christ with undying ardour all his life. He died on January 2, 1857, and up to that time it was stated that no man ever had so many of his tracts circulated as he had; in England and America some fourteen millions of them had been scattered, and they were also translated into ten other languages.

This was the man who, with an instinct that had its origin in his own walk with God, attached himself to the boy at Stambourne, asked him where he slept, so that he might waken him in the morning, called him at six o'clock the next day, and took him out to one of the yew-tree arbours in his grandfather's garden. There he told him of the love of Christ, and with arm round the boy's neck prayed for him. During the three days of his stay he sought every opportunity of winning his life for Christ, and then at morning prayer, in the presence of the whole family, he took the boy on his knee and spoke as an oracle of God. "This child will one day preach the Gospel," he said, "and he will preach it to great multitudes. I am persuaded that he will preach in the chapel of Rowland Hill." It was a singular utterance, difficult to explain, and it doubtless helped in part to bring about its own fulfilment.

---

[1] *Richard Knill's Biography.*

Having spoken, he gave the boy sixpence—that would help him to remember it—and made him promise to learn the hymn, and to see that it was sung when he preached in Rowland Hill's Chapel—

"God moves in a mysterious way
His wonders to perform."

So when Spurgeon preached at Surrey Chapel, London, and also when he ministered at Wotton-under-Edge, where Rowland Hill had his summer residence, the hymn was sung, and the preacher, filled with emotion, told the story. "To me it was a very wonderful thing, and I no more understood at that time how it came to pass than I understand today why the Lord should be so gracious to me," is his mature comment on the sequence of incidents.

In the autumn of 1849 he went as an articled pupil to the school of Mr. John Swindell, at Newmarket, Cambridgeshire. During the Christmas holidays the great spiritual crisis of his life came. He had been prepared for it, doubtless, by frequent conversations with Mary King, the cook of the Newmarket household, to whom he says that he was also indebted for much of his theology. "Many a time we have gone over the Covenant of Grace together, and talked of the personal election of the saints, their union with Christ, their final perseverance, and what vital godliness meant; and I do believe that I learnt more from her than I should have learned from any six doctors of divinity of the sort we have nowadays."

The ministry they attended was somewhat barren; once when he asked the old housekeeper why she went, she made the quaint reply that a hen scratching on a heap of rubbish does not get any corn, but it shows that it is looking for it, is using the means to get it, and is warmed by the exercise. Mr. Spurgeon had a great regard for old Mary, and in her later years made her an allowance in memory of old times.

After his enlightenment he returned to Newmarket to take up his duties and studies. He called upon the minister of the church, but was not received, called four successive days, but was unable to gain an interview; his temper may be gauged by the fact that he then wrote to him saying that he would go down to the Church Meeting and propose himself for membership. This seems to have brought things to a climax, for he was admitted to fellowship on April 4, 1850.

From the earliest days of his Christian life, after his conversion, he dwelt in the spiritual tropics. There were no half shades with him, no mists to make the grey light of dawn or gloaming, it was either day or night: a man was either for God or against Him. As for himself, he was on God's side with all the power of his being all the time.

On the first day of February 1850 (remember that the snowy Sunday at Colchester was on January 6) he dedicated himself anew to God. "O Great and Unsearchable God, who knowest my heart and triest my ways, with humble dependence upon the support of Thy Holy Spirit, I yield myself to Thee; as Thy own reasonable sacrifice, I return to Thee Thine own. I would be for ever unreservedly, perpetually Thine; whilst I am on earth I would serve Thee, and may I enjoy Thee and praise Thee for ever. Amen."

In a diary which he gave to his wife soon after their marriage, opened only after his death, there are entries from April 6 to June 20 of this year. On April 22 he writes, "Went this evening to the prayer meeting; engaged in prayer. Why should I fear to speak of my only Friend? I shall not be timid another time;" and on May 5 there is the clause, "Five of us engaged in prayer." He was evidently feeling his feet.

He had not yet sat down at the Lord's Table, for though he had never even *heard* of Baptists until he was fourteen, he had been convinced, partly by the Church of England catechism and partly by study of the New Testament, that believers in Christ should be baptised in His name after they believed, and logically enough he desired baptism before his first communion. So he cast about for a Baptist minister, and failed to find one nearer than Isleham, where Mr. W. W. Cantlow, formerly a missionary in Jamaica, ministered. Like an obedient son he wrote to his parents asking their consent, which was readily given, not without a warning from his father that he must not trust in his baptism, and a playful reminder from his mother that though she had often prayed that her son might be a Christian, she had never asked that he should be a Baptist. Just as playfully he retorted that the Lord had dealt with her in His usual bounty, and had given her exceeding abundantly above what she had asked.

It was on his mother's birthday, May 8, 1850, that he "put on Christ," when he was within a few weeks of being sixteen years of age. Up early in the morning, he had two hours for prayer and dedication, then a walk of eight miles to Isleham Ferry, on the river Lark, a beautiful stream, dividing Suffolk from Cambridgeshire, which is dear to local anglers. It was Friday, and there was not such a concourse of people as assembled when there was a baptism on a Sunday. Still, quite a respectable number were present. Never having seen a baptism, the young confessor was somewhat nervous. Two women were also to be baptised—Diana Wilkinson and Eunice Fuller, who held it a great honour ever afterwards that they were baptised the same day as Spurgeon. His own description of the scene is worth transcribing— "The wind blew down the river with a cutting blast as my turn came to wade into the flood; but after I had walked a few steps, and noted the people on the ferry-boat, and in boats, and on either shore, I felt as if heaven and earth and hell might all gaze upon me, for I was not ashamed, then and there, to own myself a follower of the Lamb. My timidity was washed away; it floated down the river into the sea, and must have been devoured by the fishes, for I have never felt anything of the kind since. Baptism also loosed my tongue, and from that day it has never been quiet."

The evening was spent in happy converse in the Isleham vestry. There was a prayer meeting, at which the newly-baptised disciple prayed; "and people wondered and wept for joy as they listened to the lad." He was back at Newmarket in the morning, and on the following Sunday he sat down at the Lord's Table and also became a Sunday School teacher.

"I did not fulfil the outward ordinance to join a party, and to become a Baptist, but to be a Christian after the apostolic fashion; for they, when they believed, were baptised. It is now questioned whether John Bunyan was baptised; but the same question can never be raised concerning me. I, who scarcely belong to any sect, am nevertheless by no means willing to have it doubted in time to come whether or no I followed the conviction of my heart." So he wrote years after.

His earliest service for the Church was the distribution of tracts: on Saturday afternoons he visited seventy people, not only handing in the tracts to the houses, but "endeavouring to draw their attention to spiritual realities." The Saturday after his baptism saw him at this work, which he had taken up some weeks earlier.

On Sunday afternoon he was in the Sunday School. Once before he had attempted to take a class, during a visit to Stambourne, but was not much encouraged. "I felt myself a failure, and I fancied that some around me were not brilliant successes." But now that he was rejoicing in Christ, and spoke of things he had himself tasted, he was able to hold the attention of his boys. When they began to fidget, he took it as a signal that he must give them an illustration. One boy at times said, "This is very dull, teacher. Can't you pitch us a yarn?" and the apprentice preacher learnt the lesson which he never afterwards forgot, that truth in a tale is often remembered when the sermon is forgotten.

But he was in deadly earnest all the time. On May 8 he, who was afterwards supposed to be the harlequin of the pulpit, wrote in his diary, "Teachers' business meeting. Too much joking and levity to agree with my notions of what a Sunday School teacher should be"!

At a subsequent teachers' meeting it was suggested that the teachers should alternate with the superintendent in giving the closing address of the school. When Spurgeon's turn came he was so successful that the superintendent asked him to speak every Sunday, but naturally he demurred. The matter was compromised by Spurgeon taking the superintendent's days, and on these afternoons the older people began to come too, so that the school almost became like a Church service.

His witness for Christ broke the bounds of the school. In season and out of season he was ready to bear testimony. Newmarket, with its racing atmosphere, was not a very congenial place for Christian service, but at any rate he could refrain from going on to the racecourse. Not content with this, he was ready to rebuke others when he thought they needed rebuke. Seeing a professing Christian about to enter a dancing booth at the village fair, he went up to him and, perhaps remembering his earnest preaching exploit at Stambourne, said, "What doest thou there, Elijah? Art *thou* going in *there?*" But this time the appeal was fruitless.

From his diary it is evident that Paul was his hero. On May 9 of this early year he writes, "Make me to be an eminent servant of Thine, and to be blessed with power to serve Thee like Thy great servant Paul." On June 7, "Could I be like Paul, how honoured I should be!"

People had not then begun to talk about the sub-conscious mind, but there is no doubt that great thoughts were even then stirring in his soul. Already he had the strong impression that he was to be a preacher, and he has told us that sometimes he even dreamt that his sermons would be printed. But his fondest dreams came nowhere near the future reality.

That ardent affection for the Lord Jesus which has been deemed extravagant in his after-life, was already evident, and it was as real to him as to Samuel Rutherford, of whom he has written: "Let it be known that Spurgeon counted Rutherford's *Letters* as the nearest thing to inspiration in all human literature." His own diary contains such sentences as these: "Beloved, Thine is enduring beauty." "Life of my soul, forgive me when I am so blind as to look on an earthly object, and forget Thy divine beauties." "Desire of my heart, keep me nearer Thy bosom."

Before we close the diary two other expressions may be noted—a confession, "Pride is yet my darling sin;" a desire, "Lord, give me much of Berean nobility."

His first speech in public, outside the Sunday School, was at a missionary meeting on Monday, September 10, 1849. It was given in the school where he was a pupil. Professor J. D. Everett, of Queen's College, Belfast, his fellow-student, recalls both the circumstance and the date, and says that "he spoke fluently." In the same place he gave another missionary speech on June 14 of the following year. Here it may not be amiss to say that in the beginning of his ministry in London he seriously faced the question whether he was not called to preach the Gospel in China, and that right through his life his sympathies were always strong with those who had gone overseas with the message of life.

In those early days young Spurgeon was accustomed to repeat, to Mr. Everett and other intimates, long passages from the open-air orations at Colchester Fair of Mr. Davids, the Congregational minister there; he could also repeat many passages from *Grace Abounding,* and he was not only a good sermon taster, but a generous critic of pulpit utterances.

In August 1850 he moved to Cambridge, to a school established by Mr. Leeding, who had been usher at the Colchester School when young Spurgeon was there, and here he remained for three formative years as assistant without a salary, learning and teaching, and, as we shall see, preaching too. With gratitude he recalled that in this home at 9, Union Road, each morning from eight o'clock, for half an hour, the members of the household returned to their rooms for prayer and meditation.

Towards the end of his time in Cambridge it became necessary for him to earn some more money, though he never sought money for its own sake. In November 1852 he wrote to his mother, "I had rather be poor in God's service than rich in my own." And there is no doubt that he was poor, for earlier in the same year he calculated that at midsummer he might have £15 in hand, to provide himself with books and other necessities.

So at the end of 1853 the following advertisement appeared in a Cambridge newspaper: "No. 60, Park Street, Cambridge. Mr. C. H. Spurgeon begs to inform his numerous friends that after Christmas he intends taking six or seven young gentlemen as day pupils. He will endeavour to the utmost to impart a good commercial education. The ordinary routine will include Arithmetic, Algebra, Geometry and Mensuration; Grammar and Composition; Ancient and Modern History; Geography, Natural History, Astronomy, Scripture and Drawing; Latin and the elements of Greek and French if required. Terms £5 per annum." Surely a very modest announcement. But that school was never started, the beginning of his great career prevented it.

When he first came to Cambridge he joined the St. Andrew's Street Baptist Church, where Robert Hall, in his day England's greatest preacher, had for some time ministered; where Robert Robinson, the author of the hymn "Come, Thou Fount of every blessing," had also been pastor. An amusing incident, revealing his sense of the equality of the saints and of the aristocracy of grace, is best told in his own language—

"When I joined the Baptist Church at Cambridge, one of the most respectable churches that can be found in the world, one of the most generous, one of the most intelligent—this was a great many years ago, when I was young—nobody spoke to me. On the Lord's Day I sat at the Communion table in a certain pew. There was one gentleman in it, and when the service was over, I said to him, ' I hope you are quite well, sir?' He said, 'You have the advantage of me.' I answered, 'I don't think I have, for you and I are brothers.' 'I don't quite know what you mean,' said he. 'Well,' I replied, 'when I took the bread and wine just now, in token of our being one in Christ, I meant it. Did not you?' We were by that time in the street; he put both his hands on my shoulders—I was about sixteen years old then—and he said, 'Oh, sweet simplicity!' Then he added, 'You are quite right, my dear brother, you are quite right; come in to tea with me. I am afraid I should not have spoken to you if you had not first addressed me.' I went to tea with him that evening; and when I left, he asked me to go again the next Lord's Day, so I went, and that Sabbath Day he said to me, 'You will come here every Sunday evening, won't you?' So old Mr. Watts and young Mr. Spurgeon became fast friends."

Soon he began in Cambridge, as in Newmarket, to address the Sunday School, and he read an essay on Sunday School work at the Teachers' Institute of the town, but he had never yet delivered a set discourse to a congregation met for worship.

There was at that time a Mr. James Vinter in Cambridge, who was President of the Preachers' Association, a Society that still continues its good work for the villages. "Bishop Vinter," the name by which he was generally known, called one Saturday morning on young Spurgeon, just as the school was dismissed, and asked him "to go over to Teversham the next evening, for a young man was to preach there who was not much used to services, and very likely would be glad of company." Evidently he knew his man. A definite request to preach would have met with a refusal, but the leader of the band of preachers knew that this young recruit had it in him, and only needed to get started. The ruse was perhaps pardonable, anyhow it was successful.

So Spurgeon, accompanied by another young man somewhat older than himself, started off in the early evening, walked through Barnwell, along the Newmarket Road, and at length the younger man expressed the hope that his companion would realise the presence of God when he preached. Aghast, the older man declared that he had never preached, could not preach, would not preach, and unless Spurgeon preached there would be no sermon. Both were perplexed, but his companion suggested that if he would give one of his Sunday School addresses it would do excellently, and they both went forward. And the Lord Himself drew near and went with them, as with the two to Emmaus. Spurgeon reproached himself for his hesitancy: "Surely," he thought, "I can tell a few poor cottagers of the sweetness and love of Jesus, since I feel them in my own soul."

His biographer may be pardoned if he expresses sympathy with the preacher of the evening, since all unexpectedly his own first sermon in England was preached in the same village of Teversham on Easter Sunday 1875, and on one of his latest visits to Cambridge he was reminded of it by one who recalled the text.

Spurgeon's text on that notable evening was "Unto you that believe He is precious," and under the low-pitched roof of the thatched cottage he spoke the praises of his Lord. When he finished, delighted with the fact that he had not broken down (so low was his estimate of his own powers), he took up the hymn-book, when an aged voice cried out, "Bless your dear heart, how old are you?" Somewhat on his dignity the preacher said, "You must wait until the service is over before making any such inquiries. Let us now sing." So they sang, and then there was a free friendly talk, during which the question was renewed, "How old are you?" and Spurgeon gave the quaint and almost prophetic reply, "I am under sixty "(he died at fifty-seven). "Yes, and under sixteen," said the old lady; to whom the preacher replied, "Never mind my age, think of the Lord Jesus Christ and His preciousness." Then he promised to come again if the gentleman in Cambridge thought him fit to come!

His fame soon spread round the countryside, and he was invited to preach both on Sundays and weekdays. He describes his methods at this time. In the early morning he was up praying and reading the Bible, then school duties until about five in the evening he set off, almost daily, to tell the villagers round about Cambridge what he had learned during the day, and he found that the things he had thought of during the day were wrought into the fibre of his being when he proclaimed them to others. He frankly confesses that he said many odd things and made many blunders, but he had friendly audiences and there were no reporters.

Toward the end of October 1851, he engaged to supply the pulpit of the church at Waterbeach, six miles from Cambridge, the village where Rowland Hill is supposed to have preached his first sermon. The chapel was a primitive structure with a thatched roof. The promise was but for a few Sundays, but he remained with the people for more than two years. At first they contributed very little towards his expenses, so he continued his week-day work at the school, but at length they gave him £45 a year. As he had to pay twelve shillings a week for the two rooms he occupied, his income was scanty, and had they not shared their produce with him he could not have continued with them. But the Lord whom he served supplied his needs, sometimes through unexpected channels.

There was a miser in the village, and somebody said to the pastor, "He has never been known to give anything to anybody," to which he replied that he knew better, for one Sunday afternoon he had given him three half-crowns, and he had bought a new hat with the money. "Well," rejoined the friend, "I am quite sure he never forgave himself such extravagance, and that he must have wanted his three half-crowns back again." Instead of that, the old man came the next Sunday, and asked his minister to pray for him that he might be saved from covetousness, for the Lord had told him to give half a sovereign, and as he had kept back half a crown, he could not rest at night for thinking of it.

Different from this was an old gentleman familiarly known as Father Sewell. A meeting on behalf of Home Missions was being held, and he was only able to get to it at the very end. The pastor said, "Our brother who has just come in will, I am sure, close the meeting by offering prayer for God's blessing on the proceedings of the evening." He stood up, but instead of praying began to feel in his pockets. "I am afraid that my brother did not understand me," Mr. Spurgeon said. "Friend Sewell, I did not ask you to *give*, but to *pray.*" To which the bluff old saint replied, "Ay! Ay! but I could not pray till I had given; it would be hypocrisy to ask a blessing on that which I did not think worth giving to."

Both pastor and people lived in a world that even then was out of the main current of English life; a rural world that preserved much of the simplicity and religious sincerity of the Puritan era, feared God and reverenced His word. The qualities of the people were well matched by the single-hearted devotion and clear-cut theology of the young preacher, who had the Lord always before him, and walked with God day by day.

Waterbeach was notorious for its drunkenness and profanity when Spurgeon went to it as God's messenger. "In a short time the little thatched chapel was crammed, the biggest vagabonds of the village were weeping floods of tears, and those who had been the curse of the parish became its blessing. I can say with joy and happiness that almost from one end of the village to the other, at the hour of eventide, one might have heard the voice of song coming from every roof-tree, and echoing from almost every heart." Which reminds us of the change wrought by Richard Baxter at Kidderminster.

A labourer's wife was his first convert, and he prized that soul more than all the multitude that came after. Early on the Monday morning he drove down to her cottage to see his first spiritual child. "If anybody had said to me, 'Somebody has left you twenty thousand pounds,' I should not have given a snap of my fingers for it compared with the joy which I felt when I was told that God had saved a soul through my ministry. I felt like a boy who had earned his first guinea, or like a diver who had been down to the depth of the sea, and brought up a rare pearl."

He was ever seeking such pearls. One night at Waterbeach he shared a room with a young man who jumped into bed without praying, and Spurgeon, seizing the opportunity, asked him how it would be if, going to sleep prayerless, he never wakened again. It ended on them both rising, and after two hours the young man was converted as they knelt together. On another occasion, in the same room, Spurgeon woke his companion to tell him that he had had such a vision of the judgment of sinners that he dare not sleep, and the next day he preached such a sermon on the fate of the lost that the faces of the people blanched and their knees trembled. For scores of years afterwards that terrible sermon was recalled by those who had heard it.

Of the deacons the young pastor spoke with much esteem. One of them, a Mr. King, instead of rebuking him openly for some unguarded statement, just stuck a pin into his Bible at Titus ii. 8: "Sound speech, that cannot be condemned; that he that is of contrary part may be ashamed, having no evil thing to say of you."

As an example of his daring utterances, one day he declared that a change of nature was absolutely necessary, for if a thief went to Heaven without it, he would be a thief still, and would go round the place picking the angels' pockets. During the week the Mayor of Cambridge took him to task, and told him that the angels have no pockets. Quite gravely Mr. Spurgeon said he had not known that, but he was glad to be assured of the fact by a gentleman who did know, and that he would put the thing right on the first opportunity. On the following Monday he walked into Mr. Brimley's shop and said, "I set that matter right yesterday, sir." "What matter?" he inquired. "Why, about the angels' pockets." "What *did* you say?" the elder man asked in despairing tones. "Oh, sir, I just told the people that I was sorry I had made a mistake, but that the Mayor of Cambridge had assured me that the angels had no pockets, so I would say that if a thief got among the angels, without having his nature changed, he would try to steal the feathers out of their wings." Upon which his critic, who had several times found fault with him, said, "Then I'll never try to set you right again"—which was exactly what young Spurgeon wanted him to say.

Such an incident lends point to the remark of Mr. Sutton of Cottenham, who said that Spurgeon was "the sauciest dog that ever barked in a pulpit." He had invited the popular preacher over to his village, and the people were arriving in all sorts of conveyances, when he was taken aback to find in his vestry one so young, nor did he dissemble his disappointment. The old minister sat in the pulpit in case the boy should break down. But the preacher was equal to the occasion. He read the chapter in Proverbs where it is written, "The hoary head is a crown of glory," and then stopped and said, "I doubt it, for this very morning I met a man with a hoary head, yet he had not learnt common civility to his fellow-men." Proceeding with the reading, he finished the verse, "if it be found in the way of righteousness." "Ah!" he said, "that's another thing. A hoary head would then be a crown of glory, and for the matter of that so would a red head, or a head of any colour." The reading finished, he preached, and as he came down from the pulpit, the old minister slapped him on the back, said he was never better pleased with a sermon in all his life, and then told him he was a saucy dog.

At Waterbeach the afternoon service followed quickly after the morning service, with but a small interval, and one Sunday after dinner, which came between, Spurgeon was quite unable to recollect even the subject of the sermon he had prepared for the second service. "Oh, never mind," said the farmer, "you will be sure to have a good word for us." Just at that moment a blazing log fell out of the fire. "There," said his host, "there's a sermon for you. Is not this a brand plucked out of the fire?" And on that text he preached, and the sermon had converting power.

Two sets of books, with floral frontispieces, containing the outlines of his earliest sermons, have been preserved, containing the "firebrand" discourse amongst the rest. Some idea of the extent of the service he rendered to the country may be gathered from the fact that before his call to London he had preached six hundred and seventy sermons.

Of these early days his brother James says, "When I drove my brother about the country to preach, I thought then, as I have thought ever since, what an extraordinary preacher he was. What wonderful unction and power I remember in some of those early speeches! The effect upon the people listening to him I have never known exceeded in after years. He seemed to have leaped full-grown into the pulpit. The breadth and brilliance of those early sermons, and the power that God's Holy Spirit evidently gave to him, made them perfectly marvellous. When he went to Waterbeach his letters came home, and were read as family documents, discussed, prayed over, and wondered at. We were not surprised, however, for we all believed that it was in him."[1]

On one occasion, the fame of the Waterbeach pastor having spread, he was invited to Isleham. The deacons hoped for such crowds that they borrowed the largest chapel in the neighbourhood, but when the day came the congregation in the morning numbered exactly seven persons. Nothing daunted, he preached one of his best sermons, with the result that in the evening there was not standing room in the place.

It was during this period that, for the Jubilee Services at Waterbeach on June 26, 1853, he composed one of his finest hymns. It is a remarkable production for a youth of nineteen.

"When once I mourned a load of sin,
When conscience felt a wound within,
When all my works were thrown away,
When on my knees I knelt to pray,
Then, blissful hour, remembered well,
I learnt Thy love, Immanuel!

"When storms of sorrow toss my soul,
When waves of care around me roll,

---

[1] *James Archer Spurgeon,* by G. H. Pike, p. 25.

When comforts sink, when joys shall flee,
When hopeless gulfs shall gape for me,
       One word the tempest's rage shall quell,
       That word, Thy name, Immanuel.

"When for the truth I suffer shame,
When foes pour scandal on Thy name,
When cruel taunts and jeers abound,
When 'bulls of Bashan' gird me round,
       Secure within my tower I'll dwell,
       That tower, Thy grace, Immanuel.

"When hell, enraged, lifts up her roar,
When Satan stops my path before,
When fiends rejoice and wait my end,
When legion'd hosts their arrows send,
       Fear not, my soul, but hurl at hell
       Thy battle-cry, Immanuel.

"When down the hill of life I go,
When o'er my feet death's waters flow,
When m the deep'ning flood I sink,
When friends stand weeping on the brink,
       I'll mingle with my last farewell
       Thy lovely name, Immanuel.

"When tears are banished from mine eyes,
When fairer worlds than these are nigh,
When heaven shall fill my ravished sight,
When I shall bathe in sweet delight,
       One joy all joys shall far excel,
       To see Thy face, Immanuel."

The question of going to a theological college for further study occurred to him again and again. He was inclined towards such a course, but did not wish to take it at the expense of other people, and besides, he says (writing to his father), "I am now very well off, I think as well off as any one of my age, and I am sure quite as happy. Now shall I throw myself out, and trust to Providence as to whether I shall ever get another place as soon as I leave College?" At which, in view of the future that awaited him, we can afford to smile.

But at length he had some definite thought of entering Stepney College, now Regent's Park College, and when Dr. Angus, the Principal, visited Cambridge on February 1, 1852, to preach at St. Andrew's Street Chapel, he expressed a desire to see the young preacher. It may be noted here that Joseph Angus for two years had been pastor of the church at New Park Street,

London, to which Spurgeon was afterwards to be called; that for some time afterwards he was Secretary of the Baptist Missionary Society, and in later years was on the Committee which issued the Revision of the Scriptures in 1881.

An appointment was made for Dr. Angus to meet Mr. Spurgeon in the house of Mr. Macmillan, the publisher. Punctually the young man called, and was shown into the drawing-room, where he waited for two hours, feeling too much impressed, as he says, by his own insignificance, and the greatness of the tutor from London, to venture to ring the bell and make inquiries as to the unreasonably long delay. At length he ventured to ring, and was informed that the Doctor had waited a considerable time for him in another room, and had at length been compelled to go to London by train. The stupid girl who had put him in the drawing-room had forgotten to tell any one in the house of the young man's arrival, and so it came to pass that the two men, anxious to see each other, were in the same house at the same time and missed each other,

Of course, Spurgeon was much disappointed, but that afternoon, on his way to a village appointment, he was walking over Midsummer Common to the little wooden bridge that used to be on the road to Chesterton, when, in the centre of the Common, the word of the Lord came to him. A loud voice seemed distinctly to say, "Seekest thou great things for thyself? seek them not." And then and there he renounced his thought of a collegiate course. Dr. Angus made a mistake, to which as a college official he was, of course, liable, when he wrote two days later to Mr. Watts, "I should regret for your friend to settle without thorough preparation. He may be useful in either case, but his usefulness will be much greater, it will fill at all events a wider sphere, with preparation than without it." Which, of course, is all true, but the writer was quite oblivious of the fact that Spurgeon was already serving his apprenticeship and learning his business in practical ways.

But he had set his face like a flint, never afterwards to seek great things for himself. Bishop Ken, in the two books he oftenest used, wrote, "Et tu quæris tibi grandia? Noli quærere;" but the words were written on Spurgeon's heart. He had no need to offer the beautiful old Moravian Litany, "From the unhappy desire of becoming great, preserve us, gracious Lord and God," but greatness came, though he did not seek it.

CHAPTER IV

THE VOICE IN THE CITY

November 28, 1853—*April* 28, 1854

WHILE the young preacher of the Fens was busy at Waterbeach, and content to stay there, a church in London was seeking, and apparently seeking in vain, for a pastor under whose ministry it might retrieve its fallen fortunes. It was one of the loading Baptist churches of the Metropolis, one of the six that had a membership of over three hundred. The churches at Edgware Road and Dorset Square excelled it in numbers, but amongst the hundred and thirteen churches of its own order at that time in London, most of them small, the church at New Park Street held an honoured and influential place, its chapel probably being the largest of all the Baptist Church buildings.

The situation of the chapel was very unfavourable, and as a consequence the congregation for years had declined. An earlier building in Carter Lane was demolished to make way for the widening of the road to London Bridge on the south side of the river, and in a fit of parsimony a new site was chosen with a very inconvenient approach. The direct road from it led over Southwark Bridge, where a toll was charged, and no hackney carriages could be hired within half a mile. It lay so low that it was frequently flooded, and when factories and warehouses sprang up all around it, naturally enough the people moved their residences elsewhere. It was, in fact, what we would now call a down-town church. "A more dingy, uninviting and repelling region than where the chapel is situated I have seldom explored," said one pastor. "It is in a gloomy, narrow street, surrounded by small, dirty-looking houses. Within a minute's walk of the chapel you see written up at the corner of a little street 'Bear Garden.'"

During its history of two hundred years it had at least three notable preachers, whose portraits may still be seen in the vestry of the Metropolitan Tabernacle. Benjamin Keach, who had suffered in the pillory for his faith, and left some writings on the Metaphors and Parables of Scripture, was pastor for thirty-six years, from 1668 to 1704. Dr. John Gill, who followed him, was minister for fifty-one years, from 1720 to 1771. Ponderous in appearance and in utterance, his learned and laborious *Commentary* is still to be found in some libraries. For a long time his pulpit, preserved in one of the rooms of the Metropolitan Tabernacle, was used by the students of the Pastor's College for their trial sermons. He was a very pronounced Calvinist, and in his portrait his nose has a distinct tilt; Mr. Spurgeon was accustomed to say that he was turning it up at Arminians. Dr. John Rippon, famous for his selection of hymns, the first issued by the Baptists, had a ministry of no less than sixty-three years, from 1773 to 1836. He came to the church when he was but twenty years old, and some of the older members left because of his youth. Subsequently three or four others ministered to the church, without distinction, until, in a building accommodating twelve hundred persons, there was only a congregation of two hundred. For three months the pastorate was vacant, and then they made the great discovery.

It was made very unexpectedly, but its genesis was quite simple. Mr. George Gould, a deacon of the church at Loughton, Essex, happened to be in Cambridge, and attended the anniversary gathering of the Cambridge Sunday School Union in the Guildhall. Young Spurgeon was one of the speakers. The manners of the time may be guessed from the fact that the two other speakers did not hesitate to declare their contempt for the young man. One of them asked why he had left his few sheep in the wilderness, and the other wished that boys would tarry at Jericho until their beards were grown before attempting to instruct their seniors. It rather looks as if young Spurgeon had been somewhat aggressive: he was certainly not lacking in confidence, for he asked permission to reply, and reminded the people that those who were bidden to stop at Jericho were not boys whose beards had not grown, but men whose beards had been shaved off by their enemies, and that an old minister who had disgraced his calling resembled them more than a young minister who was seeking to fulfil it. It was a random shot, but it hit the mark, for the description exactly fitted one of his detractors. The affair was unimportant save for the fact that it deepened the impression on the visitor's mind, which the address had made, and when, on his return to London, Mr. Thomas Olney, one of the New Park Street deacons, lamented to Mr. Gould that they could not find a suitable pastor for their church, he recalled the incident and suggested Mr. Spurgeon's name.

It was not surprising that the first suggestion of the unknown preacher was forgotten, but on their next encounter the subject came up again; Thomas Olney then consulted his fellow-deacon, James Low, and, willing to try the experiment, he wrote to Waterbeach, the only address he knew, inviting Mr. Spurgeon to preach for a Sunday.

So on his arrival at the chapel at Waterbeach on the last Sunday of November 1853, the invitation awaited Mr. Spurgeon. Such a thing was so little anticipated that, having read it, he passed the letter over to Robert Coe, one of the deacons, declaring that there must have been a mistake, the invitation was evidently meant for somebody else. But the deacon sorrowfully shook his head and replied that he did not think there was any mistake: what he had long dreaded had happened at last, but he was surprised that the Londoners had heard of their pastor quite so soon. "Had it been Cottenham, or St. Ives, or Huntingdon," he said, "I should not have wondered at all; but going to London is rather a great step from this little place." The modest doubts of the preacher were not, however, quite dispelled, so the next day, November 28, he sent a cautious answer to the invitation, expressing his willingness to come to London for a Sunday, but hinting that the invitation had probably been sent to him in error, that he was only nineteen years of age, and quite unknown beyond his own neighbourhood. A second letter from London set his mind at rest, and, still wondering, he arranged to preach at New Park Street on December 18, 1853.

It was with no sense of elation that he started for the great city. Indeed, his heart was heavy within him, and again and again he repeated to himself the text, "He must needs go through Samaria." He felt that he was being forced along an undesired path, wished he had stayed at home, and in the midst of the preparations for Christmas in the big city he was somewhat bewildered.

None of the congregation offered him hospitality on the occasion of his visit. With scant courtesy, which was the measure of their expectation, they sent their preacher to a boarding-house in Queen's Square, Bloomsbury, a neighbourhood which has since decayed and has again risen to new respect-ability, and here he was given a bedroom, more like a cupboard, over the front door. The boarders looked askance at the new arrival, who was unversed in town ways; his very clothes proclaimed his country breeding. He had a great black satin stock round his neck, and in special honour of the occasion he produced a blue handkerchief with white spots. The young men gave him some tall talk about the wonderful preachers of London, and sent him to his little bedroom so depressed that, with the added torture of the street traffic, he was unable to sleep.

It was a most unsympathetic reception, and had not the preacher been conscious of his calling, assured that he had stirred neither foot nor finger to secure the invitation, he might have been tempted, even at the last moment, to evade the appointed task. Indeed, when he arrived at New Park Street the following morning and saw the building, which appeared to him very imposing, he was amazed at his own temerity.

But once in front of the congregation, which was very sparse, about eighty people, he gained confidence, and delivered his message from James i. 17: "Every good gift and every perfect gift is from above, and cometh down from the Father of lights, with whom is no variableness, neither shadow of turning." Neither preacher nor congregation guessed that he himself was the finest illustration of the text. Quite an unusual interest was aroused during the service; one of the deacons declared after it that if the preacher were only with them for three months the place would be crowded. The news of the wonderful young man from the country spread, visits were paid to friends during the afternoon, urging them to come in the evening, and a greatly increased congregation then gathered, amongst them the lady who was afterwards to be his wife, to listen to a discourse from Rev. xiv. 5: "They are without fault before the throne of God." The very choice of texts was unconsciously prophetic; the whole life of Spurgeon lay between them like a parenthesis. From God he came, to God at length he went, and his unceasing vocation all the while was to magnify God in the eyes of the people.

The people were so excited that they would not move until the deacons assured them that they would do their best to induce the young preacher to come again, and before Spurgeon left the building he was urged to repeat the visit. His own account of the day is worth recording: "The Lord helped me very graciously. I had a happy Sabbath in the pulpit, and spent the interval with warm-hearted friends; and when at night I trudged back to the Queen's Square narrow lodging, I was not alone, and I no longer looked on Londoners as flinty-hearted barbarians. My tone was altered, I wanted no pity of any one; I did not care a penny for the young gentlemen lodgers and their miraculous ministers, nor for the grind of the cabs, nor for anything else under the sun. The lion had been looked at all round, and his majesty did not appear to be a tenth as majestic as when I had only heard his roar miles away."

Writing to his father some days later, he says, "I spent the Monday in going about London, climbed to the top of St. Paul's, and left some money with the booksellers." In his *Commentary and Commentators,* he tells us that he bought the *Commentary* of Thomas Scott with his first pulpit fee in London, though he afterwards came to think of it as "nothing but milk and water."

The London of seventy years ago was very different from the London of today. In size and population it was about a quarter of what it is now, and it lay largely on the north side of the Thames. On the west side it was practically bounded by the Edgware Road; Fulham, Hammersmith and Brompton were market gardens. On the east it reached to Stepney Green; Hackney and Bow were open country, and the lisle of Dogs a marsh seven feet below high-water mark. On the north side it included the district within a line drawn east and west from the top side of Regent's Park; Kentish Town and Hampstead were still open. South of the river, gardens lay between Lambeth and Southwark; Newington, Kennington and Stockwell were hamlets; Rotherhithe, save for a row of houses backing on to the river bank, was open; Battersea was market gardens; Camberwell and Peckham New Town were villages; and Deptford, Greenwich and Woolwich lay quite apart. Lines of villas, with fields behind, ran out beyond the city along the main thoroughfares—Clapham Road, Brixton Road, New Kent Road, Bow Road, Kingsland Road, Hampstead Road, Edgware Road, Bayswater Road, and these were chiefly occupied by retired people. The merchants of the day mostly lived in the squares of Bloomsbury, but such of them as had their homes further out rode into business on horseback, or drove in their carriages. It was estimated that about half a million workers came into the City every day.

There were stage coaches, that came into London from the surrounding suburbs in the morning and returned in the evening, and omnibuses, that ran from place to place within the limits, the front seats on either side of the driver being eagerly prized, though it was a somewhat perilous operation to clamber up the steep steps that led to them, clinging to a leather strap the while. The rotund drivers of these omnibuses, their faces generally bloated with beer-drinking, were the wits of the day, and made merry as they passed each other, or raced along the same roads. Hansom cabs were not yet invented, and the four-wheeled "growlers" were, like the omnibuses of the day, carpeted with straw.

There were no tramways, no underground railways, no tubes. St. Pancras, Liverpool Street, Victoria and Marylebone stations had no existence, and Hungerford Market was on the site now occupied by Charing Cross Station. There were no railway bridges across the river. The North-Western Railway ran into Euston, the Great Northern into King's Cross and the South-Western into Waterloo, but the Great Western Railway found its terminus at Westbourne Park, the Eastern Counties Railway at Shoreditch, the Blackwall Railway at Fenchurch Street, and the Dover, Brighton and South Coast Railway at London Bridge. There was also a station of the South-Eastern Railway at Bricklayer's Arms. There was no Holborn Viaduct. The Thames Embankment did not exist, save only the terrace of the Houses of Parliament.

That was the London to which Spurgeon came. The dull Georgian aspect of its architecture was just beginning to change, but its social condition was deplorable. Great areas of slums abounded; it was estimated that over three thousand children under fourteen years of age were living as thieves and beggars; more than twenty thousand over fifteen years of age existed in idleness, and at least a hundred thousand were growing up without education. Ragged schools were even then places of peril to their teachers, and the common lodging-houses sheltered tens of thousands, "in lairs fitter to be the habitation of hogs rather than of human beings." But people were beginning to care; Lord Shaftesbury was leading a crusade against the exploitation of the poor; it was a time of transition; the city was ready for a voice, and was not too large to be reached by it.

No other preacher who supplied the pulpit at New Park Street during the vacant months had been invited a second time, but Spurgeon came again on the first, third, and fifth Sundays of January 1854, and so great was the success of his ministry that on January 25 he was invited to occupy the pulpit for six months, with a view to permanent acceptance of the pastorate.

He had given the deacons scant encouragement from the beginning. Writing to his father after his earliest visit, he says that when it was suggested that he should come to them, he had told them "that they did not know what they were doing, nor whether they were in the body or out of the body, they were so starved that a morsel of the Gospel was a treat to them." And when the definite call of the church reached him, given with only the votes of one man and four women against it, he replied from 60, Park Street, Cambridge, that he dared not accept an unqualified invitation for so long a time. "My objection is not to the length of the time of probation," he added, "but it ill becomes a youth to promise to preach to a London congregation so long until he knows them and they know him. I would engage to supply for three months of that time, and then, should the congregation fail or the church disagree, I would reserve to myself the liberty, without breach of engagement, to retire, and you on your part would have the right to dismiss me without seeming to treat me ill. Enthusiasm and popularity are often like the crackling of thorns, and soon expire. I do not wish to be a hindrance if I cannot be a help."

His first home in London was at 75, Dover Road, in the borough of Southwark. From this address on March 2, 1854, he wrote to his Uncle James at Stambourne a witty letter, in which occurs the following paragraph: "But to joke no more, you have heard that I am now a Londoner, and a little nit of a celebrity. No college could have put me in a higher situation. Our place is one of the pinnacles of the denomination. But I have a great work to do, and have need of all the prayers the sons of God can offer for me." In a kind letter from the same address, which he wrote about the same time to the Misses Blunson, the ladies with whom he had lodged at Cambridge, he says, "I get on very well in my present lodgings, but not better than with you, for that would be impossible."

One of the earliest presents from the deacons was a dozen white pocket-handkerchiefs: a hint that it was time that the blue handkerchiefs with white spots were put away. The deacons in those days wore white cravats to be in keeping with their office, and they expected their minister to do likewise.

The suggested probation was cut short by a requisition to the deacons of the church, signed by fifty of the men members, asking for a special Church Meeting. Accordingly the church gathered on April 19, and passed a resolution in which they record with thankfulness the esteem in which the preacher was held, the extraordinary increase in the congregations both on Lord's Days and on week-days, and "consider it prudent" (mark the word) "to secure as early as possible his permanent settlement amongst us." On April 28 Mr. Spurgeon replied, "There is but one answer to so loving and candid an invitation. *I accept it.*" Then, asking for their prayers, he continues, "Remember my youth and inexperience, and pray that these may not hinder my usefulness. I trust also the remembrance of these will lead you to forgive mistakes I may make, or unguarded words that I may utter."

Neither he nor the church had any misgivings as to the future, but the Baptists of London seem either to have been unconscious of his coming, or to have tacitly agreed to ignore him. In the *Baptist Manual* of 1854 the minister of New Park Street is said to be "J. Spurgeon," evidence enough that he was considered of no importance. The Baptist ministry of London at that time included such names as Drs. Brock, Steane, Howard Hinton, Charles Stovel, Jabez Burns, W. G. Lewis, J. Aldis and C. W. Banks. Mr. Leechman was at Hammersmith, though that was not then counted as part of London. It is on record that at an early meeting, when Mr. Spurgeon was present, one of the London ministers prayed for "our young friend who has so much to learn, and so much to unlearn," and that he took it quite pleasantly.

But there were men in the Churches that had vision, amongst them Mr. Sheridan Knowles, the actor and playwriter, who had been baptised by Dr. Brock about that time, and was appointed as teacher of elocution in Stepney College, now Regent's Park. On the day a presentation was made to him by the students, he entered the class-room and immediately said, "Boys, have you heard the Cambridgeshire lad? "None of them had heard him; as a matter of fact he had only been preaching two Sundays. Mr. G. H. Davies reports what followed. "Go and hear him at once," he said; "his name is Charles Spurgeon. He is only a boy, but he is the most wonderful preacher in the world. He is absolutely perfect in oratory; and, beside that, a master in the art of acting. He has nothing to learn from me or any one else. He is simply perfect. He knows everything. He can do anything. I was once lessee of Drury Lane Theatre; were I still in that position I would offer him a fortune to play for a season on the boards of that house. Why, boys, he can do anything he pleases with his audience! He can make them laugh and cry and laugh again in five minutes. His power was never equalled." Then he asserted that Mr. Spurgeon would live to be the greatest preacher of the age, and that his name would be known everywhere.

If it were not so well attested this incident might be received with some caution; as it is, it may be put alongside the earlier prediction of Richard Knill, and counted as a prophecy concerning the prophetic voice that had just been raised in the great city.

That it was prophetic cannot in the retrospect be gainsaid. As has been already hinted, the times were ripe for a message from God, and it cannot be doubted this was the prepared messenger. Here was a man whom God had prepared, whom God could trust. He had much to learn still of the ways of men, but in the ways of God his apprenticeship was over. He was a preacher full grown—so mature, indeed, that not a few who listened to his earliest sermons in the villages imagined that they could not be his own.

If we seek to find the reason on God's side why he was so much used, "we infer that it was due to the fact that there was nothing in him necessitating delay. He could be placed in the seat of honour, for he had the spiritual grounding requisite. He could serve the relative-end, for the basis of it had been laid in his own heart. The light was there—it needed but a stand adequate to its power of illumination. And specially should be instanced this point—that he had the true Christian foil in respect of honour, namely, humility. He had, as we have just seen forsworn the search of great things for himself and what is this, in the economy of Grace, but the forerunner of promotion?"[1]

But if he had no great stalking ambition for himself, he felt within him a compulsion not to be resisted. On the previous September 27, while he was still at Waterbeach, he wrote to his grandfather: "I have a good field of labour here, but I want to do more if possible. I often wish I were in China, India or Africa, so that I might preach, preach, preach all day long. It would be sweet to die preaching." And it was not only the exercise of preaching that appealed to him, it was the result of it. "Souls, souls, souls," he said, "I hope this rings in my ears, and hurries me on."

On the human side one other quality fitted him for his great vocation. In his first letter to the London church he himself states it, when he writes with the simple emphasis of truth, "I have hardly ever known what the fear of man means." It was almost a reincarnation of the spirit of John Knox. Words written of the Scottish reformer might as truly be written of Spurgeon: "Behind him was the Cross of Christ, before him the judgment seat of Christ, and between the two he stood watching for souls as one that must give account." The spirit that inspired them was the same. W. T. Stead lamented at Melrose that England never had a John Knox in her pulpit. "Maybe not," said the old lady who acted as guide, "but you have Mr. Spurgeon."[2]

Ten years afterwards, in his great sermon on "Baptismal Regeneration," he not only named his hero, he dared to speak as his hero would have spoken. "We want John Knox back again. Do not talk to me of mild and gentle men, of soft manners and squeamish words; we want the fiery Knox, and even though his vehemence should 'ding our pulpits into blads,' it were well if he did but rouse our hearts to action. We want Luther to tell men the truth unmistakably in homely phrase. The velvet hat got into our ministers' mouths of late, but we must unrobe ourselves of soft raiment, and truth must be spoken and nothing but truth; for of all lies which have dragged millions

[1] *C. H.. Spurgeon,* by James Douglas, p. 52.
[2] *Review of Reviews,* Feb. 1892

down to hell, I look upon this as being the most atrocious—that in a
Protestant Church there should be found those who swear that baptism saves
a soul. Call a man a Baptist, or a Presbyterian, or a Dissenter, or a Churchman, that is nothing to me; if he says that baptism saves the soul, out upon
him, out upon him; he states what God never taught, what the Bible never
laid down, and what ought never to be maintained by men who profess that
the Bible, and the whole Bible, is the religion of Protestants."

Let Carlyle describe both Knox and Spurgeon. "Reality is of God's
making: it is alone strong. How many *pented bredds,* pretending to be real,
are fitter to swim than to be worshipped. This Knox cannot live but by fact;
he clung to reality as the shipwrecked sailor to the cliff. He is an instance to
us how a man, by sincerity itself, becomes heroic; it is the grand gift he has.
We find in Knox a good, honest, intellectual talent, no transcendent one, a
narrow, inconsiderable man, as compared with Luther; but in heartfelt,
instinctive adherence to truth, in *sincerity,* as we say, he has no superior. Nay,
we might ask, What equal he has? The heart of him is of the true Prophet
cast. 'He lies there,' said the Earl of Morton, at his grave, 'who never feared
the face of man.' He resembles, more than any of the moderns, an Old-
Hebrew Prophet. The same inflexibility, intolerance, narrow-looking
adherence to God's truth, stern rebuke in the name of God to all that forsake
truth; an Old-Hebrew Prophet in the guise of an Edinburgh minister of the
sixteenth century. We are to take him for that: not require him to be other."[1]

Such a courage was constantly reinforced from its Source. An early
example of the strengthening of his heart amidst human weakness, although
it slightly anticipates our story, may be given in his own words. It is
especially valuable as illustrating the thoroughness and simplicity of his
ministry, even from the beginning. In his exposition of the ninety-first Psalm
in *The Treasury of David,* perhaps the noblest of his writings, he says, "In
the year 1854, when I had scarcely been in London twelve months, the neighbourhood in which I lived was visited by Asiatic cholera, and my
congregation suffered from its inroads. Family after family summoned me to
the bedside of the smitten, and almost every day I was called to visit the
grave. I gave myself up with youthful ardour to the visitation of the sick, and
was sent for from all quarters of the district by persons of all ranks and
religions. I became weary in body and sick at heart. My friends seemed
falling one by one, and I felt or fancied that I was sickening like those around
me. A little more work and weeping would have laid me low amongst the
rest: I felt that my burden was heavier than I could bear, and I was ready to
sink under it. As God would have it, I was returning mournfully from a
funeral, when my curiosity led me to read a paper which was watered up in

---

[1] *The Hero as a Priest,* p. 137. *Heroes and Hero Worship.*

a shoemaker's shop in the Dover Road. It did not look like a trade announcement, nor was it, for it bore in a good bold handwriting these words; 'Because thou hast made the Lord, which is my refuge, even the Most High, thy habitation: there shall no evil befall thee, neither shall any plague come nigh thy dwelling.' The effect on my heart was immediate. Faith appropriated the passage as her own. I felt secure, refreshed, girt with immortality. I went on with my visitation of the dying in a calm and peaceful spirit; I felt no fear of evil and I suffered no harm. The providence which moved the tradesman to place those verses on the window I gratefully acknowledge, and in the remembrance of its marvellous power I adore the Lord my God."

PORTRAIT OF A YOUNG SPURGEON

CHAPTER V

THE PROPHET OF THE PEOPLE

May 1854—*December* 1859

FROM the beginning there were those who recognised the young London preacher as a prophet for his time, and as the weeks went on the discovery was made by increasing numbers. Their estimate was a true one, for in retrospect today no more fitting words can be found to describe him than, "There was a man sent from God." Before he attained his majority he was conscious that he was a man with a mission, and such a man always bears a charmed life.

Dr. Joseph Parker, speaking in the Tabernacle years after, at the Spurgeon Jubilee, said: "A greater Baptist than Mr. Spurgeon had to pass through all the stages he had passed through in popular estimation. A reed shaken with the wind, a nine days' wonder, a flash in the pan, a little momentary flutter —that was the first step. Then the man clothed in soft raiment, seeking for himself, feathering his own nest, making a good thing of it—that was the next step. But a prophet, yea, more than a prophet— that was the last step in the process, and to that step Mr. Spurgeon has come."[1]

But Mr. Spurgeon was a prophet all along. Like Paul, he could in his measure say that the Gospel he preached was not after man. "For neither did I receive it from man, nor was I taught it, but it came to me through revelation of Jesus Christ." Like the elder Pitt, he leaped full-grown upon the stage, an acknowledged prince amongst his fellows, wielding his tools with skill, and fulfilling his task with ease.

" He was not 'dandied and cosseted by a superfine education' into a great preacher, any more than Edmund Burke was prepared by similar advantages to become a distinguished legislator and orator. *Nitor in adversum* was the motto of both."[2] Even a Jewish writer could recognise the seal of God on such a ministry. "Spurgeon was a powerful instance of the difference between scholastic attainment and genius," he says. "There was much of the Old Hebrew Prophet about him, and, like all Puritans, his soul was saturated with the Old Testament."[3]

It was an Anglican journal that declared, at his death, that "every now and then some one takes the world by storm. Without succeeding to anybody else's post, the newcomer makes for himself a definite place in the world's consciousness, and a recognised influence, for good or for ill, in some

---

[1] *South London Press*, June 21, 1884.
[2] *Daily Telegraph*, Feb. 1, 1892.
[3] *Jewish Chronicle*, Feb. 5, 1892.

department of the world's work. He may be statesman, soldier, poet, artist or preacher, but he is unique. That is the type of man whose influence lives on, and whose figure becomes historical. If we mistake not, Mr. Spurgeon belongs to this small class of persons whose career seems independent of circumstances just as their genius is independent of training."[1]

His prophetic gift became daily more evident. Wider and wider grew the circle of his influence, steadier and steadier the light shone. While ecclesiastics debated, and journalists laughed, the people eagerly sought for the building that seemed as if it had been placed in that South London by-way to elude their search. But, like his Master, Spurgeon could not be hid. The scene when he was preaching there in those early days was recalled in a vein of friendly banter by a Society journal, famous for its caricatures, when seventeen years afterwards it selected him as its subject. "In 1853," it said, "the fame of his natural oratory won for him the position of minister of New Park Street Chapel, which soon overflowed with his audiences, so that the narrow streets were blocked, and the public houses were crowded with those who could not find room in the chapel, or who, on leaving it with an awakened sense of sin, felt it to be a relief to quench the spirit in a mug of beer."[2]

That half-humorous, half-true description by a man of the world, reflects the heterogeneous conditions of the time. After a few months it became quite evident that the chapel was all too small for the congregations that gathered in increasing volume. Not only the seats, but the aisles, and even the window-sills were crowded, and hundreds lingered at the doors in the hope of hearing snatches of the sermon. Of course the atmosphere became stifling, and from the beginning that was a thing he could not endure. "His eyes continually hungered for the sight of green fields, and his homestead in later years was always so situated that his ear could drink in the song of the morning lark, and the matin strains of the nightingale, and his heart felt the sweet and refining influence that comes from wood and vale."[3] But though he urged the deacons to improve the ventilation of the place, nothing was attempted until one morning it was discovered that some one had been round the building and had broken a good many of the windows. It was suggested in the officers' meeting that a reward should be offered for the discovery of the person who had dared to do such a thing, but Spurgeon dissuaded them from this course, and the offender was never discovered, though several persons made a shrewd guess as to his identity. If the offer of the reward had been successfully made, Spurgeon himself would, of course, have been both the winner and the culprit. The nearest he ever came to a confession was when

---

[1] *Record*, Feb. 5,1892.
[2] *Vanity Fair*, Dec. 10, 1870.
[3] *Charles Haddon Spurgeon*, by George C. Lorimer, p. 23.

he showed a stout stick "that might have done it." Anyhow, the deacons were stirred to action.

The young preacher was never scared by the assumptions of officials. Once in those early days he was somewhat late for an engagement, an exceptional occurrence, and a pompous deacon met him, severely holding out his watch, face-front, as he approached. As if quite unconscious of the implied rebuke, Spurgeon took the watch in his hand, examined it carefully, and handed it back saying that it really was a very good watch, but seemed somewhat out of repair.

But the crowning audacity was witnessed one Sunday when the preacher, turning to the wall behind the pulpit, declared that "by faith the walls of Jericho fell down, and by faith this wall shall come down too." It was certainly an entirely unconventional method of suggesting an enlargement of the premises; the deacons were aghast at the proposal, and one of them did not scruple to tell him that they must not hear of it again. In spite of that, a little later he carried the church with him, and two thousand pounds were spent in throwing schools and vestries into the chapel, and building a new school at the side with sliding windows, so that it might be used if necessary for the congregation. This work occupied from February 11 to May 27, 1855, and during the alterations the services were held in Exeter Hall.

Such a course would today cause slight comment. Then it was considered quite extraordinary that a congregation should meet for Christian worship in a public hall. If any hall might have been counted suitable for the purpose, it was the already famous gathering-place of the May Meetings, but the proprieties of the time seemed to be seriously compromised by the action. Spurgeon was not indeed the first to hold religious services in secular buildings, any more than Columbus was the first to cross the Atlantic, but previous attempts had been chiefly provincial and inconspicuous. Now in the very heart of the metropolis and under the eye of the London Press this invasion was witnessed, and the leader of the movement had to accept the honour and the opposition which are the usual lot of pioneers.

The hall was crowded from the beginning, the Strand was blocked with carriages, and Spurgeon began to be the talk of the town. Slanders and fables grew with the crowd, nothing seemed too absurd to contribute to the gossip of the hour. Some of the criticisms were amusing, many of them ill-natured, and they need not be recalled; their authors probably were afterwards ashamed of them. On March 4, 1855, he wrote to his father about one "slanderous libel," and says, "For myself I will rejoice, the devil is roused, the Church is awakening, and I am counted worthy to suffer for Christ's sake. Good ballast, father, good ballast."

To this period belong several of the most effective of the legion of caricatures that have enlivened the records of his life. One of them represents a bishop drawing a coach with two horses, "Church and State "; the other the young preacher with flowing hair seated on a locomotive engine—"The Spurgeon"—the titles being "The Slow Coach" and "The Fast Train." Another, entitled "Brimstone and Treacle," represented two preachers, one with eyes and mouth wide open and hands extended, the other in his robes with simpering smile. A third, "Catch-em-alive o'," represents Spurgeon with a tall hat of fly-paper; the people as flies. A fourth, the Archbishop of Canterbury and Mr. Spurgeon as conductors on rival omnibuses. It is evident that, at any rate, Spurgeon was counted as different from the ordinary run of preachers.

These things told upon him severely at first. He writes, for instance, to the lady who was to be his wife: "I am down in the valley partly because of two desperate attacks upon me, but all the scars I receive are scars of honour, so, faint heart, on to the battle."

The deep heart-searching that these attacks caused him may be guessed from a passage in one of his sermons two years later. "I shall never forget the circumstance," he says, "when a slanderous report against my character came to my ears, and my heart was broken in agony because I should have to lose that, in preaching Christ's Gospel. I fell on my knees and said, 'Master, I will not keep back even my reputation from Thee. If I must lose that too, then let it go; it is the dearest thing I have, but it shall go, if, like my Master, they shall say I have a devil and am mad; or, like Him, a drunken man and a winebibber.'" But soon the reproaches came so thick and fast that they wrought their own cure, and a little while after we find him in a different mood. "This I, hope I can say from my heart—if to be made as the mire of the street again, if to be the laughing-stock of fools and the song of the drunkard once more, will make me more serviceable to my Master, and more useful to His cause, I will prefer it to all this multitude, or to all the applause man can give." And to the end he was able to bear blame rather than praise. He valued the goodwill of people as much as the rest of us, and yearned for friendship, but early he had learnt the worthlessness of merely human applause or blame. In a very real sense he was hidden in God's pavilion from the strife of tongues. "I grew inured to falsehood and spite. The stings at last caused me no more pain than if I had been made of iron; but at first they were galling enough."

"I was reading some time ago," he said on one occasion, "an article in a newspaper, very much in my praise. It always makes me feel sad—so sad that I could cry—if ever I see anything praising me; it breaks my heart; I feel I do not deserve it, and then I say, 'Now I must try to be better, so that I may deserve it.' If the world abuses me, I am a match for that; I begin to like it. It may fire all its big guns at me, I will not return a solitary shot, but just store them up, and grow rich upon the old iron."

To his friend to whom he wrote at intervals during the early years, speaking of the early success at New Park Street, and the enlargement of the chapel, he says in a pithy sentence, "Our harvest is too rich for the barn." Later he writes, "Really I never seem to have an hour to call my own. I am always at it, and the people are teasing me almost to death to let them hear my voice. It is strange that such power should be in one small body to crowd Exeter Hall to suffocation, and block up the Strand, so that pedestrians have to turn down by-ways, and all other traffic is at a standstill." "I believe I could secure a crowded audience at dead of night, in a deep snow." The extent of his labours at this time may be guessed by a reference in a subsequent letter. "Eleven times this week have I gone forth to battle, and at least thirteen services are announced for next week. Congregations more than immense. Everywhere, at all hours, places are crammed to the doors. The devil is wide awake, but so too is the Master."

Voices which gave a friendly note were not wanting. One wrote: "It was a remarkable sight to see this round-faced country youth thus placed in a position of such solemn and arduous responsibility, yet addressing himself to the fulfilment of its onerous duties with a gravity, self-possession and vigour that proved him well fitted to the task he had assumed."[1] Another, "We found him neither extravagant nor vulgar. His voice is clear and musical; his language plain; his style flowing yet terse; his method lucid and orderly; his matter sound and suitable; his tone and spirit cordial; his remarks always pithy and pungent, sometimes familiar and colloquial, yet never light nor coarse, much less profane. To the pith of Jay and the plainness of Rowland Hill, he adds much of the familiarity of the Huntingtonian order of ultra-Calvinistic preachers."[2] Still another, "His appearance and labours in this metropolis have excited in all religious circles, and even beyond them, attention and surprise, if not admiration. Scarcely more than a youth in years, comparatively untutored, and without a name, he enters the greatest city in the world, and almost simultaneously commands audiences larger than have usually listened to her most favoured preachers "[3]

"Beyond a doubt," says Edwin Paxton Hood in *The Lamps of the Temple,* "the lad is impudent, very impudent; were he not, he could not, at such an age, be where he is, or what he is. It must be admitted that amongst all the popularities there is no popularity like his. Among this—remarkable or not, according to the reader's ideas—is the treatment of the young preacher by his brethren—shall we say brethren?—in the ministry. We understand they have generally agreed to treat him as a black sheep. He is said to imitate Robert Hall and William Jay. We should give him a different location. He

---

[1] *The Friend.*
[2] *The Patriot.*
[3] *The Christian Weekly News*, March 4, 1856.

has the unbridled and undisciplined fancy of Hervey without his elegance; but instead of that the drollery of Berridge and the ubiquitous earnestness of Rowland Hill, in his best days. He who determines never to use a word that shall grate harshly on the ears of a refined taste, may be certain that he will never be extensively useful; the people love the man who will condescend to their idiom, and the greatest preachers—those who have been the great apostles of a nation—have always condescended to this. Bossuet, Massillon, Hall, Chalmers, McAll, were the doctors of the pulpit; at their feet sat the refinement, the scholarship, the politeness of then times; but such men as Luther and Latimer, St. Clara and Keen, Whitfield and Christmas Evans—such men always seized on the prevailing dialect and made it tell with immense power on their auditors." As to Spurgeon, "he is the topic and theme of remark now in every part of England; and severe as some of his castigators are, he returns their castigations frequently with a careless, downright hearty goodwill."

One of Mr. Spurgeon's earliest and staunchest friends was Mr. James Grant, editor of *The, Morning Advertiser,* a paper that then ranked with *The Times* in circulation and influence. After the second service in Exeter Hall, he. wrote, "It will easily be believed how great must be the popularity of this almost boyish preacher, when we mention that yesterday both morning and evening the large hall, capable of holding from four thousand to five thousand people, was filled in every part. There can be no doubt that Mr. Spurgeon possesses superior talents, while in some of his happier flights he rises to a high order of pulpit oratory. It is in pathos that he excels, though he does not himself seem to be aware of that fact. He is quite an original preacher; has evidently made George Whitefield his model; and like that unparalleled preacher, the prince of pulpit orators, is very fond of striking apostrophes."[1]

In the following year Mr. Grant reverted to the same comparison. "Never since the days of George Whitefield," he said, "has any minister of religion acquired so great a reputation as this Baptist preacher, in so short a time. Here is a mere youth, a perfect stripling, only twenty-one years of age, incomparably the most popular preacher of the day. There is no man within her Majesty's dominions who could draw such immense audiences; and none who, in his happier efforts, can so completely enthral the attention, and delight the minds of his hearers. Some of his appeals to the conscience, some of his remonstrances with the careless, constitute specimens of a very high order of oratorial power. When pronouncing the doom of those who live and die in a state of impenitence, he makes the vast congregation quake and quail in their seats. He places their awful destiny in such vivid colours before their

---

[1] *The Morning Advertiser*, Feb. 19, 1855.

eyes that they almost imagine they are already in the regions of darkness and despair."[1]

The shrewdness of this appreciation may be admitted when we find Spurgeon himself writing in 1879, "There is no end to the interest that attaches to such a man as George Whitefield. Often as I have read his life, I am conscious of a distinct quickening whenever I turn to it. *He lived,* other men seem only to be half-alive; but Whitefield was all life, fire, wing, force. My own model, if I may have such a thing in due subordination to my Lord, is George Whitefield; but with unequal footsteps must I follow in his glorious track."

To Spurgeon we might apply the words of John Wesley, when, preaching the funeral sermon of George Whitefield, he spoke of his unparalleled zeal, his indefatigable activity, his tender-heartedness to the poor, deep gratitude, tender friendship, frankness and openness, courage and intrepidity, great plainness of speech, steadiness, integrity. "Have we read," he said, "of any person since the Apostles who testified the Gospel of the Grace of God through so widely extended a space, through so large a part of the habitable world? Have we read of any person who called so many thousands, so many myriads, of sinners to repentance?"

In the midst of these labours, it was little wonder that his voice was overtaxed; he had not learnt yet its perfect use. The services in Exeter Hall proved almost too much for him. His wife records that "sometimes his voice would almost break and fail as he pleaded with sinners to come to Christ, or magnified the Lord in His sovereignty and righteousness. A glass of chili vinegar always stood on a shelf under the desk before him, and I knew what to expect when he had recourse to that remedy. I remember with strange vividness the Sunday evening when he preached from the text, 'His name shall endure for ever.' It was a subject in which he revelled, it was his chief delight to exalt his glorious Saviour, and he seemed in that discourse to be pouring out his very soul and life in homage and adoration before his Gracious King. But I really thought he would have died there, in face of all those people. At the end he made a mighty effort to recover his voice; but utterance well-nigh failed, and only in broken accents could the pathetic peroration be heard— 'Let my name perish, but let Christ's name last for ever! Jesus! *Jesus!* JESUS! Crown Him Lord of all! You will not hear me say anything else. These are my last words in Exeter Hall for this time. Jesus! *Jesus!* JESUS! Crown *Him* Lord of all!' and then he fell back almost fainting in the chair behind him."

---

[1] *The Morning Advertiser,* Feb. 18, 1856.

When the congregation returned to the enlarged chapel on May 31, 1855, it was discovered that the expenditure on it was almost wasted, for while several hundreds more gained admittance, the disappointed crowds were greater than ever, and after a year's trial Exeter Hall had again to be requisitioned. Meanwhile as occasion served, Spurgeon, like Whitefield, took to the fields. Writing before their marriage to Mrs. Spurgeon on June 3 of the same year, he says about a service in a field at Hackney: "Yesterday I climbed to the summit of a minister's glory. My congregation was enormous, I think ten thousand, but certainly twice as many as at Exeter Hall. The Lord was with me, and the profoundest silence was observed; but oh, the close— never did mortal man receive a more enthusiastic oration! I wonder I am alive! After the service five or six gentlemen endeavoured to clear a passage, but I was borne along, amid cheers, and prayers, and shouts, for about a quarter of an hour—it really seemed more like a week! I was hurried round and round the field without hope of escape until, suddenly seeing a nice open carriage, with two occupants, standing near, I sprang in, and begged them to drive away. This they most kindly did, and I stood up, waving my hat, and crying, "The blessing of God be with you!" while from thousands of heads the hats were lifted and cheer after cheer was given. Surely amid these plaudits I can hear the low rumbling of an advancing storm of reproaches; but even this I can bear for the Master's sake."

Nor was he mistaken. His friend W. P. Lockhart, at his death, recalled some of the phases of the storm so soon to break: "One remembers that long years ago, on the occasion of some popular demonstration in London, his carriage was driven through the crowd, and when its occupant was recognised he was heartily hooted by the mob, and one remembers also the scornful notices of a portion of the Press, which drew from him one of the most striking things he over uttered—'A true Christian is one who fears God, and is hated by the *Saturday Review.*' Perhaps one of the most remarkable criticisms in those early days was that of Lord Houghton—then Monckton Milnes who said of him, 'When he mounted the pulpit you might have thought of him as a hairdresser's assistant; when he left it, he was an inspired apostle.' The people might frown or fawn, it mattered little to him, not one jot did he abate of what he believed to be the truth of God. His Pauline Calvinism, his sturdy Puritanism, his old-fashioned apostolic gospel, remained unchanged to the end."

For a year all the services continued in the enlarged chapel at New Park Street. The two outstanding occasions, when all the gatherings were wonderful, were the Watch-night Service at the end of 1855, and his marriage on January 8, 1856. One of his earliest friends was John Anderson, the minister of Helensburgh, and he visited London this year. His attention was first attracted to him by the reading of one of his printed sermons. "I had no sooner read a few paragraphs of it than I said, 'Here at last is a preacher to my mind, one whom not only I, but Paul himself, I am persuaded, were he on earth, would hear, approve and own.' I remember well saying to myself, 'I would rather have been the author of that sermon than of all the sermons, or volumes of sermons, published in my day.' I had lately before this been reading Guthrie and Caird, but here was something entirely different, and, to my mind, in all that constitutes a genuine and good Gospel sermon, infinitely superior."

By the courtesy of a police officer, Mr. Anderson, because he had come from Scotland, was admitted to the chapel, already crowded when he arrived.

"My friend and I thought ourselves happy, like Eutychus of old, in being permitted to sit 'in a window,' with a dense crowd in the passage at our feet. I asked a man near me if he came regularly; he said he did. 'Why, then,' I asked, 'do you not take a seat?' 'Scat,' he replied, 'such a thing is not to be had for love or money. I got a ticket for leave to stand.' The Church, I am told, is seated for fifteen hundred, but what with the schoolroom and passages, which were choke-full, there could not have been fewer in it than three thousand. The service commenced with the singing of a hymn. Never did I hear such singing; it was like the voice of many waters, or the roll of thunder. Then came the prayer. Phrenologically speaking, I should say that veneration is not largely developed in Mr. Spurgeon; yet that prayer was one of the most remarkable and impressive I have ever heard. He prayed for the unconverted. 'Some,' he said, 'were present who were in that state, who in all likelihood would never be in that or any other church again—who were that night to hear their last sermon—who, the next Lord's day, would not be in this world, and where would they be? There was but one place where they would be—in Hell.' He then said, or rather cried out, 'O God! must they perish? Wilt thou not save them and make the sermon the means of their conversion?' The effect was overwhelming: many wept, and I am not ashamed to say I was one of them.

"Mr. Spurgeon is equally great in the tender and in the terrible. Nor is he without humour. His taste, according to some, is bad. It is, I admit often so. But then think of the immaturity of his years. I was told he was conceited. I saw no proofs of it; and if I had, was I on that account to think less of his sermons? I do not say that I will not eat good bread because the baker is conceited. His conceit may be a bad thing for himself, his bread is very good for me. I am far from thinking Mr. Spurgeon perfect. In this respect he is not like Whitefield, who from the first was as perfect an orator as he was at the last. In respect of his power over an audience, and a London one in particular, I should say he is not inferior to Whitefield himself."[1]

---

[1] *Life and Work of Charles Haddon Spurgeon*, by G. Holden Pike, Vol. II. p. 223.

Mr. Anderson afterwards became Mr. Spurgeon warm friend, and he treasured a book presented to him in which was the following inscription—

"To my dear friend John Anderson, whose boundless generosity compels me to add an injunction to all men, women and children on the face of the earth, that none of them dare accept this volume of him when he shall offer it, seeing that this is a small token of the undying love of

"C. H. SPURGEON."

February 21, 1859.

As to the question of conceit, that criticism followed him all his life, and in later years he gave a sufficient answer. "A friend of mine was calling upon him some time ago," writes one after his death, "and happened to say, 'Do you know, Mr. Spurgeon, some people think you conceited?' The great preacher smiled indulgently, and after a pause said, 'Do you see those bookshelves? They contain hundreds, nay, thousands of my sermons translated into every language under heaven. Well, now, add to this that ever since I was twenty years old there never has been built a place large enough to hold the numbers of people who wished to hear me preach, and, upon my honour, when I think of it, I wonder I am not more conceited than I am.'" Upon which the writer remarks, "That is the kind of bonhomie that disarms criticism."[1]

Thirty-five years afterwards, Sir William Robertson Nicoll takes down the volume of Mr. Spurgeon's *Sermons* preached in 1855, and this is what he says—

"The life in Mr. Spurgeon's book, its red-hot earnestness, at once impresses the reader. Those who think of the preacher as in early days little more than a buffoon, might be challenged to find in his first volume of sermons anything to provoke a smile. The burden of all is 'Flee from the wrath to come; lay hold on eternal life.' The order is intentional, for the supreme thought in the preacher's mind is the imminent peril of his hearers. He does not shrink from the terrible pictures of the damned in their misery and despair; but the earnestness of his pleading with men is even more awful. Flee from the wrath to come; this burden is hardly found now, not even in the sermons of the same distinguished preacher. There is something soporific in the air. But if the object of preaching is to reproduce the New Testament, a change must come, and perhaps it may come from an unexpected place. Perhaps the interpreters of natural law may yet tell us that punishment is in

---

[1] *English Illustrated Magazine*, March 1892.

its nature everlasting, and then Christianity will come with its gospel declaring that the sentence of the law may be reversed.

"It goes along with this that Mr. Spurgeon's view of the world, even in his youth, was severe. Perhaps these moods come ever and anon to all greatly-endowed natures; moods produced by unsought and wringing facts; moods when love becomes anxiety, when hope sinks to misgiving and faith to hope, when it seems as if the world were indeed very evil and the times waxing late.

"The young preacher was from the first a theologian. We do not mean merely that he was a Calvinist, he was much more than that. He possessed the theological temper, without which the final message of the Holy Ghost in the Apostolic Epistles is practically useless and enigmatic.

"'I think I am bound to give myself unto reading, and not to grieve the Spirit by unthought-of effusions,' says the youth. He has been faithful to that conviction, and to this diligence the splendour of his long and high career is largely due. We have often expressed the conviction that even by his own admirers scant justice is done to Mr. Spurgeon's intellectual power; the maturity, the freshness, the range of this book, only deepen this belief. Coming from a youth of twenty, it is a miraculous production. Be that as it may, Mr. Spurgeon has never presumed on his talents, he has gone on storing up treasure, and speaks from a full and exercised mind."[1]

About this time a pamphlet was issued by a Doctor of Divinity, which caused a great stir in religious circles. It was entitled "Why so popular? An hour with the Rev. C. H. Spurgeon." It is addressed to Mr. Spurgeon himself, and says—

"Your ministry has attained the dignity of a moral phenomenon. You stand on an eminence which, since the days of Whitefield, no minister—with a single exception, if indeed there be one—of any church in this realm has attained. You have access to a larger audience than the magic of any other name can gather. You have raised a church from obscurity to eminence, perhaps I might add (rumour is my authority) from spiritual indigence to affluence.

"Nor has God given you favour with your own people alone. Blessed with a vigorous mind, and great physical energy, you have consecrated all to your Master's service, and hence you have become an untiring evangelist. East, west, north, south, in England, Wales and Scotland, your preaching is appreciated by the people, and has been blessed of God. No place has been large enough to receive the crowds that flocked to hear the 'young White-

---

[1] *The British Weekly*, June 27, 1890.

field,' and on many occasions you have preached the glorious Gospel, the sward of the green earth being the floor on which, and the vault of the blue heaven the canopy under which, you announced to uncounted thousands 'all the words of this life.'"

At length arrangements were made to return to Exeter Hall for the evening service, the morning service being continued in the chapel. The first Exeter Hall service in this second series was on June 8, 1856, and the crowds were, if possible, greater than before—so great indeed that it became clear that a larger building was necessary. So on October 6 a meeting was held to initiate the enterprise; the structure was spoken of as likely to be "the largest chapel in the world," and a fund was started for its erection. The need became all the more apparent when the proprietors of Exeter Hall intimated that it was impossible for them to let their building continuously to one congregation.

Some temporary expedient was necessary. Happily at this time the Surrey Music Hall, capable of holding ten thousand to twelve thousand people, became available. It was erected in the Royal Surrey Gardens for concert purposes, and the bold idea occurred to several people that it might be utilised for Mr. Spurgeon's services. Some thought it would be too large, others that it would be very unsuitable to hold Divine service in a place of worldly amusement. This aspect of the question would present no difficulty to us in the present day, so many ventures of a similar nature have since been made, but nothing of the kind had then been attempted.

The news that Spurgeon was to preach in the Concert Hall ran through London like wildfire. "In the squares, the streets, the lanes, the alleys, as well as in the workshops and counting-houses, and all the chief places of concourse, it has been, through each successive day, the one great object of thought and converse." On the Sunday evening, October 19, 1856, the crowds that had been gathering since the afternoon were enormous. The streets in the vicinity were packed with people. Ten thousand persons were in the Hall and another ten thousand in the Gardens unable to enter. The sight of the people at first unnerved the preacher, but he soon rallied, and took his place in the rostrum to pass through the ordeal of his life.

His friend Dr. Campbell, who was present, wrote—

"Ecclesiastically viewed Sunday last was one of the most eventful nights that have descended on the metropolis for generations. On that occasion the largest, most commodious and most beautiful building erected for public amusement in this mighty city was taken possession of for the purpose of proclaiming the gospel of salvation. There, where for a long period wild boasts had been exhibited, and wilder men had been accustomed to congregate, in countless multitudes, for idle pastime, was gathered together the largest audience that ever met in any edifice in these Isles to listen to the voice of a Nonconformist minister."

The service began before the appointed time. After a few words of greeting there came a prayer, a hymn, and the Scripture reading, with a running comment, according to the general custom. After another hymn, prayer was again being offered when suddenly there was a cry of "Fire! The galleries are giving way, the place is falling." It may have been hysterical excitement, much more probably it was the criminal work of miscreants bent on plunder. A terrible panic ensued, many of the people rushed for the doors, stumbled, fell, were piled on each other; the balustrade of the stairs broke and people toppled over. Seven lost their lives, and twentyeight were taken to hospital seriously injured.

In the midst of it all, the preacher, ignorant of the extent of the disaster, unconscious that there had been any fatal accident, endeavoured to quell the tumult. Many of the people resumed their seats when it became apparent there was no cause for alarm, and in response to repeated cries, Mr. Spurgeon endeavoured to preach. He told them that the text which he had intended to take was in the third chapter of Proverbs, the thirty-third verse, "The curse of the Lord is upon the house of the wicked; but He blesseth the habitation of the just," and asked the people to retire gradually. There was renewed disturbance, and a hymn was sung. Again the preacher urged the people to retire, and then he himself was carried fainting from the pulpit, and the next day, stunned and helpless, taken to a friend's house in Croydon that he might escape callers and in quietness recover his mental balance. As he was being assisted from the carriage at Croydon a working-man saw him, and stammered: "It's Mr. Spurgeon, isn't it? It must be his ghost, for last night I saw him carried out dead from the Surrey Gardens Music Hall."

If he had been dead his enemies would have rejoiced, but, being alive, he was traduced and slandered by almost the entire newspaper press. *The Saturday Review* excelled itself in vituperation—the wonder was that such a personage could be notable at all, it was almost useless to hold up Mr. Spurgeon as a very ordinary impostor: "We do not see why Mr. Spurgeon should have a monopoly of brazen instruments south of the Thames. Whitefield used to preach at fairs. In these days of open competition we perceive no reason why the practice should not be inverted. The innovation would only be the substitution of one set of amusements for another; or rather, an addition to our list of Sunday sports." "This hiring of places of amusement for Sunday preaching is a novelty, and a powerful one. It looks as if religion were at its last shift. It is a confession of weakness, rather than a sign of strength. It is not wrestling with Satan in his strongholds—to use the old earnest Puritan language—but entering into a very cowardly truce and alliance with the world." Nearly all the London papers joined in the chorus of condemnation.

Meanwhile Mr. Spurgeon, unconscious of most of it, spent days of depression and heart-searching in his retirement; no light shone upon him, until on walking in his friend's garden, suddenly the message came to his heart concerning his Master: "Wherefore God has highly exalted Him, and given Him a name that is above every name," and straightway he was comforted. It mattered nothing what became of Spurgeon if Jesus was exalted and praised. So with only an interval of one Sunday, he was back again, discoursing on the text in New Park Street Chapel on November 2, 1856. He declared his forgiveness of those whose malice had caused the accident, but asserted his determination to preach in the place again.

He describes these days of darkness in his first book, *The Saint and his Saviour:* "Who can conceive the anguish of my sad spirit? I refused to be comforted: tears were my meat by day and dreams my terror by night. My thoughts were all a case of knives, cutting my heart in pieces until a kind of stupor of grief ministered a mournful medicine to me. I sought and found a solitude which seemed congenial to me. I could tell my griefs to the flowers, and the dews could weep with me. My Bible, once, my daily food, was but a hand to lift the sluices of my woe. Prayer yielded no balm to me. There came the 'slander of many'—barefaced fabrications, libellous slanders, and barbarous accusations. These alone might have scooped out the last drop of consolation from my cup of happiness, but the worst had come to the worst, and the utmost malice of the enemy could do no more."

"On a sudden, like a flash of lightning from the sky, my soul returned to me. I was free, the iron fetter was broken in pieces, my prison door was open, I leaped for joy of heart. The Name, the precious Name of Jesus, was like Ithuriel's spear, bringing back my soul to its right and proper state. I was a man again, and, what is more, a believer. The garden in which I stood became an Eden to me, and the spot was most solemnly consecrated in my most grateful memory. Then did I give to my Well-Beloved a song touching my Well-Beloved. Then did I cast my burden on the. Lord. I could have riven the very firmament to get at Him, to cast myself at His feet, and lie there bathed in the tears of joy and love. Never since the day of my conversion had I known so much of Him, never had my spirit leaped with such unutterable delight. Scorn, tumult, and war seemed less than nothing for His sake. I girded up my loins to run before His chariot and shout forth His glory."

Two more Sundays elapsed, and then he was back to the scene of the tragedy. But not now in the evening; it seemed to be the safer course, although it was even more daring, to hold the morning service in the Music Hall, and from November 23, 1856, to December 1859 this arrangement was continued. The smallest acquaintance with Church matters will make it apparent that this was a far severer test of the preacher's power over the people than the service on the Sunday evening. But they came in unceasing crowds, and an entirely new set of people were touched. The matter cannot be put better than it was, thirty years later, by one of the leading London newspapers, which at the time of the accident had not a hard enough word to say of him.

"Curiously enough," it writes, "it was an accident of a serious nature that first drew the attention of the world in general to the rising influence of Mr. Spurgeon. The young preacher—he was then very young—had already secured an immense following on the south side of London. But the world on the other side, the world north of the Thames, the world of society and of the clubs and the West End, the world of Bloomsbury and Fitzroy Square, the world of Maida Vale and Highgate, all these various microcosms knew little or nothing of the powerful young preacher whose congregations had already far outgrown the capacity of New Park Street Chapel in Southwark."

But when the accident happened—

"Mr. Spurgeon became famous at once. Society went out of its way, put itself to trouble, to hear the young preacher whose admirers could not be contained in a building of less size than the Great Music Hall.

"Mr. Spurgeon, of course, would have been known to the whole public of these countries in time, even if there had never been a panic and a rush and a catastrophe in the Surrey Music Hall. But he found himself famous the morning after the accident, and he kept his fame. Naturally he met with some severe and scornful criticism. One celebrated critic, who made a special pilgrimage to the south side to hear him, contrasted him in words of melancholy scorn with Irving and Whitefield. But the critic had not heard Irving or Whitefield. Perhaps if he had been a critic when Irving was still preaching, he would have drawn disparaging comparison between him also and Whitefield. Perhaps if he had lived in Whitefield's days he would have lamented the degeneracy of the age that accepted such a man as a popular preacher. As a pulpit orator he had special advantages. He had a voice of marvellous power, penetration, and variety of tone. His voice has been compared with that of O'Connell, of the late Lord Derby, of Mr. Gladstone, of Dr. McNeile, the famous Liverpool preacher, and of various other orators living or dead. He had resources, readily drawn upon, of pathos and a certain kind of humour; and he could vivify his sermons by all manner of telling and homely, sometimes perhaps too homely, illustrations. He never preached over his listeners or at them. He always talked directly to them. He was always intensely in earnest. His emotions carried himself, as well as his congregation, away.

"The qualities by which Mr. Spurgeon secured his influence have ever since enabled him to keep it, and broaden it, and deepen it. It can hardly be said that his influence passed much outside what we may call Mr. Spurgeon's own denominational sphere. It did not overflow the obvious limitations to anything like the same extent that Mr. Beecher's influence did at one time in the United States. The various little worlds of which we have already spoken went out of their courses to hear Mr. Spurgeon, but they went back again."[1]

All that was to some extent true, but Mr. Spurgeon had compelled even the highest in the land to listen. True, his appeal was chiefly to the middle class. At the time of the accident one London newspaper seized on this point. Commenting on the ordinary congregations, it asks, and it might almost be dealing with the conditions of today—

"But where are the artisan classes? So very scanty is their attendance upon the most noted preachers, that it is their adhesion to Mr. Spurgeon which has made that gentleman a prodigy and a phenomenon. In the list of killed and wounded at the Music Hall are journeymen painters, tanners, and milliners' girls. It is worth while to ask the reason why.

"A single hearing is sufficient to answer the question, supposing that the hearer can also see. There never yet was a popular orator who did not talk more and better with his arms than with his tongue. Mr. Spurgeon knows this instinctively, and when he has read his text he does not fasten his eyes on a manuscript and his hands on a cushion. As soon as he begins to talk he begins to act; and that not as if declaiming on the stage, but as if conversing with you in the street. He seems to shake hands with you all round and put every one at his case. His colours are taken from the earth and sky of common human experience and aspirations. He dips his pencil, so to speak, in the veins of the nearest spectator, and makes his work a part of every man's nature. He does not narrate occurrences, he describes them with a rough graphic force and faithfulness. He does not reason out his doctrines, but announces, explains, and applies them. In the open air some one may interrupt or interrogate, and the response is a new effect. In short, this man preaches Christianity, his Christianity, at any rate, as Ernest Jones preaches Chartism, and as Gough preaches temperance."[2]

Dr. Campbell again spoke in defence of the young preacher—

---

[1] *Daily Telegraph*, Jan. 14, 1888.
[2] *The Evening Star*.

"Mr. Spurgeon is in all respects original," he said, "a preacher of Heaven's own formation; and hence all is nature and all is life, while that life and that nature are among the millions a power. Is he abrupt, blunt, direct? It is nature. Is he idiomatic, colloquial, playful, dramatic? It is nature. Nature is power; artifice impotence. Without nature no man can please much and please long. Nature responds only to nature; it turns a deaf ear to all that is contrary. Art may captivate the fancy; nature alone can subdue the heart. What., then, is the source of this unprecedented attraction? It is primarily in the *soul of the man,* a soul large, liberal, and loving.

"Since the days of Whitefield no man has exacted so much attention in this metropolis, and the result, as in a former age, is a great diversity of sentiment. Such things, however, would seem, as in the case of Whitefield, only to help him onward. When Foote, of unhappy memory, wrote *The Minor,* bringing Whitefield on the stage as Dr. Squintum—for the great orator was marked by that visual peculiarity—he did much to excite public attention and confirm Whitefield's hold of the better section of society. All such opposition and misrepresentation only tend to further the popularity it is sought to check. It operates like air on the furnace, which would languish and die but for the action of the atmosphere.

"Mr. Spurgeon is no negative theologian. Whitefield in this, as in other respects, had much in common with Spurgeon. Essences must not be confounded with accidents. The peculiarities which often distinguish great men have no necessary connection with the truth which they propagate in common. A firm friend of Whitefield has left it on record that, whether he looked grave or gay, it was nature acting in him. His laugh was hearty, his weeping 'loud and passionate,' and while his manner was natural, his language was simple—John Bunyan's English. It was indeed that he used 'market language.' Spurgeon, too, we repeat, is in everything a child of nature; he is everywhere at home. A master of dialogue, he is not less master of powerful declamations—the two great things for which Whitefield himself was remarkable."[1]

For three years the services in the Music Hall continued with unabated success, and the current of public opinion gradually changed. Even *The National Review* gave him a good word. Quoting one of his sayings, it said there was nothing vulgar in it, though it was grotesque as a gargoyle; and contrasting his style with much of the ornate and hazy preaching of the day, it declared—

---

[1] *British Standard*, Jan. 9, 1857.

"If we must choose between the two, we do not know whether it is not less bad to handle spiritual truths as you would handle a bullock, than to handle them as you would handle a mist."

A costermonger of Kennington, questioned in 1908, remembered Spurgeon in the Surrey Gardens days: "He was a stout man and wore a broad-brimmed hat. People used to say that he ran down the theatre, and yet he copied a lot of his antics from there."[1]

To gain entrance to the services, tickets were necessary—this in order to prevent the entrance of people bent on mischief. All sorts of folk applied for these tickets. A service in 1857 is described by "an eyewitness": "Every seat was occupied by half-past ten o'clock, when the doors were opened to the public, then there was a rush of excited and hurried people, and in ten minutes every inch of standing room was occupied. Dr. Livingstone sat on the platform, and the Princess Royal, as well as the Duchess of Sutherland, were said to be present." Lord Palmerston on one occasion secured a ticket, but was prevented attending by his old enemy, the gout. It was even said that Queen Victoria, disguised, was herself once present.

A reference in the *Greville Memoirs* has often been quoted. It bears date February 8, 1857.

"I have just come from hearing the celebrated Mr. Spurgeon. He is certainly very remarkable, and undeniably a fine character; not remarkable in person; in face resembling a smaller Macaulay; a very clear and powerful voice which was heard through the hall; a manner natural, impassioned, and without affectation or extravagance; wonderful fluency and command of language, abounding in illustration, and very often of a familiar kind, but without anything ridiculous or irreverent. He preached for about three-quarters of an hour, and, to judge by the use of handkerchiefs and the audible sobs, with great effect."[2]

Principal Tulloch, himself a famous preacher, visited the Surrey Music Hall in May 1858, in company with Professor Ferrier, the metaphysician, and in his Life, written by Mrs. Oliphant, the following descriptive passage occurs, Mr. Spurgeon being described by the authoress as "one of the wonders of society, competing with Mr. Charles Kean, if not surpassing him, in public interest."

---

[1] *The Surrey Comet*, Oct. 1908.
[2] The Greville Memoirs (Third Part), Vol. II. p. 83.

"We have just been to hear Spurgeon," Tulloch wrote, "and have both been so much impressed that I wish to give you my impressions while they are fresh. As we came out we both confessed, 'There is no doubt about *that,*' and I was struck with Ferrier's remarkable expression, 'I feel it would do me good to hear the like of that, it sat so close to reality.'

"The sermon is about the most real thing I have come in contact with for a long while. Guthrie is as sounding brass and a tinkling cymbal to it; and although there is not the elevated thought and descriptive felicity of Caird (the latter especially, however, not wanting), there is more power. Power, in fact, and life are its characteristics, and I could not help being pleased that I had hit upon the man pretty well in the notice of him along with Robertson and Guthrie, which was never published.

"The place is fully adapted for preaching, being the largest, lightest, and airiest building I ever saw. It was crammed, of course, but not in the least uncomfortable, as round all the thickly-studded benches there was a wide and open corridor, with window-doors open, out and in of which you could walk into the gardens (Surrey Gardens) as you liked; and Ferrier kept taking a turn now and then during the sermon. He began the service with a short prayer, then sang the twenty-third Psalm, but instead of our fine old version, some vile version, in which the simple beauty of the hymn is entirely lost. Then he read and expounded the thirty-second chapter (I think) of Numbers. His remarks were very good and to the point, with no display or misplaced emotion. He then prayed more at length, and this was the part of the service I least liked.

"He preached from the same chapter he read, about the spies from the land of Canaan—the good and bad spies. It was a parable, he said, of religion. Canaan is not rightly taken as a type of heaven, but of the religious life. Then, after speaking of men of the world judging religion (which, however, they had no right to do) from those who professed it rather than from the Bible— which in thought and grasp was the fullest part of the sermon—he said he would speak of two classes of people, the bad spies first., those who made a great ado about religion and did not show its power, and then the good spies. His description here was graphic beyond what I can give you an idea of, the most telling satire, cutting home, yet not overdone, as he spoke of the gloomy religionist who brought up a bad report of the land of religion, making himself and his wife and children miserable, drawing down the blinds on a Sunday, 'almost most religious when most miserable, and most miserable when most religious'; then the meek-faced fellow, who can pray all Sunday and preach by the hour, and cheat all Monday, always ready with his prayer-book, but keeping a singular cash-book, wouldn't swear, but would cheat and lie. Then, again, he showed still higher powers of pathos in describing the good spies—the old blind saint who had served God for fifty years and never found Him fail; the consumptive girl testifying of the goodness of her Saviour as the dews of death gathered on her brow. And then of all who only lived as Christians—the good wife who converted her husband by her untiring gentleness, and having supper ready even at twelve o'clock at night; the servant who, because she was religious, cleaned knives better without losing their edge; the. Christian merchant; the wife who, unknown to fame, and having no time for teaching or district visiting, achieved her household work day by day.

"In fact, the whole was a wonderful display of mental vigour and Christian sense, and gave me a great idea of what good such a man may do. The impression made upon Ferrier, which he has just read over to me as he has written it to his wife, 'is driving downright.' He improves in look, too, a little, as he warms in preaching. At first he certainly is not interesting in face or figure—very fat and podgy; but there is no doubt of the fellow, look as he may. His voice is of rare felicity, as clear as a bell—not a syllabic lost."[1]

On the day of National Humiliation on account of the Indian Mutiny, Mr. Spurgeon preached in the Crystal Palace to a congregation of 23,654 persons, counted in at the turnstiles, and up to that date the assembly was described as "the largest ever addressed by a preacher of the Gospel in Europe or the world"—which was perhaps true. The trains began to run at half-past seven in the morning, and by noon the immense congregation was ready for the preacher. The collection amounted to £675, including £200 from the Crystal Palace Company, and was "not far short of all the other collections in London put together." The text was from Micah, sixth chapter, and ninth verse: "Hear ye the rod, and who hath appointed it." The service was acknowledged to be the most memorable thing in connection with the observance of the day, but, of course, there was the. usual bout of criticism.

Three interesting incidents may be mentioned—

"Seated near the pulpit," writes one who was present, "I observed Mrs. Spurgeon take her place just before her husband appeared, and that she was visibly affected by the mighty concourse of souls, all with upturned faces, and fixed gaze upon one man, and all about to be thrilled to the core by that man's impassioned appeals to them to be saved alive. While Mrs. Spurgeon was concealing her emotion as best she might, I saw the pastor beckon far off with his forefinger to one of the deacons, a stout, greyhaired man of rubicund complexion, and with a defect in one eye. He was in very glossy black, which was the orthodox dissenting uniform in those far-off days, and walked with a limp which made his progress up the pulpit, or rather platform,

---

[1] *Life of Principal Tulloch*, by Mrs. Oliphant, p. 132.

steps tantalisingly slow. Some brief, but evidently important, instruction was at last whispered by Mr. Spurgeon in the lame man's ear, and twenty-five thousand people were agog with curiosity to know what this could possibly be at such a time, when the whole vast place was quivering with anticipated and suppressed emotional excitement. I happened to be seated so near Mrs. Spurgeon that when the worthy deacon 'made for her,' in his crab-like, ponderous way, it was unavoidable that I, at least, one of the vast and silent crowd of expectants, should hear what had delayed the pastor, and what the urgent matter was which he had at such a critical moment to communicate. In a hoarse whisper I heard this: 'Mr. Spurgeon says, please will you change your seat, so that he will not be able to see you; it ('it' was doubtless Mrs. Spurgeon's emotion) makes him nervous,' and the lady immediately moved to another seat not visible from the preacher's place."[1]

The second incident in connection with the service happened some days previous to it, when Mr. Spurgeon went to the Crystal Palace to try the acoustics of the place. Having to say something, he said something worth saying—"Behold the Lamb of God that taketh away the sin of the world." A workman busy in one of the galleries heard the words, that seemed to come to him from heaven, and, smitten with conviction of sin, he put down his tools and went home, nor did he rest until he was able to rejoice in Christ as his Saviour.

The third incident has a psychological interest. Though Mr. Spurgeon was not conscious of any special strain at the time, he went to sleep that Wednesday night and did not awake until Friday morning!

The turn of the tide in Mr. Spurgeon's favour is marked by a letter which appeared in *The Times* on April 13, 1857, supported by a laudatory leading article, both probably written by the same hand, and that hand not unfamiliar with the Editor's writing-table. *The Times* in those days was the mirror of public opinion, and its utterance is therefore the more notable. Apart from its biographical interest, the letter is worth transcribing for its literary flavour. It was entitled "Preaching *and* Preaching "—

"SIR,

"One Sunday morning about a month ago my wife said, 'Let us send the children to St. Margaret's to hear the Archbishop of ——— preach on behalf of the Society for Aged Ecclesiastical Cripples, which is to celebrate today its three hundredth anniversary.' So the children went, though the parents, for reasons immaterial to mention, could not go with them. 'Well, children, how did you like the Archbishop of ———, and what did he say about "the Aged Ecclesiastical Cripples"?' Here the children—for

---

[1] *The World*, Feb. 4, 1892.

it was during their dinner—attacked their food with great voracity, but never a word could we get out of their mouths about the spiritual feast of which they had just partaken. No! not even the text could they bring out. The more they were pressed the more they blushed, and hung their heads over their plates, until at last, in a rage, I accused them of having fallen asleep during the service. This charge threw my first-born on his defence, and he sobbed out the truth, for by this time their eyes were full of tears. 'Why, papa! we can't say what the Archbishop of —— said, because we could not hear a word he said. He is very old and has got no teeth; and, do you know, I don't think he has got any tongue either, for, though we saw his lips moving, we could not hear a single word.' On this I said no more, but I thought a good deal of 'the Aged Ecclesiastical Cripples' and their venerable advocate, and, being something of a philologist, I indulged in dreamy speculations on the possibility of an alphabet composed entirely of labials; and if my wife had not roused me by some mere matter-of-fact question, I almost think I should have given my reflections to the world in the shape of a small pamphlet entitled 'The Language of Labials; or, How to Preach Sermons without the Aid of either Tongue or Teeth; published for the benefit of the Society of Aged Ecclesiastical Cripples, and dedicated, of course by permission, to the Archbishop of ——.'

"Now listen to another story. A friend of mine, a Scotch Presbyterian, comes up to town and says, 'I want to hear Spurgeon; let us go.' Now, I am supposed to be a High Churchman, so I answered, 'What, go and hear a Calvinist—a Baptist—a man who ought to be ashamed of himself for being so near the Church and yet not within its pale!' 'Never mind, come and hear him.' Well, we went yesterday morning to the Music Hall in the Surrey Gardens. At first I felt a strange sensation of wrongdoing. It was something like going to a morning theatrical performance on Sunday; nor did a terrific gust of wind which sent the 'Arctic Regions,' erected out of lathes and pasteboard, in a style regardless of expense, flying across the water of the lake, tend to cheer a mind depressed by the novelty of the scene. Fancy a congregation consisting of ten thousand souls streaming into the hall, mounting the galleries, mumming, buzzing, and swarming—a mighty hive of bees, eager to secure at first the best places, and at last any place at all. After waiting more than half an hour—for, if you wish to have a seat, you must be there at least that space of time in advance—Mr. Spurgeon ascended the tribune. To the hum and rush and trampling of men succeeded a low, concentrated thrill and murmur of devotion, which seemed to run at once like an electric current through the breath of every one present, and by this magnetic chain the preacher held us fast bound for about two hours. It is not my purpose to give a summary of his discourse. It is enough to say of his voice that its power and volume are sufficient to reach every one in that vast assembly; of his language, that it is neither high-flown nor homely; of his style, that it is at times familiar, at times declamatory, but always happy and often eloquent; of his doctrine, that neither the Calvinist nor the Baptist appear in the forefront of the battle which is waged by Mr. Spurgeon with relentless animosity, and with Gospel weapons, against irreligion, cant, hypocrisy, pride, and those secret bosom sins which so easily beset a man in daily life; and, to sum up all in a word, it is enough to say of the man himself that he impresses you with a perfect conviction of his sincerity.

"But I have not written so much about my children's want of spiritual food when they listened to the mumbling of the Archbishop of ———and my own banquet at the Surrey Gardens, without a desire to draw a practical conclusion from these two stories, and to point them by a moral. Here is a man not more Calvinistic than many an incumbent of the Established Church, who 'mumbles and mumbles,' as old Latimer says, over his liturgy and text. Here is a man who says the complete immersion, or something of the kind, of adults is necessary to baptism. These are his faults of doctrine, but if I were the examining chaplain of the Archbishop of ———, I would say, 'May it please your Grace, here is a man able to preach eloquently, able to fill the largest church in England with his voice; and, what is more to the purpose, with people. And may it please your Grace, here are two churches in this metropolis, St. Paul's and Westminster Abbey. What does your Grace think of inviting Mr. Spurgeon, this heretical Calvinist and Baptist, who is able to draw ten thousand souls after him, just to try his voice, some Sunday morning, in the nave of either of these churches? At any rate, I will answer for one thing, that if he preaches in Westminster Abbey, we shall not have a repetition of the disgraceful practice now common in that church, of having the sermon *before* the anthem, in order that those who would quit the church when the arid sermon begins, may be forced to stay it out for the sake of the music which follows it.'

"But I am not, I am sorry to say, examining chaplain of the Archbishop of ———, so I can only send you this letter from the devotional desert in which I reside, and sign myself,

"HABITANS IN SICCO."

Broad Phylactery,
    Westminster.

In the leading article the question is asked concerning the Establishment—

"How is it, then, that the Church never has a monster preacher? The reason is that a loud voice requires its proper material to exert itself upon. The voice is notoriously the most sympathetic thing in nature. It cannot be loud and soft indiscriminately. Some things are made to be shouted, and others to be whispered. Nobody shouts out an axiom in mathematics; nobody balances probabilities in thunder—*Nemo consilium cum clamors dat.* There must be a strong sentiment, some bold truth, to make a man shout. In religion there must be something extravagant in the way of doctrine. The doctrine of conversion or of irresistible grace can be shouted, but if a man tried ever so hard to shout in delivering a moderate and sensible doctrine on freewill he would find himself talking quietly in spite of himself. It admits of question whether a little extravagance and a little one-sidedness might not be tolerated for the sake of a good, substantial, natural, telling appeal to the human heart."

This appeal to the human heart at the Music Hall drew together the crowds for three years. "Spurgeon's eloquence was not the eloquence of literary vanity, but the eloquence of moral power." There were, of course, ebbs and flows in the congregation, especially towards Christmas time, but the numbers at the end were as great as at the beginning. The end came because the proprietors of the place proposed to open the Hall for Sunday evening concerts. Their purpose was frustrated at first by the plain intimation that if they did it, Mr. Spurgeon would withdraw, and as the fee for the Sunday morning service was probably the only thing that kept them from bankruptcy they desisted. But at length the announcement was made that the Gardens would be opened on December 18, 1859, so Mr. Spurgeon preached his last sermon there on the previous Sunday morning, December 11. The Sunday concerts did not prosper, the income from the Sunday services was lost, and in trying to make the best of both worlds they gained neither, becoming bankrupt soon afterwards. The site of the gardens has long since been disposed of for building purposes, and is now covered with houses. The Music Hall was destroyed by fire. One of Mr. Spurgeon's latest acts was to open "The Surrey Gardens Memorial Hall" near the spot, and there an encouraging mission work is today being carried forward.

The year before both Westminster Abbey and St. Paul's Cathedral had been thrown open for popular services.

CHAPTER VI

THE ROMANTIC YEARS

1854-1867

MR. SPURGEON was able truthfully to boast that the doctrines of grace that he preached at the beginning of his ministry he preached to the end. But he would have admitted freely that with the years there was a change in emphasis and a development of style. Indeed, in the preface to the volume of his sermons for 1855 he draws attention to the fact that during that year he gave more place to the subject of the Second Coming of Christ than before, and he preached the doctrine consistently during the rest of his life, though he gave less place to it in later years, and never at any time committed himself to any theory of the order of events.

A friendly critic once suggested to him that the sermons preached between 1860 and 1867 were not on the high level of the earlier or later ones. "Yes, it may be so," he answered.[1] The reason is obvious; during the earlier years he was addressing the crowd, later he spoke to congregations as crowded as before, but largely to interested and converted people, and the dashing eloquence of the initial years gradually gave place to the mellower and more placid style which characterised his last quarter of a century. The years between were perhaps scarcely as effective.

But those earlier years, including the years of the transition, were full of romance. The period is quite easily marked off; it began with the London ministry, for which the previous years had been the preparation, and ended with the great services in the Agricultural Hall, Islington, from March 24 to April 21, 1867, held during the renovation of the Tabernacle. These were the fourteen romantic years.

It may be recorded here that those services in the Agricultural Hall were each attended by some twenty thousand people. Apart from the solitary gathering in the Crystal Palace they were the largest crowds he ever addressed. Drawn from all parts of the metropolis, they enabled the preacher to lay hold of a new constituency, and consolidated his influence in the city. He used to recall that a musician, testing his voice in the Tabernacle and in the Agricultural Hall, found that it was a tone and a half higher in the larger building—naturally and insensibly he had adjusted his speech to the wider range. It may also be noted that D. L. Moody, visiting London at the time heard Spurgeon in this Hall, little dreaming that he himself would one day

---

[1] *Personal Recollections of C. H. Spurgeon*, by W, Williams, p. 237.

75

preach in the same building though, owing to a difference in the seating arrangements, his audiences were scarcely so large.

Part of the experience of those romantic years has been chronicled in the two previous chapters, but only as far as it related to his pulpit work in London we have as yet taken no notice of his varied preaching services elsewhere, nor of his utterances, other than sermons, which attracted much attention. To these this chapter is devoted, leaving the early history of the Metropolitan Tabernacle, which chronologically belongs to this period, to the chapter that follows.

It was no uncommon thing for the young preacher, in the exuberance of his early days, to preach ten to twelve times a week. He was in request in all parts of London and the home counties: later he went further afield.

The. earliest of many visits to Scotland was in 1855. This was his first long journey, and it was therefore to him of very special interest. His reputation had preceded him, and he had great crowds. Outside Greyfriars Church in Glasgow it was estimated that there were twenty thousand people clamouring for entrance. The newspaper criticism largely echoed the London press, mingling praise with scorn—

"Like his great model, Whitefield, he seems blessed with 'no constitution.' He is endowed with a voice strong, clear, bell-like, which could be heard by many thousands, and with a physical frame equal to a vast amount of hard work. In contour of face, he reminds us something of John Caird, and his eye has the lustrous light of genius in it."[1]

That on the one hand; on the other: "In our estimation he is just a spoilt boy."[2]

In Edinburgh he felt himself to be a failure, he thought the Spirit of God had deserted him, and he told the people that the chariot wheels had been taken off. He was subject to such moods to the end, but a confession like that shows clearly enough that at other times, in spite of his easy eloquence, his reliance was on God's Spirit, and not on himself.

On one of these occasions of gloom "he became impressed with the idea that he was only a waiter, and not a guest, at the Gospel feast," and so he retired to a village, determined not to preach again until the question was settled. On the Sunday he went to a little Methodist Chapel, where the service was conducted by a local preacher. He tells us that as he listened "the tears flowed from my eyes—I was moved to the deepest emotion by every sentence of the sermon, and I felt all my difficulty removed, for the Gospel,

---

[1] *Daily Bulletin*, July 16, 1855.
[2] *Christian News*, July 28, 1855.

I saw, was very dear to me, and had a wonderful effect on my heart. I went to the preacher and said, 'I thank you very much for the sermon.' He asked who I was, and when I told him he turned as red as possible, and said, 'Why, it was one of your own sermons I preached this morning.' 'Yes,' I said, 'I know it was; but that was the very message I wanted to hear, because I then saw that I did enjoy the very word I myself preached.'"

This Scottish visit laid the foundation for the great influence that Spurgeon had to the end in that country, where his sermons were read more regularly and valued more greatly than perhaps anywhere else. A second visit in 1859, during the progress of the phenomenal services in the Metropolis, increased his reputation.

On April 28, 1858, in the Surrey Gardens Music Hall, a sermon was given on behalf of the Baptist Missionary Society, which was probably the most memorable in its history, for on a Wednesday morning the great building was thronged. On several other occasions Mr. Spurgeon preached again for the Missionary Society, and in 1870 he spoke for the Bible Translation Society.

Meanwhile in the summer of 1858 he visited Ireland, and the minister of my own church, Dr. James Morgan, of Fisherwick Place, who heard him thrice out of the four times he preached in Belfast, my native city, has written—

"I was not disappointed, although the mass of the people were. When he preached in the Botanic Gardens he was well heard of seven thousand persons, he was well received, and deserved to be so for his plain, honest and good preaching and deportment. I much question if his influence was as good as that of Mr. Grattan Guinness, who preceded him by a few months. There was a great contrast between them. Mr. Spurgeon was gay, lively and humorous; Mr Guinness was solemn and earnest, and very reserved. Mr. Spurgeon is by far the abler man, yet were there a poll tomorrow in Belfast for the two, it would be in favour of Mr. Guinness."[1]

It will not be forgotten that the great Irish revival came the following year, 1859. Though it could not be traced to the influence of any preacher, breaking out spontaneously in many quarters about the same time without any attributable human cause, it is not without interest to trace God's hand in sending His messengers before His face to prepare the path of His feet. In my boyhood's days the two evangelical names that were treasured in all our hearts were these—C. H. Spurgeon and H. Grattan Guinness.

In February 1860, while the great Tabernacle was being built, after a week spent in Dublin, a visit was paid to Paris. It was arranged by the Rev.

---

[1] *Recollections of My Life*, by James Morgan, D.D., p. 311.

William Blood, who escaped from the burning of the "Amazon." The visit was so great a success that a special pamphlet giving a description of it was published. Mr. Spurgeon was then preaching each Sunday at Exeter Hall, and the Paris visit was therefore strictly limited as to time. He preached three times in the American Chapel, and twice in the Oratoire. Each evening he was invited to the residence of some person of position in the city, and these *salon* gatherings were as remarkable as the public services. He also visited the College at Passy and addressed the missionary students there. Neither Scotland nor Ireland had given him such a genial reception. Dr. Frederic Monod wrote that "Mr. Spurgeon is a new proof that God does nothing by halves. If He calls one of His servants to special work, He gives him the special endowments necessary for it." Dr. Grand-Pierre wrote, "One would willingly hear him during two hours at a time. Among the requisites to oratory which he possesses, three particularly struck us, a prodigious memory, a full, harmonious voice, and a most fruitful imagination. Mr. Spurgeon is in reality a poet." And M. Prevost-Paradol, a distinguished writer of the time, a Roman Catholic, declared that he was "the most natural, and, we would willingly say the most inspired orator we have ever had the pleasure of hearing."

At this time we find a verdict calmly given that "his name is the most popular in Christendom,' and a shrewd judge of men declared that "he acts in everything as if he had been the first actor, and as if this were the first age of Christian Society, with neither ancestry nor precedent." Indeed, a High Church critic, on being asked where he would put Spurgeon, seeing that his ministry was so manifestly blessed of God, declared that he was like Melchizedek without predecessor and without successor. He was the man most talked about everywhere, beloved and despised according to circumstances. Bishop Wilberforce, on being asked whether he did not envy the Nonconformists their possession of Spurgeon gave the caustic answer, "Thou shalt not covet thy neighbour's ass."

At the end of April 1863 a visit was paid to Holland where Mr. Spurgeon preached in the chief cities with much acceptance, sometimes speaking for two hours at a stretch. In conversation long afterwards, though he lamented that he found it difficult to approach individuals on spiritual matters, he told me that one of his most encouraging interviews was when he visited the Queen of Holland, and talked with her heart to heart. This was on Friday morning, April 24. Then may be put alongside that the greeting of a peasant woman, who came with much emotion, gripping his hand at the door of the Dom-Kirk at Utrecht, and said, "Oh, Mr. Spurgeon, God bless you! If you had only lived for my soul's sake you would not have lived in vain!"

The months of June and July 1860 were given to a Continental tour, Mr. Spurgeon's first holiday in seven years. Belgium, the minor German states, and Switzerland were visited. The chief interest lies in his visit to Geneva, where he preached twice in Calvin's pulpit. "The first time I saw the medal of John Calvin, I kissed it," he says. "I preached in the Cathedral of St. Peter. I did not feel very comfortable when I came out in full canonicals, but the request was put to me in such a beautiful way that I could have worn the Pope's tiara if they had asked me. They said, 'Our dear brother comes to us from another country. Now when an ambassador comes from another country, he has a right to wear his own costume at court, but, as a mark of a very great esteem, he sometimes condescends to the weakness of the country which he visits, and will wear Court dress!' 'Well,' I said, 'yes, that I will, certainly; but I shall feel like running in a sack.' It was John Calvin's cloak, and that reconciled me to it very much."

Amongst the books he most valued were Calvin's works; in the first volume of the Commentaries in his library is written, "The volumes making up a complete set of Calvin were a gift to me from my own most dear and tender wife."

It may be said of Spurgeon, as of Calvin, that "nowhere does the whole personality stand out in such clear relief as in his sermons." The style of preaching was also very similar. The following estimate of Calvin with slight changes might have been written of Spurgeon—

" He was a born preacher. For years the spacious church of St. Pierre, in Geneva was thronged, not once or twice, but several times a week to hear him. He was the star of the Genevan pulpit, but his words carried far beyond the city in which they were spoken. Seldom has any man addressed a wider audience or received a more grateful response. His sermons became models and standards for hundreds of pastors who were confined to such help as their publication supplied.

"Admiral Coligny, warrior, diplomatist, and saint, was not the only one who made them his daily provender. It was on John Calvin's sermons on Ephesians that John Knox stayed his soul as he lay on his deathbed.

"There is something of a perennially modern note in Calvin's preaching. He was not afraid to risk the charge of vulgarising his theme by the use of the picturesque language of colloquial social intercourse. Whatever enabled him to grip the people's attention and penetrate to their consciences and hearts was legitimate. Much of his preaching was familiar talk poured forth by a man whose humanism could accord with a love for popular speech. If vernacular and classical alternatives presented themselves, the vernacular commonly received the preference.

"Proverbs tripped from his tongue as though coined on the spot for the occasion, and gave agreeable piquancy to his words. Illustrations and metaphors he drew from all sources, sometimes surprising by their unexpectedness, coming from the lips of such a man. An early translation, reproducing the flavour of the original, represents him as saying, 'We would fain live in pleasure that God should dandle us like little cockneys.' Often he indulges in quite dramatic passages, making the characters with whom he is dealing express themselves in racy soliloquy or dialogue. Instead of making Moses, on receiving the order to ascend the mountain, point out how fatiguing and dangerous that would be for one of his years, Calvin pictures him as exclaiming, 'That's all very fine! And I'm to go and break my legs climbing up there, am I? Of all things in the world! That's a fine prospect!'

"Beza tells us that he despised ostentatious, pretentious eloquence. He held it wrong to seek to give brilliance and charm to God's Word by embellishment of language and subtleties of exposition. In his case the man was the style, and the man shaped the style. All was nervous, spirited, earnest, eager, mostly level to the intelligence of the humblest man who came to hear him, with that throb of suppressed passion often beating through it which touches the fringes of one's consciousness as the sound of a distant eardrum."[1]

These paragraphs, as we have said, might almost have been written of Spurgeon. And not only did he resemble the great Reformer in style, and in the number of sermons he preached—Calvin is supposed to have preached between three and four thousand— his heart was established in the same faith in God's sovereignty. "I can recall the day when I first received those truths into my soul," he says, and from his diary we know that day was April 7, 1850, "when they were, as John Bunyan says, burnt into my heart as with a hot iron; and I can recollect how I felt that I had grown on a sudden from a babe into a man, that I had found, once for all, the clue to the truth of God. One week-night, when I was sitting in the House of God—I was not thinking much about the preacher's sermon, for I did not believe it—the thought struck me, 'How did you come to be a Christian?' I sought the Lord. 'But how did you come to seek the Lord?' The truth flashed across my mind in a moment. I should not have sought Him unless there had been some previous influence in my mind to make me seek Him. I prayed, thought I; but then I asked myself, 'How came I to pray?' I was induced to pray by reading the Scriptures. 'How came I to read the Scriptures?' Then in a moment I saw that God was at the bottom of it all, and that He was the Author of my faith; and so the whole doctrine of grace opened up to me, and from that doctrine I have not departed." "And his Calvinism was no nineteenth-century Laodicean compound."[2]

---

[1] *Life of Calvin*, Rev. A. Mitchell Hunter, M.A., Cardross.
[2] *Pall Mall Gazette*, Feb. 1, 1892.

"You may take a step from Paul to Augustine," he once said to his students, "then from Augustine to Calvin, and then—well, you may keep your foot up a good while before you find such another." In another student talk he said that John Newton put Calvinism in his sermons as he put sugar into his tea, his whole ministry was flavoured with it; then he added, "Don't be afraid of putting in an extra lump now and then."

Mr. Spurgeon was amongst the most eager celebrants of the tercentenary of Calvin's death on May 27, 1864. He agreed with John Knox, who said that in Geneva, in Calvin's day, was "the most perfect school of Christ that ever was on the earth since the days of the Apostles."

Preaching in Leeds for the Baptist Union in a Methodist Chapel on a memorable occasion, he read the tenth chapter of Romans. Pausing at the thirteenth verse, he remarked, "Dear me! How wonderfully like John Wesley the apostle talked! *Whosoever* shall call. *Whosoever*. Why, that is a Methodist word, is it not?" "Glory! Glory! Hallelujah!" came the responses. "Yes, dear brothers," the preacher added, "but read the ninth chapter of the epistle, and see how wonderfully like John Calvin he talked—'That the purpose of God according to election might stand.'" Smiles on the faces of those that had before been silent were the only response to this utterance. "The fact is," continued the preacher, "that the whole of truth is neither here nor there, neither in this system nor in that, neither with this man nor that. Be it ours to know what is Scriptural in all systems and to receive it."

Wherever he went the people thronged upon him to hear the word of life. Thousands gathered in Parker's Piece in Cambridge, and the desire to speak to him was so great that friends with clasped hands had to form a circle round him to make it possible for him to walk to the house where he was being entertained. Under Cheddar Cliffs he preached to thousands who had gathered from all parts of the district. At Trowbridge so great was the desire to hear him that, having preached in the afternoon and evening, he held another crowded service at ten o'clock at night. At Risca, in South Wales, he preached three sermons one after the other, and on a later visit, in the open air near by he again preached to thousands, the people swaying beneath the word like corn in the summer winds. At Abercarne, where some twenty thousand people gathered, there were some great persons present in their carriages who attempted to get near the speaker, upon which the preacher cried that "four horses and a carriage would occupy the ground of fifty people, so the horses and carriages must remain where they are." A similar scene took place at Melbourne, near Cambridge, when the service was to be held in a field. When Spurgeon arrived the field was half covered with vehicles, and he made a request that the horses should be taken from the carriages. "We cannot edify the horses, but the carriages will be a great comfort to the occupants."

At Castleton, in South Wales, there were enormous crowds in the open air. At Naunton, near Cheltenham, the experience was repeated. At Dunnington the hymn-sheets used for the services are preserved yet. Pepphard, near Caversham, was the scene of another great conventicle—"He do put the spade in deep, don't he?" said one of his village hearers. At Ogbourne St. George, near Marlborough, the service was to have been in the open air, but the weather became wintry, so a wealthy farmer had a tent erected; then there came a heavy fall of snow, but, nothing daunted, the farmer cut up a rick of straw, and made a path with it from village to tent, about a quarter of a mile distant. At Lymington a monster booth, holding nearly three thousand people, was crowded. At Swansea, although it was midnight when he arrived, hundreds of persons welcomed him at the railway station. The next morning was wet, so he preached two sermons in chapels, instead of one in the open air, and the weather clearing he preached again in the field to thousands of hearers. At Carlton, in Bedfordshire, there were open-air sermons afternoon and evening, with tea between in chapel, schoolroom, and booth.

At the opening of City Road Chapel, Bristol, the crowd in the afternoon was so great, and those outside so unruly, that after a brief address the service had to be concluded. At a subsequent visit in 1868 in connection with the Baptist Union meetings he was announced to preach on Thursday evening, October 15, and so great was the demand to hear him that the evening before he promised to preach also at nine on the next morning. Colston Hall was again crowded. At Halifax six thousand persons gathered in a large wooden structure three times in one day, and as the crowds were dispersing in the evening, some boards gave way, and the people in one of the galleries were thrown against each other; there were screams from the frightened folk, but fortunately no worse consequence than two broken legs. The entire structure, overloaded by snow, and beaten by a boisterous wind, fell three hours afterwards. The timbers were split to shivers so completely that most of it was rendered useless for building. It came very near to a disaster more tragic than that at the Surrey Music Hall. Little wonder that Spurgeon was always nervous thereafter about a crowd. Persons he feared not at all, a multitude of people made him tremble. But "then it is the racehorse, not the carthorse, that trembles on the verge of the task."

At Bradford the largest building was too small; at Birmingham crowds of six thousand gathered; the secretary who dispensed the tickets had so many applications that his door-bell was broken. Stockton-on-Tees gave a worthy greeting to its visitor. Dudley and Wolverhampton were not behind in enthusiasm. Liverpool, which offered a Welsh, as well as an English audience, seems to have fired the heart of the preacher to new earnestness for the rest of the year. At some of these places collections were taken for the new Tabernacle; the gifts of the people at all of them were generous; at two village places Mr. Spurgeon, preaching for poor pastors, was unconventional enough to ask an offering to purchase the minister a new suit of clothes. At Cheltenham he met Grattan Guinness, then in his prime, for the first time, both of them preaching in the town the same evening. Guinness was at that time "bidding fair to rival the renowned Mr. Spurgeon as another modern Whitefield." Brownlow North was also spoken of as "The Northern Spurgeon."

One of the most interesting of these country visits was to Stambourne on March 27, 1856. Again crowds. He also revisited Waterbeach. In 1866, when the Free Church Assembly was in session, he visited Edinburgh, and, to judge of the interest he excited by the eagerness there was to hear him, Spurgeon eclipsed the General Assembly, while at that Assembly itself he was to the majority the principal figure. People climbed over the railings of Free St. George's in the afternoon to hear him preach, and broke down one of the doors of the United Presbyterian Church in the evening. Another Scotch visit included most of the northern cities; five thousand tickets, ranging in price from a shilling to half a crown, were sold before he entered the town of Aberdeen.

Years after he said, "I cannot remember visiting a single village or town that I have visited a second time, without meeting with some who praised the Lord that they heard the Word of truth there from my lips."

A service of great interest was held on Clapham Common on July 10, 1859. A fortnight before, a tree on the Common had been struck by lightning, and a man sheltering under it killed. Ten thousand persons gathered round the stricken tree to listen to the appeal, "Be ye therefore ready also," and a collection was taken for the widow. In aid of a chapel at Epsom Mr. Spurgeon preached, on June 11, 1858, two sermons from the Grand Stand of the racecourse. One was from the text "So run that ye may obtain." When Bunyan's tomb in Bunhill Fields was restored he also spoke at length in City Road Chapel, the afternoon of May 21, 1862 being too wet for anything but the briefest service at the grave.

Truly these were romantic years. Crowds, crowds everywhere. "If crowds come to hear a preacher," he once said to his students, "some are ready to say, 'Oh! they are running after a man.' What would you have them run after—a woman?" The people had a true instinct, the old gardener leaning on his spade voiced it—"Spurgeon! Ah, there was no humbug about him!"

Here I may perhaps be permitted to quote myself in the biography of Thomas Spurgeon in illustration of the extent to which his father was venerated and almost adored—

"I know of an old man in a country district which Spurgeon was to visit who asked permission from his master to attend the preaching. The farmer insisted on the day's work being done first, and so the old man began at the first sign of dawn to use the scythe, and at every sweep of it he said Spurgeon! Spurgeon! Spurgeon!' until, having finished his task, with a glad spirit he got away to hear the man whose name had inspired his heart for years and been on his lips all the morning.

"Dr. MacArthur of New York tells that on passing the cottage by the gate of Melrose Abbey he discovered how Spurgeon was honoured there. 'I saw an old Scotch lady, with white hair, and the bloom of heather on her cheek, sitting and reading. She was the wife of the gatekeeper, and I could not help noticing, without intending to be intrusive, that she was reading one of Mr. Spurgeon's sermons. I said to her, "I am glad you are reading that sermon, for I love the man and the sermons," and I added, "Do you know, I expect to see him and hear him next Sunday." She looked at me a moment and then exclaimed, "Oh! what wadna *I* gie to see his face and hear his voice!" So she called her husband that he might look at me, because I was to look at Spurgeon on Sunday, and she said, "I dinna wish to envy ye, but I wad gie all I hae if I could see him mysel.""'[1]

"I dinna want to die," said an old North-countryman, "till I gan to London to see Madame Tussaud's and hear Mr. Spurgeon," and a traveller relates that, getting lost in a Highland glen, he found that the people who knew nothing about either Gladstone or Beaconsfield woke up at the name of Spurgeon. There was no kirk in the glen, and they just met together and read one of Mr. Spurgeon's sermons. One old man said, "I wad shoost gang on ma twa honds and knees a' the way to Glesca tae get a sicht o' him."[2]

Of course there were still contrary voices—were until the end. One doctor of divinity, in giving the ordination to his own son in Bristol, declared that he would prefer a decent dog to one that was always barking, and warned the young minister against "the Barnums of the pulpit who draw large gatherings, collect large amounts, and preach many sermons"!

There were also kindly critics. One, who remained unknown, used to send the preacher a weekly list of mispronunciations and other errors in the previous Sunday morning's sermon. These communications were always welcome. If a phrase was used too frequently, the writer would say, "See the same expression in such and such a sermon." He remarked in one letter that Spurgeon quoted too frequently the line "Nothing in my hand I bring," and added, "We are sufficiently informed of the vacuity of your hand "!

---

[1] *Thomas Spurgeon: A Biography*, p. 3.
[2] *From the Usher's Desk to the Tabernacle Pulpit*, R. Shindler, p. 251.

Mr. Spurgeon never visited America, though he was invited on several occasions. In 1859 he was offered £10,000 for some sermons in New York, but he preferred to go unfettered, and actually intended to go the following year. Meanwhile he became the centre of Anti-Slavery controversy. His sermons were being published in America, and had a large sale, but it seemed as if he had changed his views on the subject of slavery. The fact was that the American publishers suppressed all references to the topic in sermons. When this was discovered he was bluntly asked whether he had consented to the expurgation of his sermons, and in reply he drew attention to the fact that though the question of slavery had not thrust itself upon him in the ordinary duties of his English ministry, he counted slavery as a crime of crimes. He followed this with a strong denunciation of the whole system, and as a result the circulation of his sermons dwindled, especially in the Southern States, and his visit to America was abandoned. In later years he was urged to cross the Atlantic. To one of these invitations, promising him not money (for the astute pleader knew that was not the proper bait for Spurgeon), but the opportunity of preaching to ten thousand people, Spurgeon answered that he had no wish to speak to ten thousand people, his only ambition was to do the will of God.

After the first early years he renounced all idea of visiting foreign shores. Mr. John Cook, of tourist fame, once offered to take him up the Nile like a prince, without expense to him, but he declined the generous offer. When his son Thomas was in Auckland his heart almost led him to accept an invitation to New Zealand that was pressed upon him, but the impossibility of such a visit soon became apparent.

Content to exercise his ministry in London, he did not need to go afield, for representatives of all the world came to him. An American outside the Tabernacle asked another man, "At what time do they open the doors? I am a stranger from California, six thousand miles from here." "Sorry I can't tell you, but I am a little way from home myself," quietly responded his neighbour; "I come from Sydney, a little matter of twelve thousand miles from here, I reckon."

Quite early he began to lecture as well as preach. The Young Men's Christian Association sought his help in its series of "Exeter Hall Lectures," and with a spice of mischief the young, unlettered country bumpkin instantly chose a Latin title for his subject, "De Propaganda Fide." All London wanted to be there. Spurgeon was coming out in a new phase. "What could he know about Latin?" Encouraging as the attendance at the other lectures of the series had been, that night, January 4, 1859, the crowd was overwhelming, distinguished men were present in considerable number, and excitement ran high. All through it was a great success, it was cheered at the close, and characterised as being neither lecture nor sermon, and yet for that occasion better than either. The lecture strongly condemned war, and denounced the opium traffic.

One reference evoked such approval from the men in the audience that it almost seemed as if the applause would never end. "I would rather dress as a Quaker than I would wear the things some men do," he said; "and I would rather see my sisters in Christ habited as Quakers than that they should magnify, enlarge and increase themselves as they now do." In a leading article afterwards Dr. Campbell remarked, "The stroke was the most electric one ever witnessed in that Hall. The ladies who were present, and the number was not inconsiderable, were placed in a plight most pitiable. The good-natured, yet deeply derisive cheering was tremendous, and long, very long continued. If that vast assembly might be taken as a fair representation of the young men of England, the ladies of the nation stand reprehended, laughed at, and ridiculed by gentlemen from John o' Groats to Land's End."[1] A popular cartoon soon appeared representing Spurgeon inside a crinoline snapping the hoops asunder.

Though scarcely a lecture, a previous quiet talk with his own people at the Surrey Gardens Music Hall on "A Christian's Pleasures" had provoked the merriment of *Punch,* which came out with an article on "The Spurgeon Quadrille."

When the Tabernacle work was in full swing a series of Friday evening lectures was given by Mr. Spurgeon. He began with "Shrews, and how to Tame Them," followed with "Eminent Lord Mayors," "Southwark," "The Two Wesleys," "Eccentric Preachers," and several on Natural History with specially prepared diagrams. "He seems always to do best what he is doing last," says a friendly reporter. "Throughout the hour and three-quarters he frequently spoke with all the force and vehemence which distinguished his ordinary preaching; and then be it remembered that this was after four hours in the lecture-room, and the exertions of the previous Thursday night, while only thirty-six hours remained till the commencement of the overwhelming services of the Lord's Day."

Two later lectures aroused wide attention. Paul du Chaillu had recently published his *Explorations and Adventures in Equatorial Africa,* and his statements had been received with some caution, especially his account of the gorilla. His discoveries were afterwards confirmed, but Spurgeon believed in him from the beginning, and with Nineveh Layard in the chair, and du Chaillu at his side, he lectured to a crowd that filled the Tabernacle to excess. For some occult reason this aroused the fury of the Press. More cartoons appeared; one representing Spurgeon as "Greatheart" amongst a

---

[1] *The British Standard*, Jan. 7,1859.

crowd of gorillas; another "A gorilla lecturing on Mr. Spurgeon," with his hand on the head of a bust of the preacher.

A second lecture which acquired world-wide fame was "Sermons in Candles." In an address to his students Spurgeon told them that if they could see nothing in the world but a tallow candle, they might find illustrations enough to last them six months. They demurred, and so he promised to prove his words, and the Candle lecture was the result. All sorts of candles and lamps were used as object lessons, and the lecture, which continually grew, was given again and again, always with great acceptance, and it was also widely copied by others.

Mr. Spurgeon was invited to repeat his lecture on George Fox to the Society of Friends at their Institute in Bishopsgate in London. So on November 6, 1866, he was greeted by a large representation of the Society, some twelve hundred. He felt a strong desire to lead in audible prayer, but silent petition was considered more fitting. Matthew Arnold was there, and wrote afterwards to his mother: "Last night Lord Houghton went with me and William Foster to Spurgeon's lecture. It was well worth hearing. It was a study in the way of speaking and management of the voice, though his voice is not beautiful as some people call it, nor is his pronunciation quite pure. Still it was a most striking performance; he kept up one's interest and attention for more than an hour and a half, and that is a great thing. I am very glad I have heard him."[1]

When the people had nearly all dispersed one of the audience came up to speak to the lecturer; it was John Bright, with whose oratory his own has been so often compared, and who, like him, for some years enjoyed "the beatitude of malediction."

Thus the romantic years passed. Amid praise and blame he held on his way. In a time of violent criticism Mrs. Spurgeon wondered what she could do to smooth his path, so she had a text illuminated in old English type and hung in their bedroom, where every morning he could see it, and many a time his heart was calmed as he read—

Blessed are ye when men shall revile you, and persecute you, and shall say all manner of evil against you falsely, for My sake. Rejoice and be exceeding glad: for great is your reward in Heaven, for so persecuted they the prophets which were before you.—Matt. v. 11, 12.

But, like his Master, he grew in favour with God and man. A boy in America was asked in an examination who was the Prime Minister of England. His answer was "C. H. Spurgeon." This can be matched by

---

[1] *Autobiography*, Vol. III. p. 62.

something overheard at Mentone. Spurgeon was walking on the promenade, and a carriage was passing along the road. Said the coachman to the person he was driving, "Do you know who that is? that is the Pope of England!" The people too were at last on his side. On the great day, March 7, 1863, when Queen Alexandra made her public entry into London, Spurgeon drove into town in his closed brougham. There was a block on London Bridge, and one of his hearers recognised him. The news spread, those on the bridge pressed round the carriage, struggled to see his face, almost wrenched his hand off in their fervour, cheered him again and again, giving him an ovation that even the Princess might have envied.

During these years it was no uncommon thing, on Sunday mornings on the north side of the river, for the conductors of the omnibuses that were about to cross the bridges to the south, all of them converging on the Tabernacle, to entice people into their conveyances by a device more romantic than most of them guessed. With gusto they cried, "Over the water to Charlie!"

THE METROPOLITAN TABERNACLE

INTERIOR DURING WATCH-NIGHT SERVICE

CHAPTER VII

THE GREAT TABERNACLE

September 29,1856—*April* 10, 1861; *and afterwards*

THE building of the Tabernacle was itself a romance, but there was a romance within a romance which first of all deserves mention. It was known only to a few at the time of its occurrence, and was not told in public till the meeting which celebrated, on May 19, 1879, the twenty-fifth year of Mr. Spurgeon's ministry. I heard him tell it then as a notable instance of the way God encourages His servants by "hidden evidences," as well as by those that are open to all the world.

There were not wanting those who opposed the venture; they "wished to keep the eagle in a small cage, but there was no use doing that; the eagle would either break his wings or break the cage," and happily it was the cage, and not the wings, that got broken. But if the warmest exponents of the building of what even then was spoken of as "the largest chapel in the world" had known what was before them, they might have hesitated. Fortunately faith often goes to its greatest exploits blindfold.

When on Michaelmas-day, 1856, New Park Street Chapel was crowded to discuss the suggestion, a sum of £12,000, or at most £15,000, was considered adequate to provide such a structure as appeared necessary. The building actually cost £31,322. At the close of 1859 a sum of £16,868 had been collected, and about as much again was needed. Mr. Spurgeon never had any misgivings on the matter, and his spirit sustained others when they were about to faint. His faith was accompanied by works, for before the Tabernacle was opened he had contributed over £5000 to the project himself, and it was through his personal effort that much of the rest was gathered.

If he sustained the faith of others, his own faith was sustained in a remarkable way, as remarkable as the visit of the Ravens to Elijah by the brook Cherith. He was one day in 1859 driving with a friend to preach in the country, when a carriage overtook him, and the gentleman in it asked him if he would get out of his vehicle and ride with him in his gig, as he wanted to speak to him. It was evident that he had started in pursuit of the preacher. When they were together, the stranger told him that as a business man he was sure he would succeed in the great enterprise he had in hand—it was God's work and could not fail. But he added, "You will have many friends that will feel nervous about it. I want you never to feel anxious or downcast. What," he said, "do you think will be required at the outside to finish it off altogether?" Spurgeon replied, "£20,000." "Then," said he, "I will let you have £20,000, on condition that you keep only so much of it as you need to finish the building. I only expect to give £50, but you shall have bonds and leases to the full value of £20,000 to fall back upon." The securities were duly delivered to Mr. Spurgeon, and during the next two years, when many wise heads were wagging at the extravagance of the project and the hopelessness of carrying it through, Spurgeon had the means in hand to finish it if everybody else had deserted him. "They little knew," he exclaimed on that silver-wedding evening, "how much reason I had for my assurance, nor how my faith had been strengthened by this token of God's favour." The generous benefactor knew his man, for he was only called upon to give his £50; from the beginning Spurgeon had determined that he should not be required to give any more.

For a moment we may pause and ask whether in fact faith with such a token is easier or more difficult—faith, remember. George Muller on one occasion had £3000 balance in the bank, and some one asked him whether he did not now find it easy to trust God. With true insight he said, "No, I find myself apt to trust the £3000!"

> "What need of faith, if skies were always clear?
> 'Tis for the trial-time that this was given.
> Though skies be dark, the sun is just as near.
> And faith may find him in the heart of heaven."[1]

Clear sky or dark sky, Spurgeon was conspicuous for his faith, and faith evoked faith, his trust in God led others to trust *him*. In the after years it was no uncommon thing for those who wished to bestow money on worthy objects and scarcely knew what objects to choose, to say, "Let us send it to Spurgeon, he will know how to make the best use of it."

Even he had his fits of nervousness, especially when he was ill. On one occasion when his recovery was being hindered by his doubt as to whether he would be able to meet all the obligations entailed on him by the things for which he had made himself responsible, one of his deacons, after a visit to the invalid, whom he had been unable to comfort, returned in a little while to his bedside bringing with him the scrip that represented all his investments, and pouring the papers on his bed he said, "There! I owe everything that I have in the world to you, and you are welcome to all that I possess. Take whatever you need, and do not have another moment's anxiety." It was the best of medicine. "It seemed to me," Spurgeon wrote afterwards, "very much as the water from the well of Bethlehem must have appeared to David." Of course he used none of it.

---

[1] Gerald Massey.

The selection of a site for the new Tabernacle was a matter of difficulty—Holloway, Clapham and Kensington were discussed, but at length the Fishmongers' Company were persuaded to sell part of their land where there were some Almshouses "at the Butts of Newington." In the olden days, 1546 or thereabouts, three Anabaptists had been burnt near the spot. A special Act of Parliament was needed to ensure the legality of the transfer of the freehold, and Mr. William Joynson of St. Mary Cray deposited sufficient money to carry it through. The new Tabernacle was destined to be built near the Surrey Gardens Music Hall.

An architectural competition was opened for the best plans for the new building, and at the end of January 1859, sixty-two sets of drawings and one model had been received. These were exhibited for public inspection. Twenty-eight of them were described in *The Builder* of February 12, 1859, which also states that "considerable excitement, of course, prevails." The design which gained the first prize was not accepted, but the eighth in the list, by Mr. W. W. Pocock, to which the Committee allotted the second prize, after some alterations to reduce the cost, was adopted. In sitting space the accommodation was larger than the Surrey Hall, which with three galleries contained 19,723 feet, while the Tabernacle, with two galleries, contained 25,225 feet. There were thirteen tenders for the building, the highest being £26,370, the lowest that of Mr. William Higgs, £21,500. The foundation stone was laid by Sir Samuel Morton Peto on August 16, 1859, beneath it being placed a Bible, the Baptist Confession of Faith, Dr. Rippon's Hymn Book, and a declaration by the deacons of the Church. An invalid sent from Bristol £3000 to be put on the stone, with a challenge that if twenty others would give £100 each he would add £2000 to match theirs. Before many weeks his challenge was accepted and the extra £2000 paid.

"It is a matter of congratulation to me," Mr. Spurgeon said in his speech, "that in this city we should build a Grecian place of worship. There are two sacred languages in the world, the Hebrew of old, and the Greek that is dear to every Christian's heart. The standard of our faith is Greek, and this place is to be Grecian. Greek is the sacred tongue, and Greek is the Baptist's tongue. We may be beaten in our own version sometimes; but in the Greek never. Every Baptist place should be Grecian, never Gothic."[1] So, at the beginning of the sixth year of his ministry in London, this young man of twenty-five saw his dreams materialise. "Long ago," he said, "I made up my mind that either a suitable place must be built or I would resign my pastorate; you by no means consented to the latter alternative; yet I sternly resolved that one or the other must be done—either the Tabernacle must be erected, or I

---

[1] *The British Standard*, Aug. 19, 1859.

would become an Evangelist, and turn rural dean of all the commons in England, and vicar of all the hedgerows."[1]

It would have been little wonder if his heart had been lifted up in pride. Instead of that we find him one evening after the workmen had left encountering the Secretary of the Building Committee on the site. When they had walked about for a while, Spurgeon proposed that they should seek God's blessing on the work. So, kneeling down, those two "in the twilight, with the blue sky over them, and piles of bricks and timbers all around them," committed the building and the men engaged on it to God's care; and there was not a single serious accident during the whole progress of the work.

On August 21, 1860, a meeting was held on the floor of the unfinished building, when Spurgeon justified the name chosen for it. It was truly "Metropolitan," because more than a million people had contributed to it, and it was but a "Tabernacle," because God's people are still in the wilderness. On March 18, 1861, a prayer meeting was held at seven o'clock in the morning in the building, then almost completed, and a week later another. On the afternoon of that day, March 25, Mr. Spurgeon preached his first sermon in it, the text being, "And daily in the temple, and in every house, they ceased not to teach and preach Jesus Christ." In the evening Dr. Brock discoursed on the words, "Christ is preached; and I therein rejoice, yea, and will rejoice." On Good Friday, March 29, Spurgeon preached twice, and was able to announce that all the money needed for the building had been given, and that the Tabernacle was therefore ready, free of debt, for worship on the following Lord's Day, March 31. On the following Tuesday there was a Baptism; on Wednesday, April 10, a great Communion Service; and so for three weeks the opening services and meetings continued, a prelude to the marvellous ministry to be maintained there until, on June 7, 1891, thirty years later, worn out with labours abundant, with pain and weariness, Spurgeon stood in his accustomed place and preached in the Tabernacle for the last time. The building itself was burnt to the ground on Wednesday, April. 20, 1898, the facade and outer walls being the only part of the original structure left. Under the ministry of Thomas Spurgeon, one of his twin-sons, it was re-erected at a cost of £15,000, with smaller seating capacity, and was again opened for worship free of debt on Wednesday, September 19, 1900. It has been widely discussed whether, when the great Tabernacle was destroyed, it was wise to build another: whether it would not have been better to have built four or five places of worship in the suburbs. Such a question is altogether beside the mark; the attachment of the people to the old place, and the sentimental interest attaching to the site, made only one course possible.

---

[1] *Autobiography*, Vol. II. p. 318.

After the building of the first Tabernacle, an attempt was made to continue services in New Park Street Chapel, but it became apparent that there was no need for such a large church building in the district, and it was eventually sold for business purposes.

The original Tabernacle was, outside the walls, 174 feet in length, the auditorium being 146 feet long, 81 feet broad and 62 feet high. There were 3600 seats, but by side seats and flap seats in the aisles there was accommodation for about 1000 more. Times without number another 1000 somehow found some sort of accommodation within the walls. On the evening of Mr. Spurgeon's Jubilee, when Lord Shaftesbury presided, one of the deacons who had charge of the building, and who always personified it, said, "We counted eight thousand out of her; I don't know where she put 'em, but we did."

I may be permitted again to quote from my biography of Thomas Spurgeon—

"It is almost impossible for the present generation to realise how great was the renown of Spurgeon at his zenith. He was not only followed and admired, he was trusted and loved beyond his fellows. Thomas Binney was London's greatest preacher when Spurgeon arrived, and at first he was inclined to deride the boy in the pulpit as a charlatan, but he quickly saw his mistake, and to a gathering of students he said: 'I have enjoyed some amount of popularity; I have always been able to draw together a congregation; but in the person of Mr. Spurgeon, we see a young man, be he who he may and come whence he will, who at twenty-four hours' notice can command a congregation of twenty thousand people. Now I have never been able to do that, and I never knew of anybody else who could do it.'

"D. L. Moody had not then appeared upon the scene, but mighty as was his influence his verdict on Spurgeon was; 'In regard to coming to your Tabernacle, I consider it a great honour to be invited; and, in fact, I should consider it an honour to black your boots, but to preach to your people would be out of the question. If they will not turn to God under your preaching, neither will they be persuaded though one rose from the dead.' He did, however, preach in the Tabernacle afterwards, and in his London campaign he got Spurgeon to preach for him. In writing to thank him he said: 'I wish you could give us every night you can for the next sixty days. There are so few men who can draw on a week-night.' Remember that this was twenty-two years after Spurgeon had come to London, and that during all that time he was able at any time to command a crowd as great as Chrysostom in Constantinople or Savonarola in Florence, though each of them commanded it for a much shorter time.

"That was the wonder of it: he built a Tabernacle seating between five and six thousand persons, able to contain over seven thousand, and for thirty-eight years he maintained his congregation there and elsewhere in London. Francis and Bernard, Wesley and Whitefield gathered as great throngs, but they passed from place to place, while Spurgeon remained rooted to the metropolis. Henry Ward Beecher and Canon Liddon were as popular, but they did not preach so continuously nor so long. There are, indeed, not wanting some who trace back through the history of the Church and only find Spurgeon's peer in Paul."[1]

"How many thousands have been converted here!" he exclaimed at the prayer meeting on May 26, 1890, as he looked round the building. "There has not been a single day but what I have heard of two, three or four having been converted; and that not for one, two, or three years, but for the last ten years!" Surely that is a thing unmatched in the history of the Church. The membership of the Church when he came to it in New Park Street in 1854 was 232; at the end of 1891 there had been baptised and added to the Church 14,460 others; and the membership then stood at 5311. At one Communion Service 100 persons were admitted to membership and 150 at another; the greatest number added to the membership in any one year was 571, in 1872; in 1874 there were 509, and 510 in 1875. It is notable that directly the Tabernacle was occupied the additions to the Church year by year were double the additions at New Park Street, showing that the size of the fishing pond bears some relation to the number of fishes caught.

Every Sunday, with few exceptions, for thirty years that great building was crowded morning and evening, and the Thursday evening congregations, often overflowing into the top gallery, were more wonderful than all. "Somebody asked me how I got my congregation," he once said; "I never got it at all. I did not think it was my duty to do so. I only had to preach the Gospel. Why, my congregation got my congregation. I had eighty, or scarcely a hundred, when I preached first. The next time I had two hundred: every one who heard me was saying to his neighbour, 'You must go and hear this young man!' Next meeting we had four hundred, and in six weeks eight hundred. That was the way in which my people got my congregation. Now the people are admitted by tickets. That does very well; a member can give his ticket to another person and say, 'I will stand in the aisle,' or 'I will get in with the crowd.' Some persons, you know, will not go if they can get in easily, but they will go if you tell them they cannot get in without a ticket. That is the way congregations ought to bring a congregation about a minister. A minister preaches all the better if he has a large congregation. It was once said by a gentleman that the forming of a congregation was like the beating up of game, the minister being the sportsman. But," he added, "there are some of our ministers that can't shoot! I really think, however, that I could

---

[1] *Thomas Spurgeon: a Biography*, pp. 3, 4, 5.

shoot a partridge if I fired into the midst of a covey, though I might not do so if there were only one or two."

His biographer was for some time a seat-holder in the Tabernacle, and well remembers the astonishment and excitement of strangers who came for the first time. I remember especially one lady who had gained early admittance, and was quietly settling in the place I had offered her, when the doors were opened to the public, and the rush began all over the building. She rose in alarm, thinking some dreadful thing had happened, and then, realising the situation, she asked with panting breath, "Is it always like this?"

There are three realistic descriptions of Tabernacle services given by outsiders which will perhaps give a more vivid idea of them than any account written from within. The first refers to a Sunday morning in 1879—

"It was high time to go and hear Spurgeon. We had procrastinated long enough about the matter, and now it must be put off no longer. What if the Tabernacle were a Sabbath-day's journey distant? We ought to be able to manage that exertion for once in a way; and anything was better than the grave reproach under which we lay as long as it could be said of us that we lived in London and yet had never been to hear the foremost, if not the most remarkable, of London preachers. So we made the effort and went.

"We had heard so much about the magnitude of the congregations at the Metropolitan Tabernacle that we were determined, at any rate, that it should not be our fault if we missed an eligible seat. Accordingly we found ourselves in the enclosure rather more than half an hour before the stated time of service. A few people were passing the gates with us, but as yet there was no indication of 'the crush.' Congratulating ourselves on being thus beforehand, we pushed boldly forward, with a view to enter the building by one of its fifteen doors, when there confronted us no less than three scandalised individuals, whose faces wore every expression of horror and indignation. 'You cannot get in without a ticket,' was the hopeless announcement. 'Tickets,' we exclaimed, 'we have none.' 'Then take your place on the steps,' was the chilling rejoinder; 'the general public is admitted at five minutes to eleven.' It was bad enough to have our zeal thus damped at the outset, but to be reminded that we were nothing better than a portion of 'the general public' was a hard blow. We did not, however, like to forego the advantage due to our punctuality without an effort. If this had been a concert now, or a theatre, we had about us a silver key which would doubtless have gained us admission; but the janitors of a place of worship, we considered, were surely not 'tippable' subjects. While we were rather in a dilemma, a fourth individual came up with a packet of small envelopes in his hand. 'I can give you a ticket,' said he, 'if you wish to go in.' We were ready to fling our arms round his neck as we gasped 'How much?' 'We make no charge,' replied he with the envelopes, loftily, handing us one; 'but you can put what you like in this towards the support of the Tabernacle, and drop it in yonder box!' This, then, was the incantation, the 'open sesame' we had been seeking. Seizing the welcome envelope, we retired to a corner, and followed the direction given us; after which, with a proud sense of being rather better than one of the general public, we marched triumphantly forward, inwardly reflecting that whatever the fervour of the spirit animating the authorities of the Metropolitan Tabernacle, their diligence in business was exemplary.

"The great clock on the platform points to ten minutes to eleven, and then suddenly we hear three smart claps from the other end of the building. The effect of the signal is magical. We rise from our seats, and next moment find ourselves in the longed-for pew. There is a buzz of conversation, which is at first quite alarming. Is this a place of worship or a concert hall? one mentally inquires. People talk in unabated voices and even laugh; and one of the old ladies in one pew waves her umbrella affectionately to her crony in another. It doesn't seem very reverential, but we put it down to the disturbing effect of a great number of people. But all are not here yet. The clock crawls on to five minutes to eleven, and we think of 'the general public' outside. A glance shows that there are still a fair number of empty places for them; and at the thought, lo! here they come. The aisles resemble for the moment the platform of a railway station on an excursion day—at least as far as the eagerness of the candidates for the seats goes. The noise, happily for our reputation as a body of worshippers, is not quite so great. And now every seat is full. The flaps along the aisles are let down and occupied, the gangways in the galleries are packed, the back pews up in the ceiling are tenanted, and we know that at last we are here assembled. But how can any one voice make itself heard here, above this hubbub of shuffling and talking and laughing? We are within twenty yards of the platform, and even yet have our misgivings about hearing; and what of those poor 'general publicans' away there as far as one can hurl a ball?

"It is eleven o'clock. The door at the back of the platform opens, and a stout, plain man, with a familiar face, advances haltingly to the table, followed by some dozen deacons, who proceed to occupy the stalls immediately behind the pastor's seat. Mr. Spurgeon is not a young man now, and to us he looked feeble in body and not in health. We rather envied his feelings as, having spent a moment in prayer, he looked round the vast assembly, and were by no means disposed to grudge him an iota of the pride which, mingled with thankfulness, must assuredly have filled his breast at the sight. 'Now let us pray,' he said, and in an instant there fell a hush over that entire company which, had we not witnessed it, we could scarcely have imagined possible. The first sentence of Mr. Spurgeon's prayer was delivered in absolute silence; and we had no difficulty in setting at peace, once for all, our misgivings as to the possibility of hearing. Dropping coughs presently broke the stillness of the congregation, which sometimes conspired to make an absolute tumult; but from first to last Mr. Spurgeon's voice rose superior to all, nay, even seemed to gain power from these very oppositions.

"He read through the opening hymn while a tardy batch of the general public was thronging the aisles and bustling into seats, without strain or effort, and in a voice which must have penetrated to every corner of the building. Mr. Spurgeon, we understand, has on more than one occasion said that he can whisper so as to be heard in every part of the Tabernacle, and that he can shout so as to be heard nowhere. In this art lies the secret of his mechanical power as a speaker. It is not by stentorian exertion, but by well-regulated modulation and studied articulation, that he succeeds as he does in bringing all within the compass of his voice. The process is exhausting neither to his audience nor (it would seem) to the speaker—the former are talked to rather than shouted at, and the latter, instead of waging a hopeless struggle with space, is mainly concerned to keep his voice at a sufficiently subdued pitch during the service.

"To any one who has not been in a similar scene, a hymn sung by a full congregation at the Metropolitan Tabernacle has a thrilling effect. It is no ordinary thing to see four and a half thousand people rise simultaneously to their feet, still less to hear them sing. For a moment during the giving out of the hymn it occurred to us to look wildly round for the organ, which surely must be the only instrument which could lead all those voices. There is none: and we are sensible of a pang of hurried misgiving as we nerve ourselves to the endurance of all the excruciating torments of an ill-regulated psalmody. A gentleman steps forward to Mr. Spurgeon's side as the last verse is being read, and at once raises a familiar tune. What is our delight when not only is the tune taken up in all its harmonics, but with perfect time and expression! The slight waving of the precentor's book regulates that huge chorus, as a tap will regulate an engine. The thing is simply wonderful. We feel that tight sensation of the scalp and that quiver down the spine which nothing but the combination of emotion and excitement can produce. We are scarcely able for a while to add our voices to that huge sea of melody which rises and falls and surges and floods the place. If Mr. Spurgeon's powers of voice are remarkable, those of his precentor are, to our thinking, marvellous. His voice can be heard above all the others, he holds his own, and is not to be run away with, and in the closing hymn he is as unflagging as in the first. 'Now, quicker,' cries Mr. Spurgeon, as we reach the last verse; and it is wonderful to notice the access of spirit which this produced. We sit down, deeply impressed. After all, what instrument or orchestra of instruments can equal in effect the concert of the human voice, especially in psalmody?

"The reading of Scripture followed, accompanied by a shrewd, earnest running commentary, which, though sometimes lengthy, never became wearisome. Mr. Spurgeon is not one of those who believe that Holy Scripture is its own expounder, and certainly in carrying out this view he manages to present the lesson selected in a good deal less disconnected manner than many who, with less ability, attempt a similar experiment. Another hymn, chanted, followed, and then a prayer. Mr. Spurgeon's prayers are peculiar, their chief characteristic being, to judge by the specimen we heard, boldness. We do not mean to insinuate that he rants, or becomes vulgarly familiar in his addresses to the Deity. But he wastes no words in studied ornament, his petitions are as downright as fervent, and his language is unconventional. 'This is Thy promise, O Lord,' he exclaims towards the close of this prayer, 'and Thou mayst not run back from it.' We have rarely heard this style of address adopted more freely than by Mr. Spurgeon, and we must confess that it does not exactly accord with our prejudices. Still we may safely say the earnestness "of his prayer went far to atone for what struck us as the minor defects of language, which, after all, may have been the reverse of defects to the uncritical portion of our fellow-worshippers.

"The most remarkable part of the whole service, however, was the sermon. And here we may as well observe at once, that any one who goes to the Metropolitan Tabernacle expecting to be entertained by the eccentricities of the preacher is doomed to absolute disappointment. . . . We could not help admiring his choice of words. It is pleasant to hear once more half an hour of wholesome Saxon all aglow with earnestness and sparkling with homely wit. You yield yourself irresistibly to its fascination, and cannot help feeling that after all this is better stuff than most of the fine talking and Latin quotations and elaborate periods heard elsewhere. Mr. Spurgeon told a story in the course of his sermon. It was an extremely simple one about a simple subject, but the effect was remarkable. The coughing gradually died away, or became very deeply smothered, and a complete silence fell on the audience. With masterly skill the speaker worked up the narrative, omitting nothing that could give it power, and admitting nothing that would weaken it. You saw the whole scene before you; you heard the voice of those who spoke; you shuddered at the catastrophe; you sighed when all was over. 'And so it is with us,' said the preacher, and not another word was necessary to apply the moral.

"While the sermon was going on, we could not resist the impulse to look round and see how our old ladies were enjoying it. It did one good to see one nodding her approval of each sentence, and sometimes lifting her hand to her tell-tale eyes. Other two sat close together, and we are certain that their ribs must have ached by the time it was all over from the amount of mutual nudging that went on. Indeed as we looked round galleries and basement, and saw that sea of attentive faces, we felt reproved for our own inattention, and gave over taking observation, to listen.

"Punctually to the time (and nothing can exceed the punctuality of everything connected with the Tabernacle) Mr. Spurgeon closed his Bible, and with it his address. As if relieved from a spell, the congregation coughed and fidgeted and stretched itself to such an extent that, for the first time that morning, the preacher's voice seemed at fault. But the concluding hymn gave ample opportunity for throwing off the pent-up energies of his listeners, and the final prayer was, like the first, pronounced amid a tense silence."[1]

The second description is of a Sunday evening when the regular congregation vacated their places, as for some years they did once a quarter, to give outsiders a better opportunity of hearing Mr. Spurgeon. The writer says—

"At 6.15 we find ourselves in Newington, opposite the most stolid and matter-of-fact-looking place of worship. Nothing can be more practical-looking than this vast edifice. Not an inch of space is devoted to idle ornament, not a ton of stone is sacrificed to effect. There is a Greek portico, no doubt; but the portico of the Greeks was useful to keep the sun from the philosophers who taught, and the portico of the Tabernacle is useful to keep the rain off those who come to learn.

"People are crowding in at about the rate of two hundred a minute, quite as fast as the business-like doors can swallow them up. Tram-cars and omni-buses come up to the gates, set down their swarm of serious-looking folk and pass away empty. Now and then a hansom cab rattles up, drops a common-place bride and bridegroom, or a commonplace elderly couple, and departs. But the vast majority of those who come arrive on foot, and toil up the steps with laggard feet, as though they had walked from a great distance. We do not observe any of the very poor. The waifs and strays of many shires remote from London, and the usual visitors from the two cities, twelve towns, and the one hundred and forty-seven villages that go to make up the metropolis, appear all to be in the social zone between the mechanic and the successful but not fashionable tradesman. We find no one as low as a working man, no one who follows any liberal or learned profession," (Here the narrator is wrong, but not so wrong as if it had been a morning service.) "There is a steady persistence in the way these people come up these steps, as though they were quite sure of finding within exactly what they seek. There is no hesitancy or loitering. Each one has come to hear Spurgeon preach, and each one is resolved to get as good a seat as possible. The congregation does not

---

[1] *Leeds Mercury*, Nov. 15, 1870.

look super-spiritualised or super-depraved. It is Sunday, and its worldly work for the week is over, and this day has been laid aside for rest and the business of the other world, and this congregation has come to look after its work for the other world or to rest.

"At twenty minutes past six we enter. All places on the floor have been occupied for some time; all seats on the first tier are full, so we climb up the steep, high stone steps through the square, desolate-looking stair-well. Everything here, as outside, is practical, except the steps, which are so high as almost to be impracticable. In a moment we are in the spacious body of the church. Beyond all doubt, this is one of the most novel sights in London. The vast lozenge-shaped space is paved with human heads and packed 'from garret to basement' with human forms. 'Over the clock' there is a little room to spare, but in less than five minutes the seats there are appropriated, and for fully five minutes before the hour at which the service is announced to begin there is not a vacant scat in the church.

"Inside, too, all is practical and business-like in the arrangements. The light is capital, the colour is cheerful, the seats are comfortable and commodious. There is no attempt to produce a dim religious light, no subduing or dulling of spent tertiary colours, no chance of any one posing as a martyr because of occupying one of the seats. When the acoustical properties of the building are tested they are found to be most admirable. The place was evidently designed and built that the congregation might sit in comfort, and hear and see without strain to the senses.

"Fortune favoured me, and we got a place in the first row, about half-way down the left-hand side of the platform. Upon the seat to be occupied by each person is a half-sheet of paper, printed on one side, and bearing the heading 'Hymns to be sung at the Metropolitan Tabernacle on Lord's Day evening, August 11, 1878.' Under the heading comes the following paragraph preceding the hymns: 'It is earnestly requested that every sincere worshipper will endeavour to join in the song, carefully attending to time and tune; and, above all, being concerned to worship the Lord in spirit and in truth. The hymns are selected from "Our own Hymn Book," compiled by Mr. Spurgeon. It is a special request that no one will attempt to leave the Tabernacle until the service is quite concluded, as it creates much disturbance, and renders it difficult to hear the preacher.' For the present, each person has the half-sheet of paper folded up, or is studying it, or using it as a fan.

"On a level with the first tier of seats is Mr. Spurgeon's platform. It protrudes into the well of the amphitheatre, so that it is visible from all parts of the church. Upon it are a table, chair and sofa. On the table rests a Bible. From the platform to the floor runs down each side a semi-spiral flight of stairs leading to a lower platform, situated immediately under and in front of the higher. The carpet of the platform and the cover of the sofa are of the same hue—deep red, approaching plum colour.

"Precisely at thirty minutes past six several men come down the passage directly behind the platform. First of these is a stout, square-built, square-jawed man of between forty and fifty. Although most of those present this evening are strangers, there is no commotion upon the entry of the famous preacher. There are two reasons for the apparent insensibility, one physical, one mental. The physical reason is that the building is so admirably constructed, so successfully focussed upon the small patch of platform, that every man, woman and child in the house can see the preacher from the moment he reaches the parapet of his balcony. The mental reason is that at the root of the attendance of this vast concourse here this evening lies the business idea. There is no personal enthusiasm toward the preacher. The people have come on business, and are too good business people to jeopardise their business-like calm by a disturbing interest in anything whatever but the subject-matter of the evening's service. It is rarely that a preacher of such wide and lasting popularity exercises so little personal magic over a congregation.

"The service opens with a prayer. Looking down from the height at which we sit, the great number of bright-coloured hats and bonnets of the women on the floor of the house look like a parterre of flowers, and, higher up, the first tier, sloping from the back to the front, presents the appearance of flowers on a vast stand. At the beginning of the prayer the whole multitude bend forward with one impulse, the bright hats and bonnets and bald and grey heads are lost to view, and in their stead appears a dark grey surface, made up of broadcloth-clad backs of the men and dark shoulder articles of the women.

"When the prayer is concluded there is a faint rustling sound, and looking down again we see the heads are now uplifted, and close to each head a half-sheet of paper held at a convenient distance for reading. We glance carefully round, and as far as we are able to see no one is without a paper and every one seems studying his own. There are four hymns in all, and one is about to be sung. Mr. Spurgeon gives it out slowly and with enormous distinctness. The effect of his voice in giving out the hymn is very peculiar. The words come separately and individually, and take their place, as it were, with intervals between them, like men who are to assist at a pageant, arriving one by one and marching to their posts. The first stanza having been read over and the first line repeated, all rise to their feet by one act of accord. The choir start the hymn" (a special band of singers for this particular evening), "and between five and six thousand voices take it up with great precision as to time and great accuracy as to tune. The vast volume of sound does not deafen or disgust. It is mild and suppressed. You know it has the strength of a giant, but you feel it is not using it tyrannously. At our back is a poor, slender-looking man with a red-brown beard. He is like a shoemaker out of work. His voice comes in with clear, sharp edge, a counter-tenor. By our side is a woman, a maid-of-all-work we guess her to be. She strikes in only now and then with a few low contralto notes she is sure of; she never risks a catastrophe up high. She has only about three and a half notes, but she never loses a chance of contributing them when the occasion offers. On our other side is a fresh-coloured schoolgirl home for the holidays. Her voice is a thin soprano, and seems to roughen the edges of the counter-tenor's. But when this happens there floats in upon our exercised ears the dull, low boom of a rolling bass. Who the owner of the bass is we cannot find out. We look around vainly endeavouring to discover. Now we fix on one, now on another, but this *ignis fatuus* of a voice eludes our most exhaustive efforts to run it to flesh. Meanwhile abroad in the hollow roof of the building the confluent concord of five thousand voices swells the hymn to an imperial pæan."[1]

Ten years later, we find a description of the preacher, rather than of the service, which is worthy of being quoted—

"Mr. Spurgeon's text was, 'I will give you rest,' and he got a number of headings out of and by means of an ingenious device well known to grammarians, by a changing of the emphasis in this way—

"I will give you *rest*.
I will give *you* rest.
I will *give* you rest.
I *will* give you rest.

"Besides that, he got a fresh effect in the course of his sermon by reading it very staccato, in the manner of Uncle Tom, who had to spell painfully through his Bible, thus: 'I—will—give—you—rest.' Indeed, from what he said, he appears to think that if we could unlearn our spelling lessons we should get a better idea of what we read by being forced to go more slowly over it, an idea which is not to be ridiculed. I know that on the same principle I often seem to get a clearer view of the inner meaning of a passage in a foreign author, which I have had a difficulty in translating. What seemed to hold the interest of his audience most was Mr. Spurgeon's frequent *ad captandum* little touches of pathos, such as, 'If your mother—ah! you have no mother now—were to give you a little book with her name in it you would not part with it for its weight in silver.' Then there were little personal touches, as when he told of the sleepless nights he had spent through

---

[1] *The Hornet*, April 4, 1878.

headaches, and how he got rid of worries—'God knows,' he added, 'I have more than most.' And there was a touch of romantic sadness, the sadness of age which looks back on youth, as he told how merry he used to be in the early days of his Christian life, and how a grave comforter had said, 'The black ox has not gored you yet,' and truly, I thought to myself, *atra cura,* the grim, haunting figure behind the horseman, grows more constant in his attendance as we grow older, be we Christians or not. And again, when relating a touching little incident about an old friend who had 'gone home,' he said that among that huge congregation there were some who would be gone before they met again, and he added, with a sadness that drove home his previous reflection, 'I could wish it were my lot to go first among you.' But I cannot say that his personal appearance gave the impression that these gloomy thoughts came from bad health; on the contrary, except that he is a little stiff in the legs, the preacher looks as strong and energetic as ever he did, and made, as he spoke, all the usual marchings and countermarchings between the rails of the platform, the Bible stand and the chair, which he now and then balanced on his hand."[1]

It would be impossible to recall all the associations of the sanctuary which to so many was as the very gate of heaven. It became the rendezvous of seeking souls as well as one of the show places of the metropolis. Visitors to London went as naturally "to hear Spurgeon," as they went to St. Paul's or to Westminster Abbey. "To far the larger number of Americans who crossed the Atlantic there were two desires; one was to visit Shakespeare's tomb in the lovely church by the river at Stratford-on-Avon; the other to listen to Spurgeon in the Metropolitan Tabernacle." One of these distinguished Americans who came over prejudiced against the preacher told me recently, that in a few minutes after the service at the Tabernacle began he was completely won over in his favour, and with a wide knowledge of American life, he added that the only voice he ever heard comparable to Spurgeon's was that of James G. Blaine, once candidate for the Presidency of the Republic. General Garfield, recalling his visit in 1867, wrote in his diary: "God bless Mr. Spurgeon! He is helping to work out the problem of religious and civil freedom for England in a way he knows not of."

"For a generation no country trip to town has been complete," writes a friendly critic, "without a visit to the great religious theatre—we use the word in no invidious sense—where Mr. Spurgeon so completely filled the stage. And yet the man who wielded and maintained this tremendous influence was at no pains to accommodate his teaching to new light, to soften its inexorable conclusion, to shade off its pitiless dilemmas. The web of his speech was as simple as that of John Bright's, and the effect he produced on his hearers

---

[1] *The Globe*, March 4, 1889.

strikingly similar. The mere mental refreshment of such a method to men and women must have been enormous, apart from the moral stimulus. The sight of the strong face, and the homely figure moving easily about the platform, the flow of simple Saxon speech, the rich, deep voice, that penetrated to every spot of the vast oval of the Tabernacle, one can recall, but never completely realise the attraction they had for thousands and tens of thousands of Englishmen."[1]

The place the Tabernacle had in English life may be guessed from the fact that at the Crystal Palace on August 2, 1877, it was the great set-piece in the firework display, and there was included a "Fire-Portrait" of C. H. Spurgeon.

"He was one of the two most delicate elocutionists I have ever heard," writes a visitor, "the other is Lord Coleridge. What made the elocution of both so extraordinary is that they both spoke without the slightest apparent effort. There was no motion of the body, scarcely even a visible movement of the lips; yet the voice penetrated to the remotest fringe of the audience; not a cadence, not a half-tone, was lost."[2]

"While they were worshipping with him," wrote R. W. Dale, "the glory of the Lord shone round about them, and this has never been to the same extent their experience in listening to any other man. Never again will they listen to a preacher at whose word God will become so near, so great, so terrible, so gracious; Christ so tender and so strong; the Divine Spirit so mighty and so merciful; the Gospel so free; the promises of God so firm; the troubles of the Christian man so light; his inheritance in Christ so glorious and so real. Never again. It is wonderful that such large numbers of Christian men should, in the Divine order, be made so dependent on one man."

Two men from the same country town once encountered each other under the portico of the Tabernacle as they waited for the doors to open. The one, an avowed Christian, expressed to the other, a person whose life was apparently engrossed with the things of this world, his astonishment at meeting him there. "Ah!" he answered in a tone of unfeigned solemnity, "every man has his own tale told here."

In the after years Moody himself commanded no greater crowds when he conducted a Mission in the Tabernacle. In company with Manton Smith, I also conducted several Missions there, and on occasion had crowds that blocked the road and stopped the tramcars, and at the Watch-night services for many years saw the great building thronged, but that was only occasional, and was, of course, the reflex of Spurgeon's own influence. The only photograph of the congregation filling the Tabernacle was taken at one of

---

[1] *Daily Chronicle*, Feb. 1, 1892.
[2] *Irish Times*, Feb. 16, 1892.

those midnight meetings, the photographic plate being exposed under the gaslight for the half-hour during which I was speaking. It is reproduced opposite page 144. A popular Temperance Mission, too, was once held in the building, the audience cheering for many minutes when Spurgeon donned the blue ribbon. Missionary meetings often attracted overflowing congregations, and for many years the Liberation Society drew crowds there for its annual demonstration, until Lord Morley was one year announced as a speaker, and, feeling that the religious character of the movement was compromised, the Tabernacle was denied to the Society.

Two of the greatest occasions, apart from the preaching services, were at the silver wedding of pastor and people, and at Mr. Spurgeon's own Jubilee. On the first, on May 20, 1879, as the result of a great bazaar, a sum of £6470 was presented to the pastor, the bulk of which he promptly gave as an endowment to the almshouses long connected with the Church, and the balance to other good works. The Jubilee meetings were held on June 18 and 19, 1884, and again a presentation was made; this time the sum reached £4500. It would, no doubt, have been considerably more if it had been known that it might have been for the pastor's own use; but people expected that he would give it all away—as he practically did, paying first for the Jubilee house behind the Tabernacle, sending some help to his son toward the building of his Tabernacle in New Zealand, giving Mrs. Spurgeon some for her Book Fund, making a donation to St. Thomas' Hospital, which so often received poorer members of the Church, helping the almshouses again, the Colportage Association, the fund for poor ministers, and so on. This action was only in keeping with his whole career: "Literally he gave away a fortune, walking through life from day to day with open heart and open hand."

From the beginning of 1868 until the end Mr. Spurgeon had the help of his brother, Dr. J. A. Spurgeon, in Church, College and Orphanage, indeed in everything to which he put his hand his brother was there to second his efforts. A very deep affection existed between the two. James Archer Spurgeon was pastor at Southampton for some years, then at Notting Hill, and while he helped at the Tabernacle he established the Church at West Croydon, one of the most flourishing Churches near London today. For two years after his brother's death he remained as acting-pastor at the Tabernacle, resigning in favour of his nephew when he was called to the pastorate.

So the years passed. At the Tabernacle there was almost a monotony of success: thither the tribes came up on great occasions, until there came the day—Tuesday, February 8, 1892—when only the body of the great preacher was on the platform, his voice silent, and his eye unseeing, as the crowd of sixty thousand people passed in solemn procession before his coffin. Other crowds filled the building four times the next day, and once again on the 10th for the funeral sermon, preached by Dr. A. T. Pierson, whose presence there, for months before and after, attracted crowds as great as even Spurgeon commanded.

For seven years the Tabernacle also witnessed the ministry of Thomas Spurgeon: the great scenes associated with his welcome, the services bravely sustained in spite of bodily weakness, the Spurgeon tradition constantly upheld, until the fire demolished the structure that had been founded in faith and had so fully answered the purpose for which it had been erected. It would have been scarcely fitting if so revered a structure had ended in an ordinary way.

CHAPTER VIII

AN INTIMATE INTERLUDE

IT was scarcely to be expected that Spurgeon, different from other men in so many ways, would act like an ordinary lover. Nor did he. We have seen that the lady who was to be his wife, Miss Susannah Thompson, was present at his first Sunday evening service in London, and that she was scarcely prepossessed in his favour. She was already seeking to follow Christ, and the ministry of Mr. Spurgeon was much blessed in leading her to fuller devotion to His service, and naturally enough her early prejudices soon vanished.

She has herself told the story.[1] One day there arrived at her home, 7 St. Ann's Terrace, Brixton Road, an illustrated copy of *The Pilgrim's Progress,* inscribed "Miss Thompson, with desires for her progress in the blessed pilgrimage, from C. H. Spurgeon—April 20,1854." It was a sign of growing interest, as well as of pastoral care, and her own deepening sentiment gradually led her to consult Mr. Spurgeon as to her state before God. So the friendship steadily grew.

When the Crystal Palace was opened on June 10, 1854, a party of friends, including Miss Thompson and Mr. Spurgeon, were present at the inauguration, sitting on some raised seats where the great clock is now fixed. They were in a merry mood, and while they waited for the ceremony Mr. Spurgeon handed a copy of Martin Tupper's *Proverbial Philosophy,* open at a passage to which he pointed as he asked her the question, "What do you think of the poet's suggestion in those verses?" She read—

> "Seek a good wife from thy God, for she is the best gift of His providence;
> Yet ask not in bold confidence that which He hath not promised;
> Thou knowest not His good will: be thy prayer then submissive thereunto,
> And leave thy petition to His mercy, assured that He will deal well with thee.
> If thou art to have a wife of thy youth, she is now living on the Earth;
> Therefore think of her, and pray for her weal."[2]

It was a singular wooing. "Do you pray for him who is to be your husband?" he softly whispered to the trembling, blushing girl at his side, who said nothing, could say nothing, and saw nothing, but with beating heart felt that heaven was coming near. When the ceremony was nearly over, another whisper came, "Will you come and walk round the Palace with me?" and breaking away from the others, who perhaps were not so obtuse as they looked, the two went out into the enchanted ground. He was wise enough to

---

[1] *Autobiography*, Vol. II. p. 7.
[2] *Proverbial Philosophy*, seventeenth edition, p. 213.

delay the definite proposal of marriage for some weeks, until, on August 2, 1854, in her grandfather's garden, they gave themselves to each other, she with her adoring heart, and sweet face framed in the curls that fell on each side of it, he with his clear eye, swift brain, high collar, white tie, and protruding tooth.

In anticipation of Church membership she addressed to her pastor a letter setting forth her Christian experience, to which he responded in a letter dated January 11, 1855, couched in old-world phraseology. Here is a sentence: "Dear purchase of a Saviour's blood, you are to me a Saviour's gift, and my heart is full to overflowing with the thought of such continued goodness." He baptised her at New Park Street on February 1, 1855.

The courtship lasted another year, but the lover was a busy man and sometimes absent-minded. He generally spent Monday morning with his fiancée, revising his sermon, she keeping quiet the while, and perhaps thinking the more. Once when she accompanied him to a service he forgot all about her, and left her struggling with the crowd while he slipped into the vestry. She went home indignant, but when the service was over he came running to the house seeking her, and after remonstrance by her mother, the lovers were reconciled.

During the year they collaborated in choosing the selections which were afterwards published under the title *Smooth Stones taken from Ancient Brooks.* On December 22 he sent her a copy of *The Pulpit Library,* the first published volume of his sermons, with the inscription, "In a few days it will be out of my power to present anything to *Miss Thompson.* Let this be a remembrance of our happy meetings and sweet conversations.—C. H. SPURGEON."

The wedding day was January 8, 1856. About two thousand persons were crowded into the chapel, the adjoining streets were thronged. Dr. Alexander Fletcher of Finsbury Chapel performed the ceremony, and then bride and bridegroom left for a brief visit to Paris. Twelve days later the preacher was back in his pulpit, and subsequently Mr. and Mrs. Spurgeon were publicly welcomed by the congregation.

The union was a joy in both lives, though for most of her married life the wife was an invalid, and the husband was at frequent intervals tormented with gout. "Put your foot in a vice," he said, "and turn the screw as tight as you can—that is rheumatism; give it an extra turn, and that is rheumatic gout." These physical troubles and his incessant labours kept them a good deal apart, but the love that bound them together never slackened, indeed, it grew in beauty and tenderness with the years. To the "Tirshatha," as she called him, Mrs. Spurgeon ever gave a reverent homage, even when for his good she ruled him with a gentle despotism. To him, she was ever "our angel and delight," and he was never happier than in inventing some new method of giving her joy.

Twin sons were born to them on September 20, 1856, in their first London home, 217 New Kent Road. The elder was named Charles, after his father, the younger Thomas because he was the twin. Thomas once gave a different reason; he said that as his mother's maiden name was Thompson, it was quite natural that he should be Son Tom. The story that their father, when he heard of their birth, exclaimed, "Not more than others I deserve, but God has given me more," is apocryphal; probably somebody suggested that it was what he might have said. But he was quite elated at the event; his father to the end laughed when he recalled that on the letter his son sent him announcing the birth of his twin boys, the figure 2 was written five times outside the envelope.

The Sabbath month after the boys' birth was not over before the home was shadowed by the tragedy at the Surrey Gardens Hall. Their father, as we have seen, spent a while at Croydon, and when at length he overcame the horror that had enwrapped him, mother and boys joined him there, and the parents joyfully dedicated their children, as far as they might, to the Lord and to His service.

In the family Bible there is an entry in their father's writing that his twin sons were born at Bengal Place, New Kent Road, September 20, 1857, and then below, in another ink, "By some strange I mistake I have put 57, it should have been 56.—C. H. SPURGEON." Even Jove nods sometimes.

At the beginning the young couple had to stint themselves a good deal in order to support the College, which was then in a state of embryo, but things became easier, and they were able to move, in 1857, to their second home, Helensburgh, Nightingale Lane, at that time quite rural in its surroundings. It was an old house, originally an eight-roomed cottage, but altered and enlarged by its previous owners, and it had a garden which greatly delighted its new occupants.

Here in 1858 came John Ruskin, who was a frequent attendant at the Surrey Gardens Music Hall, to inquire after Mr. Spurgeon, who had been seriously ill. It was the first day of the patient's convalescence, and Mr. Ruskin "threw himself on his knees and embraced him with tender affection and tears." He had brought two charming engravings and some bottles of wine of a rare vintage to comfort the sufferer, though whether the wine was the best medicine for the gout may be doubted. On the occasion of another visit, having brought nothing, he left the invalid for a while, and returned with a volume of Tennyson, all he had been able to buy in the neighbourhood. He also sent him an original set of *Modern Painters,* and he contributed £100 to the Tabernacle Building Fund.

Two letters that passed between these two men show the footing on which they stood towards each other. J. Ruskin, "affectionately yours," wrote from Denmark Hill on November 25, 1862—

"MY DEAR FRIEND,

"I want to have a chat with you. Is it possible to get it—quietly—and how, and where, and when? I'll come to you—or you shall come here—or whatever you like. I am in England only for ten days—being too much disgusted with your goings on—*yours* as much as everybody else's—to be able to exist among you any longer. But I want to say 'Good-bye' to you before going to my den in the Alps."

Upon which "yours ever most truly and affectionately, C. H. Spurgeon," replied—

"MY DEAR MR. RUSKIN,

"I thought you had cast me off; but I perceive that you let me alone when all is right, and only look me up when you are getting disgusted with me. May that disgust increase if it shall bring me oftener into your company!

"I shall be delighted to see you tomorrow, here, at any time from ten to twelve, if this will suit you. I wish I had a den in the Alps to go to; but it is of no use for me to grow surly, for I am compelled to live among you sinners, and however disgusted I may get with you all, I must put up with you, for neither Nature nor Providence will afford a den for me."

Of the disgust with things in general which Ruskin felt during those years a sample is given by Mr. Spurgeon himself. He says, "Mr. Ruskin came to see me one day, and amongst other things he said that the Apostle Paul was a liar and that I was a fool! 'Well,' I replied, 'let us keep the two things separate; so first of all tell me how you can prove that the Apostle Paul was a liar!' 'He was no gentleman, and he was a liar too,' answered Mr. Ruskin. 'Oh, indeed,' I rejoined. 'How do you make that out?' 'Well,' he said, 'there was a Jewish gentleman came to him one day, and asked him a polite question—"How are the dead raised up, and with what body do they come?" Paul began by saying to him "Thou fool,"—which proved that the Apostle was no gentleman; and then he continued, "That which thou sowest is not quickened except it die," which was a lie.'

"'No,' I answered, 'it was not a lie. Paul was speaking the truth.' 'How do you prove that?' asked Mr. Ruskin. 'Why,' I replied, 'very easily. What is death? Death is the resolution into its elements of any compound substance which possessed life.'

"Mr. Ruskin said, 'That is the most extraordinary definition of death that I ever heard, but it is true.' 'Yes,' I said, 'it is true, and that is what happens to the seed when it dies; it is resolved again into its original elements, and the living germ which is within it becomes the centre and source of the new life that springs out of it.'

"'Then,' said Mr. Ruskin, 'what do you mean when you talk of the death of the soul?' 'I mean,' I replied, 'the separation of the soul from God; it was originally with God, and when it is separated from Him it dies to God; that is its death, but that death is not non-existence. The separation of the soul from the body is the separation from itself of that which quickened it, and it falls back into its original condition.'

"'Well,' said Mr. Ruskin, 'you have proved that Paul spoke the truth, but you have not proved him to be a gentleman.'

"'At all events,' I answered, 'the Apostle was as much a gentleman as you were just now when you called me a fool.'

"'So you are,' said Mr. Ruskin, 'for devoting your time and talents to that mob of people down at Newington when you might employ them so much more profitably upon the intellectual and cultured few, like that Jewish gentleman who came to Paul, and others that I might name.'

"I replied, 'I always like to be the means of saving people whose souls are worth saving, and. I am quite content to be the minister of that mob down at Newington, and let those who want to do so look after the cultured and refined.'"

The early students at his College used to come to his house an hour or two on Saturday mornings for informal talk, and many a person in trouble came to him for comfort. In 1869, by the kindness of some friends, the house was rebuilt, and while the work was in progress the family removed to Brighton. Here, in the hope of restoring Mrs. Spurgeon's health, an operation was performed by Sir James Y. Simpson. He journeyed twice from Edinburgh, and when questioned as to his fee answered: "Well, I suppose it should be a thousand guineas, and when you are Archbishop of Canterbury I shall expect you to pay me; till then let us consider it settled by love."

Leaving the boys at school at Brighton, Mrs. Spurgeon returned to Nightingale Lane, much better in health, to find that in the renovation and refurnishing her every desire for herself and her husband had been anticipated. A room adjoining her husband's study had been specially fitted up for her, the lawn had been laid out so that it was suitable for the game of bowls, always a favourite pastime of Mr. Spurgeon's. In one of the trees the old pulpit from New Park Street had found a resting-place, the stairs leading up to a quiet eyrie where the preacher could retire when he wished to be quite alone.

Mr. Spurgeon was in those early days often away from home. One morning, as he was preparing to start on a journey, he noticed his wife in tears, and asked her a question which startled her. It was whether any of the children of Israel, when they brought a lamb to the Lord's altar as an offering to Him, wept when they saw it laid there. "Why, no," she replied. And then he suggested that she was giving him as they gave their sacrifice, and so the tears were dried. If ever afterwards there was a sign of sorrow at his absence, he would bring the smiles instead of tears by the question, "What! crying over your lamb?"

On one of these occasions he asked her if there was anything he could bring her on his return, and, with the whim of an invalid, she replied that she should like an opal ring and a piping bullfinch. He laughed as he bade her good-bye; there was little likelihood of her desire being granted. But the Lord is very pitiful to His tired children. An old lady whom Mr. Spurgeon had once visited had meanwhile sent a note to the Tabernacle that she wished some one to call on her, as she wished to send Mrs. Spurgeon a present. When it arrived, behold it was the opal ring, and he brought it back to her with triumph. Soon afterwards came the visit to Brighton, and one day, on his return from London, Mr. Spurgeon brought a cage containing the piping bullfinch. He had visited a dying man who was somewhat disturbed by the piping of the bird, and his wife had begged him to take the bird to Mrs. Spurgeon, declaring that she would entrust it to nobody else, and hoping that its songs would cheer her when she was so often left alone. So the Lord condescends not only to meet the needs of His children, but also their wishes!

During the last twelve years of his life, Mr. Spurgeon had his home at Westwood, Beulah Hill, Upper Norwood. It was somewhat singular how the change was made. Some business took him to the new district, and in passing over the hill he noticed that the house, which could not be seen from the road, was for sale. It had been suggested to him that perhaps if he lived on higher ground his health, and possibly his wife's health, might be better. On his return, in repassing the house, his secretary alighted, read the bill, and discovered that cards were necessary to view the premises. But the impression on his mind was so deep that he sent a message giving his name, and asked whether he could see the house without having a card. His name was enough. When he saw the house he exclaimed that it was too grand for him, and yet he could not get the thought of it out of his mind. But he did not send any one to the sale. On that very day, however, the builder of the house at Nightingale Lane called on him, inquiring whether he had ever thought of selling his present residence, for his next-door neighbour would like it for his son-in-law, who was returning from abroad. Then it was learnt that "Westwood" had not been sold, and after some further inquiry it appeared that it could be almost bought for the price his neighbour was willing to give for Helensburgh House, and without further delay the two bargains were completed. The new home was charming, not too extensive, with garden, lawns, lake, and some small fields beyond, where Mrs. Spurgeon afterwards found grazing for two or three cows. There was a fernery, a rosery, a vinery and some other glass, two large rooms looking on to the garden, one of which made a capital study, and the other an admirable library. As Mr. Spurgeon in the earlier home had fitted up a room for his wife, she, during one of his visits abroad, had a little room, opening off the study, built for him. In the study he did most of his work, Mr. J. L. Keys, his amanuensis, at one side of the long table, and Mr. Joseph Harrald, his "Armour-bearer," at the other, he himself at his own table crosswise at the top. The door to the little inner sanctum furnished by his wife was just behind him, so that he could slip in and out as he liked.

His working books were in this room, the biblical volumes arranged in Bible order. The top shelves contained "dummy "volumes, with fancy titles, a number of them suggested by the names of his students. Eastward Ho! by A. G. Brown; Cuff on the Head; Pains and Aches, by Feltham; Tydeman on Cleanliness; Gange's Rivers. Others were just witticisms: Jonathan on Exaggeration; John Bull on Bragging; The Elevation of Parliament, by Guido Faux; Hints on Honeypots, by A.B.; The Composition of Milk, by A Dealer; Absalom on the Mule; Balaam on the Donkey; Gilpin on Riding Horses.

Earl Cairns had a similar conceit. When his library door in Bournemouth was shut it seemed to be part of the shelves. Here it was only dummy backs of books which made the room look as if it had no door at all. It will not be abusing the privilege of a guest, and may be interesting as the fancy of a great man, if I record some of them: Five Minutes in China; Gaelic, the Language of Eden; Gladstone's Great Impostures; The Dog, by Barker; Natural History of Bores; Bores of St. Stephen's; Hansard's Drowsy Evenings; Silliman's Private Thoughts; Jonah's Account of the Whale; History of the Middling Ages.

Spurgeon delighted in his garden; he did not botanise, but he knew most of the flowers and plants. A frequent visitor says, "We went into the vinery one day when the tree was in full leaf. He said, sniffing the odour from the branches: 'Well done, Solomon, the vines do give a *good* smell, there is no fragrance, no perfume, nothing will describe it but good. You instinctively feel it is healthy to take in the scent of the vine.'"[1]

Between the library and the dining-room was Mrs. Spurgeon's bookroom, from whence the parcels of books were despatched to ministers by means of her "Book Fund." Mrs. Spurgeon continued to reside at Westwood till her death on October 22, 1903, and from the beginning of the Book Fund

---

[1] *Personal Recollections*, by W. Williams, p. 68.

until that time she distributed over 200,000 volumes, as well as countless copies of her husband's sermons.

The Fund began when Mr. Spurgeon handed his wife the corrected proof of the first volume of his *Lectures to My Students*. When she had read it she declared that she wished she could place a copy in the hands of every minister in England. "Then why not do it?" her husband said, and with his practical mind he added, "How much will you give?" Although she was scarcely prepared for such a challenge, it suddenly occurred to her that she had some money at her disposal, accumulated by her hobby of saving every five-shilling piece that came to her. On counting her hoard she discovered that she had enough money to send out a hundred copies, and so the "Book Fund" was born. When its inauguration became known there was a rush of applicants from all parts of the country, as well as from all sections of the Church, and the work so approved itself to God's stewards that means were generously forthcoming. It is a question whether there was more joy in the hearts of those who received the books than in the heart of the gracious lady who counted the sending of them her bit of service through her twenty-eight later years. The story is gracefully told in two volumes, *Ten Years of My Life* and *Ten Years After*. Mrs Spurgeon was much helped by her companion, Miss Thorne.

Occasionally Mrs. Spurgeon would invite her neighbours to a service on Sunday evening in the study. I remember addressing them one Sunday. Once the window was opened to freshen the room after one of these services, and it was forgotten. During the night a burglar discovered it, entered and stole a few things, the most valuable being a goldheaded stick presented to Mr. Spurgeon by J. B. Gough. As the gold bore Spurgeon's name it was afterwards the means of identifying the burglar, as he sought the next day to dispose of it. He then wrote to Mr. Spurgeon, saying, amongst other things, that he did not know it was the "horflings' Spurgeon "who lived there, and ending up by the pithy advice, "Why don't you shut your windows, and keep a dog? "This led to the advent of "Punch," the pug- dog who gave his master unending pleasure and very greatly interested his visitors.

The news of the robbery led *Punch* (the journal, not the dog) to publish a humorous page entitled "The Diary of a Burglar." Various exploits in his profession are chronicled: "Last night did a stylish little piece of work. Robbed Spurgeon's house. Not so much for the swag as to create a sensation. Have always been a follower and admirer of his, but shouldn't have been if I'd known how precious few valuables he keeps on the establishment. Nothing but tracts and reports and 'Notes for Discourses.' Returned these, of course, after reading one or two— especially one very elegant discourse on 'Theft.' Returned the whole lot—with compliments on the very elegant language of the one I have mentioned— apologising for the temporary abstraction. Shall really think of giving up my pew—quite disgusted."[1] A piece of fooling which was given and taken in excellent part.

No account of the home could be complete without a reference to "Old George," the faithful servant of many years, who anticipated his master's wants, and often insisted on things that were for his benefit. His second name was "Lovejoy"—the fruit of the Spirit, he would say—"Love, joy."

In addition to his winter furlough at Mentone, of which we will speak later, Spurgeon generally secured two or three summer weeks in the Highlands. For one or two years he was guest of Mr. John Anderson, but generally he was entertained by Mr. James Duncan at Benmore, taking a friend or two with him. On these occasions he preached each Sabbath at Rothesay, Dunoon, or on the lawn in front of the house. One year I was a privileged visitor. The first Sunday thousands of people came, and a homely sermon was given, which one of the Glasgow papers the next day criticised somewhat severely, but not unjustly. Spurgeon answered the criticism the next Sunday. On the Monday he telegraphed to his publishers to see whether his last sermon in the Tabernacle had been published; the answer was in the negative, so he preached it again. The text was "Mercy shall be built up for ever." The effect in his own pulpit had been great; given in the open air, with an immense crowd drinking in every word, it was astonishing. As the sermon progressed mercy was built higher and higher, until it pierced the heavens, and sat down on the throne of God. The preacher excelled himself. That was his answer to the newspaper.

There is a record of another great service during his summer furlough. He was announced to preach on Sunday morning, July 28, 1878, at Rothesay. On the Saturday crowds came to the place and every available room was occupied. About three o'clock Mr. Duncan's yacht arrived in the bay, and anchored amongst the many others that had been attracted there. In a few minutes the news of his arrival had spread over Rothesay. The next morning Spurgeon preached to a crowd of fifteen thousand to twenty thousand persons. After the service he rested for a while in the Provost's garden to give the crowds time to disperse, but Mr. A. G. Short, who tells the story, says that they evidently did not intend to leave him quite in that fashion. They knew he would have to leave in a boat to reach the yacht, and they gathered in thousands along the sea-wall. When Mr. Spurgeon stepped into the boat, and the sailors began to ply their oars, as one looked along the crescent shaped front, it seemed as if every person in that vast gathering had brought a white handkerchief for the special purpose of waving it in his honour. That was Scotland's way of bidding a Sabbath adieu to the great and good man

---

[1] *Punch*, Oct. 80, 1880.

she loved so well; and not until he was on board the yacht did the farewell signals cease to flutter in the evening breeze.

Adjacent to the house at Benmore Mr. Duncan had built a picture gallery, with the same ground space, approximately, as the Tabernacle, and had gathered a great collection of paintings, many of Dore's amongst them. Here an hour would be spent each evening. During the day there would be walks round the estate, and talks on all sorts of topics; occasionally there would be an excursion.

At one place—Colintraive—a party of four of us found only two rooms available in the little inn, and drew lots to fix our places; mine was with our host, and Mr. Higgs was placed with his pastor. I recall the excitement of a good woman as we walked that evening along the beach. She came running up to two of us, crying out, "Spurgeon's here! Spurgeon's here! "One especial day I remember when we went out in the launch fishing in Loch Eck, caught a salmon, cooked it on the lakeside, and feasted in royal picnic fashion. How these memories abide! One Sunday morning I preached at Kilmun. I went upstairs to prepare, and he was amongst the others downstairs. As I sat in my room I heard a gentle knock at the door, and when I opened it found him outside; he had climbed the stairs, no very easy task for him, to help me. "I have come to pray with you before you go," he said. Then we knelt down, and he prayed as he might have prayed for himself, that I might be helped to preach in power. But there was the human side to the incident too, for the next day Spurgeon pointed out the house next door to the church, with a notice exhibited, "Mangling done here," and insisted that that was where I had preached.

The home life was ideal, chastened indeed by frequent sufferings, but never fretful nor constrained. It was a deep joy to the parents when the sons were baptised, a great gratification when they began to preach in a cottage at Wandsworth. Both had entered upon business careers, one in a City merchant's office, the other as an engraver on wood, but their preaching power developed. Charles, the elder, after pastorates at Greenwich, Nottingham, Cheltenham and Hove, has now become his father's successor at Spurgeon's Orphanage; Thomas, the younger, after his ministry in Australia and New Zealand, became his father's successor at the Tabernacle, carried on the work there for fourteen years, and on October 20, 1917, died. Two years afterwards, his son Harold, in unveiling the stained glass window at the Orphanage, showed in his speech some Spurgeonic power.

If we may venture to observe the inner life of this man so greatly honoured of God in the world, we shall not find Spurgeon often on his knees; and that not because he did not pray, but because he prayed incessantly. In the New Jerusalem there is no temple, because it is all temple. Between the closing of one book and the opening of another with Spurgeon there were the shut eyes and the moving lips. "I always feel it well just to put a few words of prayer between everything I do," he once said to an intimate friend. He seldom wrote a letter without raising his heart to God for guidance. Archibald G. Brown tells how in a railway journey with him they knelt down and spent a time in prayer. Dr. Wayland Hoyt says, "I was walking with him in the woods one day just outside London, and, as we strolled under the shadow of the summer foliage, we came upon a log lying athwart the path. 'Come,' said he, as naturally as one would say it if he were hungry, and bread were put before him, 'Come, let us pray.' And kneeling beside the log, he lifted his soul to God in the most loving outpouring and yet reverent prayer. Then, rising from his knees as naturally, he went strolling on, talking about this and that. The prayer was no parenthesis interjected. It was something that belonged as much to the habit of his mind as breathing did to the habit of his body." Dr. Cuyler bears a similar testimony. In one of the Surrey woods they were conversing in high spirits when suddenly Spurgeon stopped and said, "Come, Theodore, let us thank God for laughter." That was how he lived. "From a jest to a prayer meant with him the breadth of a straw."

His idea of prayer was the passing over the counter of a cheque bearing an honoured name. There was no need for pleading, the name pleaded; it was only necessary to wait till the money was paid. And he acted his faith; there was a calm serenity about him in spite of the burdens he bore. Once when dining with a gentleman in the neighbourhood of Regent's Park, it transpired that £1000 was needed the next morning to pay the builder of the Orphanage. Mr. Spurgeon said he had prayed about it and had confidence it would come. Dr. Brock, who was also a guest, said he thought that they should speak with caution about such things, and he had scarcely said it when a telegram was handed in saying that somebody had called at the Tabernacle and left £1000!

He told me himself that he never got so near to God as on the Tabernacle platform when he prayed; this was the reason that so many were impressed by his public intercessions even more than by his sermons, though they were all of a piece. This the reason, too, why when he preached he preferred to take the whole service himself; in his homely way he said, "I like to get the juice out of the meat."

"It was marvellous to hear his soliloquies at the Lord's Table—his language there would have been considered extravagant if one did not know how perfectly real it was. From praying he would take to talking, and from talking he would stand and soliloquise about his Lord, and the audience felt that he was simply enraptured with Him."[1] How he would weep when he was in close communion with his "Well-Beloved," the name he oftenest used for

---

[1] Archibald G. Brown in his Memorial Sermon.

his Saviour! One of his friends even says that he sometimes needed to drink water to supply his fount of tears.

Only twice in his life did he spend a whole night in prayer. The second time was when, on October 2, 1879, he hade his son Tom good-bye as he went to the Antipodes, never expecting to see him again. The hopes that he had cherished of his sons standing by his side were shattered. He preached in his pulpit that evening about Hannah, "a woman of a sorrowful spirit "— the sermon is in the 1880 volume— and then he went home to agonise in prayer, and he got the victory, made the renunciation gladly, and never turned back. The other occasion is too sacred for us to intrude upon it, but here too he triumphed. "There are dungeons underneath the Castle of Despair as dreary as the abodes of the lost," he once said, "and some of us have been in them."

Once in time of physical suffering the pain became almost unendurable, and his prayer became a direct challenge to God. He told Him that he, an earthly father, could not bear to see any child of his suffer so intensely, that if he saw him tormented as he himself then was he would at any rate put his arms under him to sustain him. He dared to chide the Almighty, and in doing it stilled his own heart. When the nurse returned to his room, he declared that he would soon be easier, and sure enough the pain ceased.

He had his ambitions, but they were worthy ones. "I beseech you," he once said, "to dive not only for this age, but for the next also. I would fling my shadow through eternal ages if I could."[1]

In the secret of his own spirit he was a mystic, but he never dared to preach beyond what was written. He thundered out the message of the wrath of God, but in an intimate moment he ventured to say, "While I believe in eternal punishment, and must do, or throw away my Bible, I also believe that God will give to the lost every consideration, consistent with His love. There is nothing vindictive in Him, nor can there be in His punishment of the ungodly." In fact, though he contended earnestly for the truth in Jesus, he was no bigot, nor did he ever imagine that any finite mind could comprehend, much less systematise, the whole of divine truth. But he knew what he knew, and would not be moved from it. He gloried in the Cross, and in the sacrifice of Christ as a Substitute for guilty men, but he recognised the mystery of Redemption that lies beyond man's understanding. He often quoted that phrase in the litany of the Greek Church, "Let thine unknown sufferings atone for our unknown sins."

In one of his morning sermons in 1886, entitled, "The Three Hours' Darkness," he said some memorable words. Some of them have been quoted

---

[1] *Personal Recollections*, by W. Williams, p. 27.

by Dr. Robertson Nicoll in his charming book on Mysticism:[1] "The great modern teacher of substitution, the apostle Spurgeon, in his sermon on the Miraculous Darkness, says that 'this darkness tells us all that the Passion is a great mystery into which we cannot pry. I try to explain it as a substitution, and I feel that where the language of Scripture is explicit, I may and must be explicit too. But yet I feel that the idea of substitution does not cover the whole of the matter, and that no human conception can completely grasp the whole of the dread mystery. It was wrought in darkness because the full, far-reaching meaning and result cannot be beheld of finite mind. Tell me the death of the Lord Jesus was a grand example of self-sacrifice—I can see *that* and much more. Tell me it was a wondrous obedience to the will of God—I can see *that* and much more. Tell me it was the bearing of what ought to have been borne by myriads of sinners of the human race, is the chastisement of their sin—I can see *that,* and found my best hope upon it. But do not tell me that this is all that is in the Cross. No, great as this would be, there is much more in the Redeemer's death. God veiled the Cross in darkness, and in darkness much of its deep meaning lies, not because God would not reveal it, but because we have not capacity to discern it all.''

This breadth of heart was revealed on another occasion when in his prayer at a Thursday evening service he dared to go far beyond his creed, and in his passion for the souls of men cried, "Lord, hasten to bring in all Thine elect—and then elect some more."

---

[1] *A Garden of Nuts,* by Sir W. Robertson Nicoll, pp. 54-55; *Metropolitan Tabernacle Pulpit,* 1886, p. 217.

CHAPTER IX

A WORD PORTRAIT

1851-1892

THE earliest word picture of Spurgeon we possess is one drawn by himself of the days when he began preaching in Cambridgeshire, in the year 1851. "I must have been a singular-looking youth on wet evenings," he says, "for I walked three, five, and even eight miles out and back again in my preaching work, and when it rained, I dressed myself in waterproof leggings and a macintosh coat, and I carried a dark lantern to show me the way across the fields."

One of his Cambridge pupils says that "the prevailing fashion and dress never troubled young Spurgeon; whether people were reminded by the cut of his coat or the shape of his stock of a former generation or of the present was a matter of no concern. Thus on a certain dark and damp winter afternoon, just before breaking-up time, the door of the room opens, and the figure who enters, laughing merrily at what he supposes may be his own somewhat odd appearance, is none other than young Mr. Spurgeon, in the costume of an itinerant preacher of the Fens. Completely enveloped in an oilskin suit, the junior tutor had looked in just to show Mr. Leeding and the lads at their desks what he appeared like when fully equipped for the rain. "Here I am, going off to light the battles of the Lord," he remarked, and away he went to keep a preaching appointment in a village.[1]

As that deals with clothes, it may be said at once that he was never very particular about what he wore, as long as he was comfortable. He generally dressed in broadcloth and wore a frock-coat, but he never went to a fashionable tailor. In one of his scrapbooks there is an advertisement taken from a tailoring journal in which he is represented in an immaculate and perfectly-fitting frock-coat, the contour of his body being adapted to the necessities of the case. It represents him as he never was. In a familiar talk, I remember with what mirth he enlarged on what he considered to be the most comfortable garment for travelling in cold weather—a good rug with two cuts crosswise in the centre through which the head could be thrust when warmth of body

---

[1] *Life and Work of C. H. Spurgeon*, by G. Holden Pike, Vol. I. pp. 82, 79.

was needed, while the rug could be spread over the knees just the same for warmth of leg. He declared that he once drove over London Bridge into the city thus arrayed!

Still pursuing the philosophy of clothes—on one of his visits to the Continent with several of his friends, he brought up the rear as they entered their hotel in Paris. The others were somewhat stylishly garmented, he, as usual, carried his wide-brimmed soft hat in his hand, and the porter of the hotel, remembering that he had seen him before, and mistaking him for the courier of the party, beckoned him to his side and asked in a whisper, "Who are these gentlemen you have brought with you this time?"

Mrs. Spurgeon, who as a girl heard him on his first Sunday evening in London, says that "his countrified manners and speech excited more regret than reverence; the huge stock, the badly-trimmed hair, and the blue pocket-handkerchief with white spots attracted most of my attention, and, I fear, awakened some feelings of amusement."

One of his warmest admirers wrote in 1859: "His figure is awkward, his manners plain, and his face, except when illumined by a smile, admittedly heavy." Another on a subsequent occasion writing of him said: "The features so often described as heavy were lighted by a sunny, beautiful smile, that seemed to shed over his figure a radiance comparable only to the silver sheen on the bosom of a glassy lake. His form, though not tall, and somewhat rounded at the shoulders, was still erect enough to suggest considerable physical vigour, and was remarkably compact; and when he stood up to speak his feet were solidly placed on the ground, and his entire bearing was such as to indicate a man of firmness and determination."[1]

Professor Everett, his companion at Newmarket, says of him in his early days: "He was rather small and delicate, with pale but plump face, dark brown eyes and hair, and a bright, lively manner, with a never-failing flow of conversation. He was rather deficient in muscle, did not care for cricket or other athletic games, and was timid at meeting cattle on the road."[2]

He was, as has been indicated, under medium height, short from loin to knee, so that he never sat far back in a chair, but with body well developed, chest deep and wide (forty-one inches over the waistcoat),

---

[1] *Charles Haddon Spurgeon*, by Dr. George C. Lorimer, p. 16.
[2] *Christian World*, Feb. 11, 1892.

head massive (twenty-three inches round) and covered with thick dark hair, which afterwards turned iron grey; the ear being remarkable, its orifice opening to the front, instead of to the side, like most other ears. From his youth he was stout in build. When he first went to Waterbeach they thought him too pale and too young to be much of a preacher, and, later on, an observer, describing him in the Surrey Gardens Music Hall, said: "He was pallid, without whiskers, with his hair parted down the middle." But one of the earliest ballads about him when he came to London had a refrain which embodied the popular estimate: "O my plump, my rosy Spurgeon."

"The very build of this man, as in the case of John Bright, marks him out as a man of the people. Physically he has no angles. Note men of this make. Notwithstanding their diversity, they have this in common—they require no introduction anywhere. Whatever the company, they are at their ease. There is no putting them out. This applies whether there be education or not. Where there is education and intelligence, as in the case with which we are now concerned, we see perfect naturalness and facility of movement; the power to rise or stoop to the occasion without the least suspicion of stiffness; the ability to give out and take in, whatever the circumstances or situation might be!"[1] Amongst living examples of men of this sort, Mr. Will Crooks in some manners and movements strangely recalls Spurgeon.

But his personality was so many-sided that as far as outward characteristics went there were many Spurgeons. During his stay at Mentone in 1888 a celebrated portrait painter called at the Hotel Beau-Rivage and suggested that he might be favoured with some sittings. Mr. Spurgeon smilingly replied, "You cannot paint me," and then, mentioning the name of another artist, he added, "I sat several times at his urgent request. On the fourth or fifth occasion he threw down his brush with the remark, 'I cannot paint your portrait, Mr. Spurgeon. You have sat to me all these times, and you have never looked twice alike. Your face seems quite altered on each occasion.'" Upon which his Mentone visitor exclaimed, "Well, if he could not paint your portrait, I am sure I cannot"—and that was the end.[2]

A Scotch writer, after Mr. Spurgeon's death, said that he "had a strong resemblance in his earlier days to John Macdonald of Ferintosh,

---

[1] *The Prince of Preachers*, by James Douglas, M.A., p. 77.
[2] *Personal Recollections*, by W. Williams, p. 79.

whom Scottish Highlanders called the Apostle of the North. Dr. Macdonald was the handsomer man, and had especially a fine pair of eyes. But their ways of standing in the pulpit, of rolling out their words in natural and musical intonation, and of filling each paragraph with matter which did not crowd it, were singularly alike. And there were deeper resemblances. Both were Pauline theologians, both had a natural expansiveness and *bonhomie,* both were born preachers and rulers of the multitude, both believed in preaching, in preaching incessantly, and in not only preaching, but unfolding Christ. The only time I ever met Spurgeon I could not help telling him of his resemblance to the great Highlander and to—John Bunyan. He could not quite deny the latter. The former he had to take on faith."[1]

Paxton Hood draws his portrait in the early days: "We were greatly amazed, as we stood at his chapel doors waiting to enter, to see him as he came and passed along to the vestry respectfully lift his hat and bow again and again to his waiting auditors; there was so much audacious, good-natured simplicity, both in the act itself and on the face of the actor, that we could not help smiling right heartily. It was evident he was not indisposed to appropriate to himself a certain amount of personal homage. His face is not coarse, but there is no refinement in it; it is a square face; his forehead is square; we were wishing, although we are not phrenologists, that it had indicated a little more benevolence of character."[2]

On one occasion a phrenologist did interview him, and published his opinion, giving a table of the comparative sizes of the various organs, Comparison, Size, Weight, Benevolence, Approbativences, Firmness, Hope and Individuality being most developed; Cautiousness, Veneration, Conscientiousness, Imitation, Eventuality and Awe coming next and being equal to each other; none of the characteristics being small. This is noted for what it is worth. "I infer," said the phrenologist, "that he is not pugnacious, but desires distinction. Mr. Spurgeon's success is attributable in no small measure to laudable ambition."

"He had a remarkable face and head," Dr. Parker wrote. "The head was the very image of stubbornness: massive, broad, low, hard; the face was large, rugged, social, brightened by eyes overflowing with

---

[1] A. B. in *The British Weekly,* Feb. 4, 1892.
[2] *Lamps of the Temple,* by E. Paxton Hood, p. 545.

humour and softened by a most gracious and sympathetic smile." Dr. Cuyler, in comparing him with Henry Ward Beecher, said there were only two things they had in common, "both were fat, and both were humorous."

He once playfully remarked to me that he had not a single redeeming feature in his face, but the face itself was eloquent to those who could see. Again quoting my friend, and his friend, James Douglas: "Look then at the portrait of Charles Haddon Spurgeon, and what do you find there? Caution marked, certainly, but candour more. You will look a long time on the countenance before you find a trace of reserve. Concealment, in this case, is not one of the fine arts. Where concealment dwells, the lips are not parted in this fashion, but tightly compressed, nor could the eyes, as here, lie so calm in repose.

"Could any face more fully suggest geniality, friendliness, warmth of affection and overflowing hospitality? His greeting was as warm as sunshine. It mattered not what might be the shadow on the spirit, or the trouble of the heart—it vanished away at the voice of his welcome. There was a light on his countenance that instantly dissipated all gloom.

"Lavater has placed language in the eye, but what may we not place there? The whole soul looks out of her windows. Mr. Spurgeon's eye denoted repose, and at the same time intense observation. His is not the dreamy or contemplative eye in the least degree. He is wide-awake, he sees everything there is to be seen. He can tell at a glance who are present and who are absent in his great congregation. His is an eye that in conscious hours never slumbers. He is as quick in perception as he is ready in speech!

"Another thing strongly marked in his eye is his mirth; but no photograph can bring this out, for it appears in the twinkle. His is the laughing, gleeful eye. His love of fun stood him to the end, and no saddening of experience could tone it down one jot."[1]

He could not sing at all, and yet his voice was music. Everybody who tried to describe it spoke of it as silvery. There were both quality and ease in its tones, comparable most of all to the clear voices of a company of choir-boys. His first notes stilled the largest crowd, and his whisper, which could easily be heard over all the great Tabernacle,

---

[1] *The Prince of Preachers*, by James Douglas, M.A., pp. 82-4.

thrilled his hearers. Modulation and compass, enunciation and emphasis were perfect.

"We remember four beautiful voices," said a West-country writer. "Mr. Gladstone's had, and still has occasionally, the sound of a trumpet. Mr. Bright's was like the 'Vox Humana' on a fine organ. Professor Maurice, when reading the Lessons, was as one inspired, though we can scarcely find a comparison for the pathos of his elocution. Mr. Spurgeon's voice, however, was probably the finest voice that was ever heard in the pulpit—it was like a flute."[1]

He could never understand any one needing to be taught elocution, to him it all came naturally. The only flaw I ever detected in his speech was the quite usual Saxon habit of pronouncing "ah" at the end of a word as if it were "re" a fault so common that in the modern science of phonetics it is accepted and taught. But there should surely be a distinct difference between the pronunciation of "Noah" and "Nore."

In his early preaching there was a good deal of gesture and movement. Once, in the 'seventies, I saw him rush across the Tabernacle platform as he spoke of Joab fleeing to the Temple and clutching hold of the horns of the altar. For the moment he was Joab, and as he cried out to Benaiah that he would not come forth to the sword—"Nay, but I will die here," the people caught their breath as they looked and listened and felt. But such outbursts were infrequent, entirely absent toward the end. Even at the beginning he was credited with a great deal that never happened. He never slid down the rail of the pulpit stairs to show how easy it was to backslide. One reason was that there were no pulpit stairs visible to the congregation at the time the story was told, although it was actually vouched for by supposed eye-witnesses. In later years he often preached with one knee on a chair, the back of which he held with a hand.

When he came to London first there was an odd mixture of shyness and self-assurance in his character. He dared to say the most astounding things, yet shrunk within himself when he was misunderstood. This meant a great deal of silent suffering, and it was only a sense of his vocation which kept him strong. He says: "My success appalled me; and the thought of the career which it seemed to open up, so far from elating me, cast me into the lowest depths, out of which I uttered my miserere and found no room for a 'Gloria in Excelsis.' I hope I was not

---

[1] *Western Morning News*, Feb. 1, 1892.

faithless, but I was timorous, and filled with a sense of my own unfitness. I dreaded the work which a gracious Providence had prepared for me. I felt a mere child, and trembled as I heard the voice which said, 'Arise and thresh the mountains and make them as chaff.'"

To the end he was timid to a degree in things which most people face quite easily. For example, he hesitated to cross a road without some one to help him. Yet he used to tell that one day, near the Bank of England, a blind man caught his arm and asked him to guide him over what is probably one of the most dangerous crossings in London. He told him that he was afraid to venture across himself. "But you can see," said he. "Oh yes, I can see," said Spurgeon, "but I am afraid." To which the blind man responded, "If you can see, I'll trust you," and the trust banished the timidity, and helped both Spurgeon and the blind man across. "I knew I could trust you," the blind man said when they were over, and Spurgeon declared that to be trusted so completely just lifted him out of himself—he dared not fail such confidence: and then he urged the people to trust Christ and count Him as doubly bound to His promise by their trust.

"It was no trouble to him to clothe his thoughts, and to give them in doing so eloquent expression. Words trooped to his service as required, and the thought he had to enunciate shone forth clear as crystal. He was extempore in the true sense of the term, for his notes were but the barest bones of his thought. On the spot he mused and the fire burned. If the thought was sublime, he would give it sublime expression; if homely, he bedecked it accordingly.

"He had mental faculty far in excess of the average. He did with ease, and spontaneously, mental feats which men of name struggle in vain to accomplish. Besides, he had what every large brain has not, large method and power of concentration. He could grasp the bearings of a subject, hold his theme well in hand, and display his thought like troops in a tactical movement."[1]

He has testified that one instant result of his conversion was that the heterogeneous knowledge that he possessed before, jumbled in his brain "in glorious confusion," as he described it, seemed afterwards to be ranged on shelves, so that he was able to lay his hand upon

---

[1] *The Prince of Preachers,* by James Douglas, M.A., p. 86.

everything just when he needed it; and this power continued through his life.

"Further, historic memory was about as perfect with him as it could well be, and no tale that he ever had to tell suffered in the telling of it. While he elaborated with ease his ideas, he made them portable and easy to bear away by a happy epigrammatic finish. It is marvellous how, when he had expounded a thought, he could thus make it live for ever in a few terse, pithy words. The same faculty shines forth in his correspondence. He had the power—a power in daily exercise, a power of impromptu, of loading language to a degree we have never seen approached."[1]

During his early days in London he invited Mr. J. D. Everett to his home, and they spent half a day together. To him he spoke simply and without affectation of himself, and told him that he could always say exactly what he intended, in the time which he intended. His visitor brought away the impression that his great power was to him a simple matter of fact, of which he had no more reason to be proud than a bird of its power to fly or a fish of its power to swim. One of his most marked characteristics was the consummate ease with which he did his work. This was at the root of what was called his irreverence. "I remember suggesting to him," Professor Everett says, "that a man ought to feel and show some sense of awe in the presence of the Master," and his reply was to the effect that such awe was foreign to his nature—that he felt perfectly at home with his Heavenly Father.[2]

Principal Edwards of Bala notes this quality as specially distinguishing him: "In an address on preaching I ventured to say that Mr. Spurgeon was the only preacher I ever heard from whose lips the preacher's language seemed to me at the time quite adequate to express the truths of the Gospel. Great preachers seem often themselves to be oppressed with an uneasy sense of inability to convey to their hearers the depth and richness of Christian thoughts. It betrays itself sometimes in an exaggerated action, sometimes in the repetition of the same idea in different words. Nothing of this appeared in Mr. Spurgeon. His theology was the hardest of all theologies to couch in ordinary language. One step beyond, it would have plunged him into scholastic metaphysics. Yet he was perfectly at his ease, and seemed to revel in

---

[1] *The Prince of Preachers,* by James Douglas, M.A., p. 87.
[2] *Life and Work of C. H. Spurgeon*, by G. Holden Pike, Vol. I. p. 107.

preaching the profoundest mysteries of Christianity to the common people. It was Mr. Spurgeon's transcendent greatness as a preacher that he could do with apparent ease what many other great preachers cannot do without a painful appearance of effort. What is the explanation of his masterful repose? For one thing, though he was very original in his way, he was not a speculative theologian, struggling to give tongue to new thoughts. What he saw, he saw as clear as sunlight, and what he did not see with perfect clearness, he did not see at all. He was like Chalmers, who could walk round an idea, not like Edward Irving, whose ideas 'loomed.' Again, he was steeped in the language of the seventeenth century. Whether the Calvinism of the Puritans is true or not, it is a great theology, and Mr. Spurgeon believed it to be not only true, but the whole truth of God. Not, certainly, that he spoke to his own age in the cumbersome if majestic phraseology of Hooker or Howe, but his beliefs were thought and hammered out in the language of a past generation, and whenever the English of Mr. Bright would not express satisfactorily a theological idea which Mr. Spurgeon felt he must preach, he found ample stores to his hand in the Puritan divines. He was really master of two languages: the language of a theological past, and the non-theological language of the nineteenth century."[1]

This brings us up against the oft-quoted opinion that Spurgeon was the last of the Puritans. It might with equal assurance have been said before he came, that the Puritan day was already past. We may content ourselves by remarking that whatever the outward guise, there are abiding elements in Puritan thought and practice which are bound to re-appear whenever the problems of life, and the relation of man to God, are seriously considered. For "the Puritan conception of life on the earth has always been that of a battle and a march, under watchful heavens, towards superlative issues, with great destinies involved."[2]

A student of his time has expressed Spurgeon's debt to the Puritans in words that are worth reading, whether we agree with them or not—

"Spurgeon was the one great teacher of the century whose mind was steeped in Puritan ideas, theology and literature. In fact this remarkable man knew more about Puritanism than any of the Puritans themselves. His vast learning consisted almost entirely of this kind of erudition, and in this field he was one of the greatest of masters. This

---

[1] *British Weekly*, Feb. 4, 1892.
[2] Richard S. Storrs.

was at once the chief strength, and also the only weakness, of his splendid ministry. His mind was early surrendered to the Puritan hermeneutics, and all his homiletic power was modified by the impress of the mediaeval mould in which he preferred to cast his youthful thought. A curious and beautiful study will be furnished for those who are interested in this noble life. They will mark a problem in the higher psychology which will not admit of easy solution. Here was a great soul, a Master in Israel, who used to say, as he profoundly felt, that as every man must have some infallibility, his infallibility was the Bible. And yet, all unconsciously, this great student in the greatest realm of study failed just at this very point; for it was Puritanism, after all, and not absolutely and solely the Bible, which was really the rock of infallibility for his reliance. He never emancipated his intellect from the fascination exercised over him by Charnock, and Owen, and Coles."[1]

"The Puritan writers were to him what the Primitive Fathers are to trained theologians," says another critic, whose colour can easily be guessed. Once when sitting together on a Scotch hillside I told him a story of Moody, to whom a young preacher came complaining of the difficulty he had in finding texts. Holding up the Bible, Moody said, "That's not my difficulty, I've a book full of them; my difficulty is to find the sermons to put behind them." Spurgeon heard the story with interest, and then he said, "My difficulty is to find the text, for when a text grips me I have found the sermon."

"I confess," he once wrote, "that I frequently sit hour after hour praying and waiting for a subject, and that this is the main part of my study: much hard labour have I spent in manipulating topics, ruminating upon points of doctrine, making skeletons out of verses, and then burying every bone of them in the catacombs of oblivion, drifting on and on over leagues of broken water, till I see the red lights, and make sail to the desired haven. I believe that almost every Saturday of my life I prepare enough outlines of sermons, if I felt at liberty to preach them, to last me a month, but I no more dare use them than an honest mariner would run to shore a cargo of contraband goods."

On that same Scotch hillside I quoted to him some bits of Dr. Joseph Parker's sermons, and then recalled the story, probably apocryphal, that when the City Temple was being planned the minister of the Old

---

[1] *Christian Commonwealth*, Feb. 4, 1892

Poultry Chapel, on being asked what sort of building he wanted, replied, "Build me a church that when Queen Victoria passes down Holborn she will point to it and ask, 'What place is that?' and they will say, 'That is where Joseph Parker preaches.'" Spurgeon was silent for a minute, and then said, looking at me quizzically, "That is just what I should have felt, but I should have been too proud to say it."

Perhaps that half-humorous estimate of himself had some hidden truth in it. He was proud rather than vain. On March 23, 1855, as a very young man, he wrote: "My pride is so infernal that there is not a man on earth who can hold it in, and all their silly attempts are futile; but, then, my Master can do it, and He will." At the beginning of his ministry he accepted the title "Reverend"; in middle life he chose to be known without any title; but in later years he suffered himself to be called Pastor C. H. Spurgeon, in deference to a fashion that had then a vogue amongst Pastor's College men. Several University degrees were conferred upon him, but he put them aside, and he did not encourage his students to seek academic honours. He did not even attempt to give his sons the opportunity of a University career, though he urged them to seek theological training. The honours of the world, including the intellectual world, he held cheap; intellect he valued, and he was always a book-lover, but he ever felt after the eternal things rather than the temporal. His chief ambition might have been phrased in the ancient stanza—

> " Oh, would I were graduate in that College
> Where love is known that passeth knowledge,
> Where saints do comprehend and dwell
> In love incomprehensible."

Two questions are raised by one of the early criticisms on his work in one of the leading papers. After some rather ill-natured remarks about his success, the writer uses him as a foil for some exhortations to the clergy of that day. "Mr. Spurgeon is doubtless sincere, but surely the success of such a person in drawing large audiences to listen to him, in rousing them to attention, and in exciting their imaginations and feelings, ought to prove to the clergy of a higher grade who are educated as gentlemen, and have the tastes and manners of their class, and who are accustomed week by week to address congregations boasting of greater refinement than those of Mr. Spurgeon, that if they would cease to drawl and drone, as so many of them do, and infuse a little more life and spirit into their discourses, they would greatly increase their own popularity and usefulness. Dulness is almost as fatal a defect in a preacher as in an author, and Mr. Spurgeon, if all accounts be true, is anything but dull. The success of any preacher who would break in, as Mr. Spurgeon has done, upon the prevailing monotony and listlessness, would not be diminished by his being a gentleman and a scholar."[1]

The questions raised by this paragraph are whether or not Mr. Spurgeon was a scholar and a gentleman. Judged by University standards it can scarcely be contended that he was a scholar, and he never assumed that pose. But Dr. William Wright of the Bible Society, formerly of Damascus, himself a scholar, and Spurgeon's neighbour at Norwood, has told us how he has found him preparing his sermon with a Greek Lexicon on one side of his table and a Hebrew Lexicon on the other. The fact was that he had a great weight of learning, but it was never his habit to parade it. He was an omnivorous reader, had something like Macaulay's faculty for swift reading, and had an eye so rapid and a mind so acute that he could take in paragraphs as most readers take in sentences, and he could remember what he read. But he was not a technical scholar, nor ever pretended to be, and he had no patience with scholarly pretensions.

"He knew so much," says Dr. Lorimer, "that it was unnecessary for him to make a parade of knowledge, and he saw so deeply into the springs of the human heart and the sources of social changes, and acquired information with such rare facility that he easily out-ranked most of his enlightened contemporaries. As Thomas Carlyle expressed it, he very early in life acquired strength to stand by himself, and live without and above praise."

He reminded a man who with great air of learning had told him he was an Agnostic, that the Latin equivalent was "Ignoramus." Spurgeon was neither Agnostic in the spiritual sphere, nor Ignoramus in the intellectual.

It may also be freely conceded that judged by aristocratic standards Spurgeon was not a gentleman. He came of plain people, and he never gave himself airs. But even *The Saturday Review* at last acknowledged that, "if not very well bred, he was not in the least ill-blooded." From the beginning he had fine instincts, and early learnt the ways of men,

---

[1] *Illustrated London News*, Oct. 5, 1856.

developing with the years in matters of taste. He mixed with the highest as their equal, put the humblest at ease in his presence, said the right word at the right moment, took pains to remember people, was generosity itself, both in thought and action, and if "a gentleman is one who does not put his feelings before others' rights, or his rights before their feelings," then Spurgeon, the democrat, was a gentleman.

As was said of Wendell Phillips: "His high chair was placed in a Puritan household, which means that he was reared in an atmosphere of high thinking and holy living. It also meant that at the most plastic period of his mental growth he was familiarised with ideals of grave and decorous conduct, that he was taught to esteem lightly the frivolities and pleasures of the time, that he was impregnated with sharply- defined principles of right and wrong, and filled with an almost oppressive sense of personal responsibility for the use made of life and its opportunities."[1]

He was the soul of courtesy. Could anything excel in dainty rebuke the answer he sent to Miss Lydia Thompson, the actress, when, having introduced a song about Mr. Spurgeon into her play, and finding the newspapers inclined to protest, she wrote to him on the subject?

"Dear Madam," he wrote in reply, "I am very grateful for your courteous inquiry, and feel sure that I may leave what is purely a question of taste in your hands." The song was immediately withdrawn.

An answer as apt was once given to a person who called at his house without an appointment, and when refused an interview, would not take a denial. He sent a second message that "one of the Master's servants wanted to see him on the Master's business." Spurgeon sent a reply that he was very sorry, but at that very moment he was engaged with the Master Himself, and had no time for the servant."

A third retort may find a place here. A self-important individual introduced himself one day, and declared that the Lord had told him that he was to preach in the Tabernacle. "That is singular," said Spurgeon, "for I am in daily communication with the Lord, and He has said nothing to me about it." There was nothing more to be said.

He appreciated nice things, delighted in his flowers, admired fine scenery, was proud of his horses and took good care of them. He always said they were Jews, for though they took him to the Tabernacle

---

[1] *Black and White*, Feb. 6,1892.

on Sundays, they always rested on Saturdays. He loved to show his friends round his gardens and then sit in a summer-house and converse with them, or occasionally play a game of bowls. His tastes in fruits was peculiar: he never tasted a strawberry, but peaches made a strong appeal to him. He insisted on his garden being properly kept; one gardener who professed to have attained religious perfection had to be dismissed for carelessness, and Spurgeon declared that he would have a sinner next time. He had no patience with cant.

Which recalls another incident illustrating his instinct in mingling rebuke with gentleness. When Dr. David Thomas published anonymously his book, *The World of Cant,* he held up to ridicule the Reverend Falcon Small. The shafts of his somewhat bitter wit were evidently meant for his neighbour, Dr. Newman Hall, who bore it patiently for some time, but as the book gained currency wrote a pro-testing letter in reply, which in strength of invective outdid anything in the book. Having written it, he took it to Spurgeon to ask his opinion. Spurgeon read the letter carefully, and handing it back declared it was excellent, and that the writer of the book deserved it all. "But," he added, "it just lacks one thing." His visitor, quite gratified, was all attention. "Underneath the signature, 'Newman Hall,' you ought to put the words, 'Author of *Come to Jesus.*'" I should like to have been there as the two saintly men for a few minutes looked at each other. Then Newman Hall tore the letter in pieces.

Though gentle, Spurgeon was not pliant. He would go great lengths in friendship, but he could at times be stern. It was his dictum that if you had to kill an insect it was best to crush it with one effort. He could be blunt and severe, and though naturally trustful, could be indignant and strike hard. His own transparency of character made him liable to be imposed upon, but woe to the deliberate impostor when he was discovered. To the unwitting offender he was all tenderness and grace. The son of one of his deacons, after a prolonged absence from the services at the Tabernacle, returned, and meeting the Pastor soon afterwards, declared that his conscience would not let him stay away any longer. "Ah!" said Spurgeon, calling him by his first name, "you have a good conscience," and then he banished the answering smiles of the young fellow by adding, "almost as good as new, for you haven't used it much."

In his character there was a blend of humility and dignity. "To him C. H. Spurgeon was less than the least of all saints, but the minister of the Metropolitan Tabernacle was one of the leaders of the Lord's hosts, and was not a person to be trifled with. That was the secret of the apparent inconsistency."[1]

His generosity knew scarcely any bounds. What he once said about Hugh Stowell Brown might have been said of himself: "There was room enough in his heart for all the fleets of Europe to anchor." That was because the love of God was shed abroad so abundantly in his heart. Punshon's estimate of the American divine might have been used of Spurgeon too: "Sweep a circle seven feet around the Cross, and you take in all there was of Alfred Cookman."

My friend Benwell Bird tells that when in the early years he invited Spurgeon to Birmingham, where he was minister, a young photographer in his congregation desired him to ask his guest to allow his photograph to be taken. Spurgeon seemed disinclined to grant the request, so Mr. Benwell Bird pressed it, told him that he would be driven to the studio and back again, and that if he consented it would help the young man and give a great deal of pleasure to others. This forced Spurgeon to declare that he devoted the profit from the sale of his photographs to the support of a widow, and that he did not want to interfere with their sale.

In keeping with this was his offer in 1866 to devote the profits on his magazine, *The Sword and Trowel,* to the encouragement of his students to insure their lives, the money to go to the reduction of the premiums. But this plan came to nothing. Many a five-pound note was sent to his correspondents when they sought his help in need. During one of his visits to Mentone some one sent him a gift of £5 to help in his expenses. The same day he met a minister who had been ordered there for his health, and knowing something of his circumstances he handed the cheque to him, saying that his own expenses had already been met. He knew the value of money, and was not careless in the spending of it, but there was not a streak of meanness in his nature: he gave with both hands to those in need, and never in niggard fashion.

At one time he was offered a competence if he would join a mercantile firm in the City, but he refused. At another, one of the leading publishers in the City offered him £30,000 for the copyright of his works; but he was disinclined to change from his old firm, though it would have been very much to his financial advantage if he had done

---

[1] *C. H. Spurgeon,* by One Who Knew Him Well, p. 118.

so. Once he was left a handsome legacy, but finding that there were relatives of the testator in need and unprovided for, he did not accept it.

"It was he who made life for his disciples a more august thing in contact with him, and made them capable of higher efforts and nobler sacrifices. But even those who stood further away knew as if by instinct that Mr. Spurgeon was a man of the stuff of which saints are made. They knew that whoever else might sink into self-seeking, or fall down before the golden image of the world, that he would never. They knew that religion was always the prevailing and mastering idea of his life. He was one of those elect few to whom religious cares and interests were what secular cares and interests are to most men. He was self-controlled, observant, and wise, and he had a homely shrewdness and humour which were very refreshing. Mr. Spurgeon played his part well in the practical world, but his life was not there. The growth of the Kingdom of Grace was his prosperity; the opening of a new vein of spiritual life was his wealth. The one road to his friendship was a certain like-mindedness. This spirituality is so rare in men of great powers that it is invariably the way to influence. It inspires a kind of awe. Men bow before it, feel themselves in the presence of the eternal world, think wistfully of their own state, and are touched for a moment at least by a certain sense of wonder and regret."[1] It was not for nothing that he was known as "The Governor," but the title was more an indication of love than of authority.

His soul was seen best when he was listening to some one else speaking the praises of his Lord. He would clasp his hands, catch his breath, the tears would fill his eyes and overflow, his face would shine with a radiance other than of earth, and his rapture would communicate itself to those around. The speaker would be touched with the contagion, and at the end Spurgeon would rise to announce a hymn or to lead in prayer. At such times you saw the real man, the man to whom the Lord Jesus Christ was more dear than all the universe, whose boast was in the name of the Lord all the day long.

A rhapsody written in his later years is truer of him to the life than anything else I know.

> "All my soul was dry and dead
> Till I learned that Jesus bled —

---

[1] Sir W. Robertson Nicoll, in Preface to Nelson's *Volume of Sermons*.

Bled and suffered in my place,
Bearing sin in matchless grace.

"Then a drop of heavenly love
Fell upon me from above,
And by secret mystic art
Reached the centre of my heart.

"Glad the story I recount,
How that drop became a fount,
Bubbled up a living well,
Made my heart begin to swell.

"All within my soul was praise,
Praise increasing all my days;
Praise which could not silent be,
Floods were struggling to be free.

"More and more the waters grew,
Open wide the flood-gates few,
Leaping forth in streams of song
Flowed my happy life along.

"Lo, a river clear and sweet
Laved my glad, obedient feet!
Soon it rose up to my knees,
And I praised and prayed with ease.

"Now my soul in praises swims,
Bathes in songs and psalms and hymns:
Plunges down into the deeps,
All her powers in worship steeps.

"Hallelujah! O my Lord,
Torrents from my heart are poured!
I am carried clean away,
Praising, praising all the day.

"In an ocean of delight,
Praising God with all my might,
Self is drowned. So let it be.
Only Christ remains to me."

A CONTEMPORARY CARTOON

From a drawing in "The Hornet"

CHAPTER X

SPURGEON'S "SERMONS"

1855-1917

GREAT as was the influence of Mr. Spurgeon's preaching, it may be questioned whether the influence of his printed sermons was not greater. The series was begun the year after he came to London, and was continued during his life and after his death. There are sixty-three volumes of them in all, each containing from fifty-two to sixty sermons, except the last volume, which is incomplete owing to war conditions. If it is asked how it was possible to print so many sermons after Mr. Spurgeon's death, it must be remembered that, except during his holidays, there were three sermons preached every week and only one published. From early years all were reported, so there remained a great number of manuscripts available when the preacher's voice was silent. The publication of the sermons almost synchronises with the combined ministry of father and son at the Tabernacle, and in the biography of Thomas Spurgeon I have ventured to call those years "The Spurgeon Era."

The chief difficulty in appraising the sermons is the number of them. Nobody can sit down of set purpose and read them all, and even the most regular Spurgeon readers only know their own years. But there the volumes are, sixty-three of them, with perhaps another dozen containing sermons on connected subjects, a great monument of the fertile heart and brain that produced them, and a great legacy to the Church of Christ that only needs working over to have its riches revealed. If, instead of issuing his sermons hot from his heart, Spurgeon had published only a few volumes of selected discourses containing the purple patches scattered so plentifully over the whole field, a great sermonic literature would have been the result, but the world-wide influence of the sermons on human lives would have been missed.

"Mr. Spurgeon's power is diffused. He has given us no masterpiece like *The Pilgrim's Progress,* and few will read enough of Mr. Spurgeon in future generations to know what manner of man he was, even as few read Bunyan's *Sermons.* But there is spread over the great surface of his innumerable productions what might have made him famous if he had sought fame, and, as Mr. Haweis has discernment enough to see, the comparatively narrow range to which the Baptist confines himself makes his wonderful fertility and freedom unmistakably the result of genius.

"The chief desire amongst Christians is to gain an assurance of God's Love, and to this subject Mr. Spurgeon constantly recurs, not discussing it with a wave of the hand, but taking it up fully and elaborately. Many excellent sermons act merely as a mental stimulus: they instruct, and even to some extent excite, but they do not meet the deep needs of the soul. It is, we believe, one of Mr. Spurgeon's chief sources of power that he devotes himself almost entirely to the great concern. It is this that has made his writings so dearly prized by the dying. There is no more enviable popularity than the popularity this eminent minister has amongst those who are in the presence of the profoundest realities. When cleverness and eloquence have lost their charms, the dying often listen hungrily to Mr. Spurgeon's writings, when nothing else, save the Word of God, has any charm or power."[1]

"Said Dr. Pusey once: 'I love the evangelicals because of their great love for Christ.' And multitudes of educated Christian men loved Charles Spurgeon, in spite of intellectual differences, for that reason. From the days when Samuel Rutherford so preached his Master as to compel the Duke of Argyll once to cry out, 'Oh, man, keep on in that strain!' no one, we may safely say, has set forth the claims of Christ to men's love and service with such winning sweetness, and such melting pathos, with such eloquence of the inmost soul, as Charles Spurgeon. It may be that the dark background of his theology, to which the mind of this age could not by any effort accommodate itself, threw into greater relief this side of his teaching. The outside darkness of unbelief and irreligiousness was, indeed, made very terrible. But the inner world of spiritual experience was wondrous fair. And no human computation will be able to reckon the number of weary toilers in the working and lower middle classes whose narrow surroundings have been brightened and idealised by the glow from the realm of faith to which he introduced them. It was a great thing which this man achieved, to convince multitudes of struggling people, in the midst of a life which everything tended to belittle, that their character and career were a matter of infinite concern to the Power who made them, that they could not afford to treat sin lightly, or to throw themselves away as though they were of no account."[2]

A review of the sermons demands a volume rather than a chapter, and a great reward awaits the investigator patient enough to compile that volume, but even without such guidance as a volume might give they are invaluable. The wise preacher or writer on religious subjects will do well if, after mapping out his own course, he sees "what Spurgeon has to say about it." Sir William Robertson Nicoll, finding himself short of books in his first Highland parish, discovered that a shoemaker in the village had a set of Spurgeon's *Sermons,* and he set himself to read them all, with the result that he became one of Spurgeon's warmest admirers. Let not the reader be deceived by their apparent simplicity—it is the ease of genius, there is depth

---

[1] *British and Foreign Evangelical Review*, April 1877, and *British Weekly*, Feb. 17, 1888.
[2] *Christian World*, Feb. 4,1892.

as well as clearness; Spurgeon was, in fact, one of the great Doctors of Divinity. He had an intuitive knowledge of the ways of God, and of the needs of the human heart, and in all his preaching his one object was to commend God to men. Robert Louis Stevenson, in writing to a friend in London, says: "I wish you to get *Pioneering in New Guinea.* It is a missionary book, and has less pretensions to be literature than Spurgeon's *Sermons.*" But even if Spurgeon's *Sermons* had no claim to be considered as literature, it would be wise advice, "I wish you to get them." A distinguished professor in one of our theological Colleges was accustomed at times after his divinity lectures to read one of the sermons to his students, and he generally introduced it by saying, "Now let us have some of Spurgeon's heart-warming mixture."

"Honest Hugh Latimer, in the middle of the sixteenth century, has probably more in common with the great Baptist preacher than any of his contemporaries. It was surely a wise remark, and as it was made by a Jesuit it is not likely to be unfairly favourable to Mr. Spurgeon, that no one really loves his religion unless he is able to make a joke of it. Mr. Spurgeon may, as Matthew Arnold has said of Socrates, 'be terribly at ease in Sion.' But, then, a man to whom the spiritual is equally realised with the material is not likely to speak with bated breath of the truths of religion."[1]

For that testimony *The Daily News* is responsible; this from *The Times:* "Mr. Spurgeon laid his foundation in the Bible. His utterances abound with Scriptural text, figure, metaphor and allusion. Whatever he says sends his hearers to the sacred record. But starting from this basis, he has added to it a stock of reading such as few men can show in their talk or in their writing. He cannot be accused of not being a man of the world, or of not knowing the ways of the world, for he reads the Book and the book of nature too. His style is illustrated with almost pictorial brightness. What remains? The very tail of the matter. He occasionally drops a phrase to provoke a smile from the soft cheeks of ladies and gentlemen, and to make them think for the moment that they could say the thing better. We are not sure that Latimer and Ridley's sermons would not jar on modern refinement quite as much, but they never would have reformed the Church of England with smooth words and a pure classic style"[2]

The Bishop of Ripon, in his Cathedral, after Mr. Spurgeon's death, went further: "It was once said of Hugh Latimer, that towards the end of his career he spoke invariably from the same text. Whenever he spoke he opened his Bible and addressed the people from the words of St. Paul, 'Whatsoever things were written aforetime were written for our learning, that we, through patience and comfort of the Scriptures, might have hope.' The reason was

---

[1] *Daily News*, May 22, 1879.
[2] *The Times,* June 19, 1884.

that the text gave him the opportunity to speak of all things which were written in the past which he believed were for the learning and education of men in the present. Mr. Spurgeon once quoted that fact in Hugh Latimer's life; but he added that, were he to choose one text on which he would always be bound to preach, he would chose, 'To know the love of Christ that passeth knowledge, that you may be filled unto all the fulness of God;' for there, he said; his theme would be inexhaustible." Then the Bishop added significant words, which indicate perhaps the wise method of proclaiming the Word of God to the men of today. "The power of Mr. Spurgeon lay in this, that though from a critical standpoint he did not understand the Old Testament, yet being so much imbued with the spiritual conception he had drawn from patient and careful study of the Bible, he often escaped the very mistakes which from a critical standpoint he might have fallen into."

He preached from every book of the Bible, from some texts several times. It is remarkable that the sermons unpublished at the time of his death, no less than the published sermons, even when they deal with the same theme, avoid repetition. Of course, on occasion, when preaching away from home, he would repeat a sermon, generally the sermon of the previous Sabbath, but even in such cases, such was the productiveness of his mind that he would sometimes prefer to preach an original sermon.

"What a storehouse the Bible is," he once said at a meeting of the Bible Society, "since a man may continue to preach from it for years, and still find that there is more to preach from than when he began to discourse upon it. What pyramids of books have been written upon the Bible, and yet we who are students find no portion over-expounded, but large parts which have been scarcely touched. If you take Darling's *Cyclopaedia* and look at a text which one divine has preached upon, you will see that dozens of others have done the same; but there are hundreds of texts which remain like virgin summits, whereon the foot of the preacher has never trod. I might almost say that the major part of the Word of God is still in that condition: it is still an Eldorado unexplored, a land whose dust is gold." "For twelve years most of my sermons have been reported and printed," he said to the students at New College on October 26, 1866, "and yet in my search for something new I pace up and down my study, embarrassed with the abundance of topics, not knowing which to choose."[1]

"While reading the penny sermons of Joseph Irons, which were great favourites with me, I conceived in my heart," he says, "that some time or other I should have a *Penny Pulpit* of my own."[2] His earliest attempt was a series of *Waterbeach Tracts,* published the first year he was in London. The

---

[1] *Autobiography*, Vol. IV. p. 264.
[2] *Ibid.*, Vol. II. p. 154.

next year, 1854, his sermon preached on August 20 was published in *The Penny Pulpit* (No. 2234 of the Series), and in September 1854, expositions by Spurgeon were given in *The Baptist Messenger*. These excited so much interest that in 1855 the dream of a separate publication was realised, and *The New Park Street Pulpit* was started on January 7, the first sermon being on the text, "I am the Lord, I change not; therefore ye sons of Jacob are not consumed." Spurgeon always swam in deep waters. For seven years these eight page, small-print sermons, continued; then the abolition of the paper duty made it possible to have twelve pages and larger type, and the title was changed to *Metropolitan Tabernacle Pulpit,* and so continued until the end.

Sermons preached on Sunday and Thursday evenings still continued to appear in *The Penny Pulpit,* and as an outcome three volumes of the Pulpit Library were published, which are now very rare. The first printed sermon on the text, "Is it not wheat harvest today?" is included, and it is a wonderful production for a young man of twenty. "I think how surprised some of God's people will be," he exclaims, "when they get to heaven. They will see the Master and He will give them a crown. 'Lord, what is this crown for?' 'That crown is because thou didst give a cup of cold water to one of My disciples.' 'What, a crown for a cup of cold water?' 'Yes,' says the Master, 'that is how I pay My servants. First I give them grace to give the cup of water, and then, having given them grace, I will give them a crown.'" The first sermon in Volume II of the Pulpit Library, "Prove Me Now," was preached on the morning of the day when the disaster occurred at the Surrey Gardens Music Hall in the evening, and contains the almost prophetic sentence, "See what God can do, just when a cloud is falling on the head of him whom God has raised up to preach to you." In this volume also is "The Parable of the Ark," in which the deliverance from the Flood is cleverly allegorised.

Considerably more than a hundred millions of the weekly sermons have been sold, and they have been reproduced in numberless other ways. On one occasion the publishers received an order for a million copies, on another a quarter of a million copies were bought to be distributed in volumes of twelve or more to the students in the Universities, Members of Parliament, the Crowned Heads of Europe, and the householders in Ireland. So highly were they valued that one gentleman paid for their insertion in several of the Australian papers week by week as advertisements in order to reach the people in the Bush. At one time an enterprising American newspaper syndicate cabled the Sunday morning sermon across the Atlantic, and continued it until it was discovered that a rival newspaper had managed to tap the wires. Upon which Mr. Spurgeon wrote the characteristic paragraph: "The sermons were not long telegraphed to America, so that our friends who feared that the Sabbath would be desecrated may feel their minds relieved. We are not sorry, for the sermons which we saw in the American papers may have been ours, but they were so battered and disfigured that we would not have owned them. In the process of transmission the eggs were broken and the very life of them was crushed. We much prefer to revise and publish ourselves." The sermons were also frequently reported and reproduced in the religious press, and were translated into scores of other languages. A special edition in German was printed for the Leipsic Book Fair of 1861. Though they have ceased to be published week by week, the demand for them still continues, and possibly if the publishers could rearrange a selection of them according to topics, or in Bible order, they might yet have a great mission to fulfil. At Spurgeon's request I once made a selection of his sermons on "The Holy Spirit," which appeared to me worthy to be put beside Owen on the Spirit; but it involved the reprinting of the sermons, and his publishers postponed the matter.

The first day I was in London he captured me. Both morning and evening I was at the Tabernacle, and I sat enthralled as he discoursed on "The full soul loatheth an honeycomb; but to the hungry soul every bitter thing is sweet." I was the hungry soul and the things were not bitter. And as from the furthest corner of the top gallery later in the day I heard him talk on the text, "By this shall all men know that ye are My disciples, if ye love one another," I felt I was part of a great family. I heard him often afterwards, and have many memories of those golden days; two must suffice, both of the first sermon after his return from Mentone in different years. On the first occasion he was in splendid vigour, and his subject was, "I have yet to speak on God's behalf." As he developed his message, he seemed like a lion in his royal consciousness of strength and his scorn of all opponents. The next time he was tender and almost pensive, but never have I known more what "unction" means than then in his subject, "Supposing Him to be the Gardener."

Two collections representative of his ministry have been made, one by himself in the "Preachers of the Age" Series—he chose the title, *Messages to the Multitude,* the month he died; and another by Sir William Robertson Nicoll for a volume containing twenty-four sermons, published by Thomas Nelson & Sons. Both of them contain the sermon, "Supposing Him to be the Gardener," and both another which roused a great interest at the time, and was several times redelivered—"There go the Ships."

"Roughly the volumes may be divided into three classes," the Editor of the second compilation says. "There are those that represent the period of extreme youth. Then there is the period of his greatest powers, running perhaps up to 1876. The glow is unabated; the force, the grip, the strenuousness of appeal he himself never rivalled. Then come the later sermons. They are more full, perhaps, than their predecessors of mellow wisdom, of the wisdom of a deeply exercised spirit, and they are perhaps more touched with a growing gloom. For Spurgeon in his later days believed that he saw around him and before him a decay of faith." It was the sermons

Harry Furniss

in the middle period that appealed most strongly to Dr. James Denney. He was inclined, like some others, to despise Spurgeon, but by his wife's influence was induced to read him, with the result that "it was Spurgeon, perhaps, as much as any one, who led him to the great decision of his life— the decision to preach Christ our righteousness."[1]

Here a story by my former comrade in mission service, Manton Smith, a story at which Spurgeon was greatly amused, may be interpolated. One Monday morning he started from Burnham, in Essex, to get to Creeksea Ferry, in order to catch the omnibus to Southend. When he crossed the Ferry he found that the omnibus had gone, so he had a walk of twelve miles before him. It was very early in the morning. Soon he overtook an old man on the road and they fell a-talking. The old man, in answer to a question, told him that he had a Bible, but it was not much use to him nowadays, for the print was so small, but he said, "I'se got three old trac's, and they is beautiful, they is; they's a kind o' sort o' sermon-trac's, sir." "Where did you get them?" said my friend. "Why, sir, from the werry village where I am going to this morning, from a barber there. I called in one day when I was over this way, and he gave me them, and real nice they are too. I reads one and the t'other, and then the t'other, and then I begins again. They are written by a Mr. Spurgeon: I don't know if you have ever heard of him." He was assured, and it seemed a pity that he could not have more of the tracts, so a sixpence was given him and he was advised to ask for one called "There go the Ships," and to get it if he could; as he lived at the seaside it would be sure to interest him. When Manton Smith told the story at the Tabernacle Mr. Spurgeon laughed until he cried. "Is it summat about ships, sir?" "Yes, it is all about ships, and it will interest you very much, I am sure." "I should like to get that," he said; "I'll be sure to ask him. Let's see—what do you say they call it?" "'There go the Ships'; now don't forget!'" 'No, I won't forget. What did you say it was?" Before they parted he asked the title again, and as it was evident that the old man's memory was somewhat treacherous, the name was written on a slip of paper for him, and off he went to get some more "kind o' sort o' sermon- trac's."[2]

A third volume of sermons, entitled *Grace Triumphant,* was issued by the Religious Tract Society. None of them appears anywhere else. I had the privilege of editing it. The proof-sheets were read among the Alps, and the sermons are Alpine in thought and diction.

Mr. Spurgeon's method of preparing his sermons is not to be recommended to others who are without his gifts. Generally he had a number of friends to see him on Saturday afternoons, and after tea he would

---

[1] *Preface to Dr. Denny's Life,* by Sir W. Robertson Nicoll.
[2] *Stray leaves from My Life Story,* by J. Manton Smith, p. 177.

frequently conduct family worship with them. They all understood that they must leave at seven o'clock sharp. Then, as he used to say, he began to get some food for his sheep. Sometimes the Sunday morning sermon came easily, and in an hour or two he had completed his preparation, having his notes written on half a sheet of ordinary notepaper, possibly overflowing to the other side of the sheet. The fact was that he believed in preparing himself rather than the sermon, and, as he wrote so much, his power of accurate expression was exceptional. The Sunday evening sermon was generally prepared on Sunday afternoon. He was a rapid worker; his thoughts had the speed and the vividness of lightning. That was one reason why he never spent long in private prayer—he said to me more than once that he thought of twenty things in five minutes. He went to the pulpit with the assurance that he would be able to clothe his ideas appropriately at the moment, and many of his illustrations came to him during the delivery of the sermon.

The early sermons were but slightly revised, but the preacher became more exacting with himself as the years advanced. It was his custom to begin the revision of his Sunday morning's discourse early on Monday. The words used in speech have not the same force in type, and a sermon to be read with the same acceptance as it was heard must be pruned and amplified, balanced and arranged. It would astonish many of his readers to know what care he bestowed on his sermons. By constant practice he was able on Sunday mornings to preach long enough to fill just the twelve necessary pages, but at other times than Sunday mornings sometimes he preached longer, and sometimes shorter. During his long illness and the subsequent convalescence before his death, it was given to me to revise his sermons, and I was gradually emboldened to make large alterations in them, to develop a seven-page sermon into twelve pages, to take a piece from a long sermon and put it in a short one, and to add illustrative paragraphs here and there. Mr. Spurgeon himself, when he was able to scan the sermons of these ten months, was both interested and baffled when he tried to separate his own words from those of his editor.

The sermon to which greatest testimony has been borne of converting power was preached in the revival year, 1859. The text was "Compel them to come in." It is said that some hundreds afterwards joined the Church as a result of its influence, and from the ends of the earth scores of others have declared that it was the means of their salvation. Two other sermons preached in the Surrey Gardens Music Hall were specially blessed. One entitled "Looking unto Jesus," is, as Mr. Spurgeon himself confessed, "one of the most simple of the series, and likely to be overlooked by those who are seeking anything original and striking," but it is evidently a fit vehicle for God's Spirit, for in its printed form it has led many to the Saviour, as it did when it was preached. The other, "The Shameful Sufferer," has also had abundant testimony borne to its usefulness. In 1861 a sermon on "Simeon," twenty-four pages long, was printed in gold, and sold for a shilling, in aid of the building of the Tabernacle. Has any other sermon been deemed worthy of golden type?

The sermons numbered 500, 1000 and 1500 are all of them simple statements of the Gospel, and have been largely used in bringing people to Christ. The same may be said of No. 2000, issued after Mr. Spurgeon's death. Interesting meetings were held to celebrate the issue of the first three, and thank- offerings were given on behalf of the College, that other men might be trained to preach the same Gospel. It is singular that the sermon chosen a month before for publication during the week of Mr. Spurgeon's funeral was on "David serving his Generation by the Will of God." It had an immense sale.

A distinguished minister has given it as his judgment that "the sermon entitled 'Things that Accompany Salvation' is the most eloquent, and exhibits greater mental power than any Mr. Spurgeon ever delivered." It is certainly a most picturesque discourse, but it can, I think, be matched by others. The leap-year sermon on February 29, 1880, which was a Sunday, aroused much attention. The text was "One born out of due time."

There was a remarkable experience in connection with the sermon No. 74, in the second volume of *The New Park Street Pulpit.* On the Saturday evening Mr. Spurgeon's mind was directed to the text, "Thy people shall be willing in the day of Thy power," but the sermon would not come, although he worked late. Worn and dispirited he appealed to Mrs. Spurgeon. She advised him to go to rest, and promised to wake him early in the morning that he might have time enough then to prepare. He had scarcely got to sleep before he began to talk in his sleep and to preach in his talk a sermon on the text. Mrs. Spurgeon noted the points as he gave them, and, overjoyed, determined to keep awake repeating them. But at length she fell asleep too, and neither husband nor wife woke until the usual hour. With a start he rose, wondering what he should do, when his wife quieted him by telling him what he had preached in his sleep. "Why, that's just what I wanted!" he exclaimed. "It is wonderful!" he kept saying, and at the appointed hour he stood in his pulpit and preached it, though he gave the people no hint that he was preaching it for the second time.

An experience of quite a different kind came to him after a week of great depression. He felt that the only text he could take was "My God, My God, why hast Thou forsaken Me?" and he poured out his soul's bitterness as he spoke to the people. At the close of the service there came to him a man on the verge of despair, who began to hope because there seemed to be one man at least who understood him, and from that day he walked in the sunlight, bearing testimony years afterwards that the change was abiding. The preacher at once understood his own experience, and counted his week's eclipse of joy a small price to pay for the privilege of leading another soul back from the horror of thick darkness.

When Bishop Welldon went as a boy to Germany, his grandmother, much to his benefit, gave him some volumes of Spurgeon's *Sermons* as a stay to his faith. A newspaper correspondent during the South African War wrote that in passing through Cape Colony he generally found in Boer households a piano and a copy of Spurgeon's *Sermons* in Dutch; and Dr. Andrew Thomson declares that he has "seen Spurgeon's *Sermons* again and again in Christian homes in the continent of Europe, and not least in the manses and chalets of the Waldenses among the Cottian Alps."

David Livingstone carried through Africa the Sermon "Accidents, not Punishments," No. 408; it was returned at length to Mr. Spurgeon with a note along the top "Very good. D. L.," and was treasured by the preacher. Alongside Livingstone's pathetic copy there lay in his house a copy of the French edition of the same sermon, printed from lithographic plates on writing paper, in order that it might look like manuscript as it was read from the pulpit.

In Serbia for some time the priests did not preach, but the Bishop issued an order that preaching was to begin on a certain day, and the Minister of Finance, to make it possible, translated three of Spurgeon's sermons and sent them to six hundred and fifty priests; so on the particular Sunday in which they were called to preach they were equipped for the task. It would be interesting to know what happened afterwards. In Russia the sermons were frequently issued "by authority."

"I am aware that my preaching repels many," he said. "If a man does not believe in the inspiration of the Bible, for instance, he may come and hear me once, and if he comes and hears me no more that is his act, not mine. My doctrine has no attraction for the man, but I cannot change my doctrine to suit him." George Eliot in scorn wrote of him: "This Essex man drove bullock wagons through ecclesiastical aisles; his pulpit gown was a smock-frock." But the seal of God was on his ministry all through. A man once came to take a sitting at the Tabernacle, and hesitatingly said to its Pastor, "I may not come up to all that you expect of me, for I have heard that if I take a sitting here you will expect me to be converted, and I cannot guarantee that." "I do not want you to guarantee it," was the reply; "I do not mean the word 'expect' in that sense at all; but I do hope it will be so." "Oh," he said, "and so do I; I am going to take a sitting with that very view." "And it was so," adds Spurgeon, "of course it was so."[1] Many a time he uttered his belief that

[1] *Autobiography*, Vol. IV. pp. 88, 48.

there was not a seat in the Tabernacle but somebody had been converted on it.

He preached for conversions, and without conversions there was no welcome to the Church. A man once came offering £7000 to any object connected with the Tabernacle on condition that he might be accepted as a member. Astonished at the refusal which was kindly given to him, he pressed his claim. "No," said Mr. Spurgeon, "nor if you offered me seventy times seven thousand pounds." Years afterwards he returned in chastened mood to thank Spurgeon for his rejection, and was then received as a simple believer in Christ Jesus.

When Mr. Gladstone visited the Tabernacle on January 8, 1882, the preacher gave one of his simplest Gospel sermons on the text "Who touched My clothes?" The friendship between the two men was not in the least affected by Mr. Spurgeon's strong opposition to the first Home Rule Bill.

Very seldom he preached on public affairs, but on a few special occasions he did so with effect. His sermon on the Crimean War, entitled, "Healing for the Wounded," had a prodigious sale, and contributed materially to calm the public mind in the darkest moments of the Siege of Sevastopol. A notable sermon during the cholera visitation in 1866 was preached on August 12 of that year from Amos iii. 3-6. In 1862, when a collection was taken for the sufferers from the disaster at the Hartley Collieries, an effective sermon had as its text, "If a man die, shall he live again?" The death of the Prince Consort called forth another sermon which was widely appreciated. "Londoners will remember the way in which they were moved by the loss of many lives in the sinking of the *Princess Alice,* a pleasure steamer which went down in the Thames. The sermon preached by Spurgeon at the time served to give the disaster a vividness of spiritual meaning which affected many." The text on the occasion was, "He sent from above: He drew me out of many waters."[1]

The record of blessing on the printed sermons is apt to grow gloriously monotonous. A woman whose husband had fled the country consulted the preacher, and after he had prayed with her, he dared to tell her that her husband would be converted, and yet be a member of the Tabernacle Church. About that time on board ship the husband stumbled on one of the sermons, became a changed man, and a few months later was in triumph introduced by his wife to Mr. Spurgeon.

On a ship coasting to Oregon some one produced a volume of the *Sermons,* and after some pressure induced one of the passengers to read a sermon aloud. Nearly all the rest of the passengers, and as many of the crew as were at liberty, gathered round the reader. Some time afterwards at San Francisco he was accosted by a man who declared that he had heard him

---

[1] *The Times,* Feb. 1, 1892.

preach. "I am not a preacher, my friend," he said. Then it turned out that he had heard the Spurgeon sermon read, and the sailor added, "I never forgot that sermon: it made me feel that I was a sinner, and I have found Christ, and I am so glad to see you again."

In a South American city there was an Englishman confined for life in the prison. A fellow-countryman visited him and discovered that some years before another Englishman had called upon him in a similar manner, and left behind him two English novels, but between the leaves of one of the novels was a sermon of Spurgeon's entitled "Salvation to the Uttermost." It referred to the murderer Palmer, and gave the prisoner such hope in Christ that, though he never expected to be liberated, he was able to rejoice in his Saviour.

In an assembly at Chicago a plea was made for a missionary in the Far West, on the ground that through the reading of Spurgeon's *Sermons* no less than two hundred people had been converted there. A woman in Scotland tried to burn her Bible and a copy of one of the *Sermons;* twice it dropped out of the fire, the second time half-consumed, and, her curiosity excited, she read the fragment and was converted through it. A man keeping sheep in the Bush near Ballarat picked up a sheet of a newspaper, one of those in which the sermons were inserted as advertisements; had it been in sermon form he declared he would not have read it, but seeing it in the newspaper, he became enlightened and changed. Only a month ago I travelled with a man who in his youth had been engaged in a printing office. One day he picked from the waste-paper basket a crumpled paper, which turned out to be a Spurgeon sermon on the Atonement, and it opened to him the way of life and led him to an honourable Christian career.

In describing a service at the temporary Hall erected for Mr. Moody at Bow Road on one of his visits to London, a reporter says of the evening when Mr. Spurgeon preached, his text being, "The poor committeth himself unto Thee": "We have attended pretty regularly the services of Moody and Sankey, but were quite unprepared to find such a surging crowd of people outside the barriers after the announcement that the Hall was full." Carey Bonner, who as a young man was present that evening, speaks of it as the turning-point in his life.[1]

Of course there are not wanting humorous incidents in connection with the sermons. One of them was so blessed to a lady that she bought twenty copies of it and had them bound in a volume; and in Holland there was a person who read the sermons with pleasure until he was told that Spurgeon was a carnal and worldly man who wore a moustache, and then he was not able to read them any longer.

---

[1] *Christian Globe*, June 1, 1879.

SPURGEON'S "SERMONS"

Ian Maclaren's story of the Scotch wife who gave the parting injunction to her husband going to town, "Dinna forget Spurgeon," is memorable, as his own testimony is like that of thousands of others, "I cannot forget."

NOTES FOR THE SERMON "THE BEAUTY OF THE OLIVE TREE."
(Preached April 17, 1879.)

149

CHAPTER XI

"SPURGEON'S COLLEGE"

MR. SPURGEON spoke of his College as "his firstborn and best beloved." "This is my life's work, to which I believe God has called me," he said at another time, "and therefore I must do it. To preach the Gospel myself, and to train others to do it, is my life's object and aim." It has often been debated whether in the name he gave his College the apostrophe should come before the final "s" or after it; whether he intended it to be "The Pastor's College" or "The Pastors' College "; the College appertaining to the Pastor, or the College for the training of pastors. Doubtless it was the first, the personal tie was its chief distinction. The College centred in Spurgeon; his helpers did well in the training of the men, but he was the life and inspiration of it all. It was not the Tabernacle College, much less the Metropolitan College, as it is now named in *The Baptist Handbook*. It was Spurgeon's own. It is still in existence, and doing excellent work along Spurgeon's lines, but it is idle to say that it is just the same. It is no longer the Pastor's—Spurgeon is not there; the apostrophe is now shifted to the end of the word.

Spurgeon introduced a new directness in preaching, and he communicated it to his students. He taught them to speak plainly and to articulate clearly. Dr. Binney had prepared the way; he followed, and attracted many others to his standard. Before his day Dr. Vaughan tells us "the great object of educated preachers has been to acquit themselves learnedly, or to acquit themselves elegantly."[1] Carlyle said that "the most enthusiastic Evangelists did not preach a gospel, but keep describing how it should and might be preached."

"Suddenly a change sprang up," said a great London paper, "numbers of young men, inspired by the teaching of Mr. Spurgeon, went out into the villages and hamlets, preaching a crusade against indifference. Eyed contemptuously by the dignitaries of the Church, and coldly by the leaders of Dissent, they were yet warmly received by the people to whom they appealed. The preachers were 'hot gospellers,' it is true, but they spoke the language of the heart. The pathos of the unlettered sermons, the wild melody of the tunes they taught the people, their palpable sincerity, their undying zeal, soon attracted the villagers in throngs, and excited everywhere curiosity on the part of those—Churchmen and Dissenters alike—who considered themselves as the regular depositories of the Gospel. The movement spread; young men, hearing of the success which had already attended those who had first taken the field, went out in shoals; and there was very soon not a village

---

[1] *The Modern Pulpit Viewed in Relation to the State of Society.*

but had its local preacher, or a hamlet that could not boast its tiny meeting-house.

"Fired by the example of the peripatetic preachers and of the young disciples of Mr. Spurgeon, who, proceeding from his College, have baptised right and left the converts to their views, the old-fashioned Nonconformist minister has roused himself to greater activity, and bestirred himself to maintain the position that was, for the moment, imperilled."[1]

It all began quite naturally. A young man—Thomas William Medhurst—was converted by Spurgeon's ministry, and at once began to preach. Through his preaching two members were added to New Park Street Chapel, and this led Mr. Spurgeon to suggest that he should prepare himself for pastoral work. Accordingly, in July 1855, he was sent to a Collegiate School at Bexley Heath. Once a week he spent several hours with Spurgeon, and on March 21, 1857, he took up residence with the Rev. George Rogers of Albany Road, Camberwell, a Congregational minister, who afterwards became the Principal of the Pastor's College.

On September 22, 1855, Mr. Spurgeon wrote a letter to him in which occurs the following prophetic sentence: "I have been thinking that when you are gone out into the vineyard, I must find another to be my dearly loved Timothy, just as you are."

Soon after his studies started the first student became temporary pastor of a church at Kingston-on-Thames, Mr. Spurgeon arranging that, in addition to the amount Medhurst was receiving for his services, he should be paid what was being expended on his tuition at Bexley Heath. At the end of the first quarter this money was offered by Mr. Spurgeon to the student, with the remark that the deacons would not have given that extra if it had not been put in that way to them. Medhurst would not take the money, so the second student was installed.

"The work did not begin out of any scheme," Mr. Spurgeon said, "it grew out of necessity." The importance he attached to adequate training for the ministry may be judged by the sacrifices he made to secure it. "When we think of a young man who had recently married, who was still under twenty-three years of age, devoting a main part of his means to such service, his wife in the meantime practising the most rigorous economy in the household in order to enable him to do it, we shall not doubt his enthusiasm."[2]

It was said of him at the time, "He is not by any means the foe of learning, but he is more the friend of souls," and it was this love for the souls of men that he sought by word and example to instil into his disciples. He said to his own students often what he once said to those at Cheshunt College: "You are

---

[1] *Daily Telegraph*, May 9, 1879.
[2] G. Holden Pike in *Life and Work of C. H. Spurgeon*, Vol. II. p. 282.

preparing for the ministry, but do not wait till you have entered it—you may never live to do that. Win your highest honour, secure your best diploma now. Begin with speed, with fire, with learning, and live to save men now."[1] I sought to follow his advice and preached with some frequency while I was in College. When objection was taken to this course, Spurgeon one day said to me that that was just what he himself had done; what he learned during the day he preached in the evening, and those who poured cold water on my efforts were little aware that he was pouring on oil.

The breadth of his sympathy may be inferred from the fact that he had a Pædo-Baptist as Principal— and many a friendly tirade those two have had on the subject of baptism; his adherence to principle gauged by the crest he chose for the College, a hand grasping a cross, with the motto "Et teneo, et teneor."

The number of students grew apace. In 1861 he had twenty, the next year thirty-nine, the year following sixty-six, and in some subsequent years there were more than a hundred. Besides the College men, evening classes were initiated for those in business, and these were attended by numbers varying from a hundred to two hundred, the income of the College rising in 1863 to £4,400. Sometimes funds were low. On one occasion Mr. Spurgeon offered to sell his carriage and horses to sustain the effort, but the College commanded increasing confidence, so that in 1866 it had a third of the students in the nine Baptist Colleges in the kingdom and a third of the income.

It was, of course, objected that too many men were being turned out, and that many of them were of inferior quality, to which the President responded that "the muffs are the men who will preach; if you do not educate them they will be worse than ever"; and he was quite content if he could get one first-class man out of every eight. The result has been that many of the most useful and distinguished men of his denomination have been Spurgeon's men. There have only been two students received into the College who were not Baptists. At his death in 1892, nearly nine hundred men had been trained for the ministry.

They came to him from all parts of the kingdom—one walked all the way from the Highlands of Scotland—and gradually they arrived from all parts of the world. On one occasion there were two young men applicants for the College, and he put the same questions to both as to the other man's qualifications and merits, on the supposition that he had but one place to offer. In each case the man was so disinterested that he praised the other, and said that he ought to have the preference, and Spurgeon was so pleased with

---

[1] Dr. Reynolds to Holden Pike, *Ibid.*, Vol. V. p. 99.

their conduct in recognising the merits of the other that he decided to take both.

But wherever the men came from, it was clearly understood that the College did not exist to make ministers, but to train them. Unless a man could show some evidence that he was called to preach, and had already proved that he was able to fulfil the calling, there was no welcome for him, however great his gifts in other directions; but if he commended himself as a preacher, there was no barrier, however deficient he was in learning or in station. This meant, of course, a graduation in the College classes, for some students needed to acquire the rudiments of English, and it implied also a lowering of the average of scholarship. But it raised up a race of pulpit men, and not a few of Spurgeon's students gathered crowds round them, filled empty places of worship, built new ones, and found their way into the leading churches of their own denomination. Some of them occupy prominent places amongst the Baptists of today.

When the Tabernacle was built the College classes were held in rooms underneath it, but as the numbers increased a separate building became necessary, and the College block was erected at the rear of the Tabernacle on freehold land purchased from the Ecclesiastical Commissioners. It had once been the rectory garden, and Spurgeon declared that he intended to grow dissenters in it instead of cabbages. The foundation stone was laid by Mr. Spurgeon himself on October 14, 1873, and the College was opened by a series of special invitation meetings during September 1874. The building and furnishing cost over £15,000, and in course of time funds were accumulated which might, if occasion required, be used to wind up the Institution, and meanwhile could be lent out to help in the building of chapels. The premises also serve admirably for part of the Sunday School.

From the beginning the ultimate object of the College was the conversion of the people. The first student, Mr. Medhurst, once came complaining that he had been preaching for three months without knowing of a single soul having been converted. "Why," said Spurgeon, "you don't expect conversions every time you open your mouth, do you?" "Of course not," was the answer. "Then that is just the reason you haven't had them," he replied. But Spurgeon himself was once caught out in the same way. He preached in a large shed in connection with Mr. Howard's works at Bedford. Tea followed; and after tea an old gentleman said to him: "There was one thing I did not like this afternoon. You prayed that the Lord might be pleased to bring, here and there, one or two men out of the throng. I could not pray that. I wanted all of them." "You are quite right, sir," replied Spurgeon in all humility.

In the College the great event of the week was the Friday afternoon lecture by the President. Not that it was always a lecture. There would be readings from the poets on occasion. Young's "Night Thoughts" was a favourite, as were Milton, Cowper, Wordsworth and Coleridge, and Dr. Hamilton's "Christian Classics"; often Puritan writers were laid under contribution; and always the reading or the lecture was in itself a lesson in elocution. Two volumes of *Lectures to My Students* have been published, and they are as valuable today as when they were issued. They have had a great circulation and deserve it. In the second volume there are two lectures on "Posture, Action and Gesture," with illustrative pictures which may make the preachers wish that they could see themselves as others see them. A critic of wide experience and sound judgment has told me that he considers the lecture on "The Holy Spirit in Connection with our Ministry," in the second volume, the finest thing he has ever read on the Spirit's work.

The "College Series" also included a volume on *The Art of Illustration,* with examples; the famous book on *Commenting and Commentaries,* which is a monument of research, full of practical sagacity (Mr. Spurgeon said that he had read tons of books in its preparation), and a volume containing eighteen "Speeches." Many a man would be content with these nine volumes as a life work.

But the things that abide in the memory of his students are not those that can be printed in lectures. There were more intimate words, words that might have been spoken by a father to his sons, words uttered when reserve was cast aside, and the mind and heart freely opened to those whom he loved in the Gospel.

"Now you will have a brief holiday," he said with a smile on one occasion before the summer vacation. "If you talk at meetings, talk sense. If you preside, preside as well as you can. Your chief business, however, will be to take things remarkably easy. And don't get courting—that is not good for students. Keep yourselves to yourselves. Come back, as some one puts it, with your hearts and manners uncracked. Walk in the fields, like Isaac, by all means, and meditate, but don't lift up your eyes for Rebecca, she will come soon enough."

"Run a steam-roller of tremendous faith over the holes made in the roadway of Christianity by the sceptic," he advised. "It will then be a better road, and you may expect happier and increased traffic."

As to the attitude of the Pastor to the deacons he argued: "A minister is to take the oversight of the flock. Deacons are not shepherds, but part of the flock, therefore a minister must take the oversight of the deacons."

"It is a great mercy to be a minister," he said on one occasion; "preaching has often driven me to my knees, and chained me to my Bible." But at another time his word was: "I like to go into the pulpit saying 'God be merciful to me a sinner'; Luther trembled before he went into the pulpit, so did John Welsh and John Newton."

"Christ's presence with you in the service will fill it with more than the fragrance of a thousand flowers."

"The grace of God will teach you to be exact and circumspect in little things. I believe it will teach a boy to play marbles without cheating."

"Matthew Henry says that if religion has done nothing for your tempers, it has done nothing for your souls."

"Many sinners seem bullet proof, but we must get at them somehow. Go to their houses and dine with them and get familiar with their joints."

"Thomas Adams was a divine moralist rather than a theologian. Be sure you get his exposition of second Peter. He was the Shakespeare of the pulpit, and he says some wonderful things."

"Read Bunyan much; his *Holy War* for religious experience. Have *The Pilgrim's Progress* at your "finger-ends.""

"Richard Baxter is the most forceful of writers. If you want to know the art of pleading, read him, especially his sermon on 'Making Light of It,' and his *Reformed Pastor.*"

"Study successful models. I made Whitefield my model years ago. Buy his sermons, published by Milner and Sowerby: there are other editions which do not faithfully represent him."

"The Epistle to the Romans is the loftiest piece of writing in the human tongue."

"Whenever I meet a young Spurgeonite—and I do not know where it is possible to go without meeting one—I find him bouncing about like an india-rubber ball, as irrepressible as John Brown; whatever he may have in his knapsack, he goes marching on."

"A large church is to be preferred to a small one: the latter has many attractions, but it is not unlike a row-boat which a man is in danger of upsetting if he moves about, whereas the former is like an ocean steamer, on which he can parade without the possibility of upsetting the whole concern."

A London newspaper having said that Mr. Spurgeon's sermons of the previous Sunday were not at all striking, he remarked: "I have read the account with great amusement; it is not the work of a shepherd to strike his sheep, but to feed them."

"The best preacher is the man who charges his gun with all he knows, and then, before he fires, puts himself in."

"There is raw material in a Publican which you seldom find in a Pharisee. A Pharisee may polish up into an ordinary Christian; but somehow there is a charming touch about the pardoned sinner which is lacking in the other."

"I would like to see churches erected as the booksellers' shops are in Paternoster Row. If anybody wants to build a chapel next door to me let him come forward. I am not afraid of any of them. I am getting old and greyheaded, but if some one starts a coach and horse near me, I will start another horse to my coach."

"Be 'High Calvary' preachers, as one in mistake described 'High-Calvinistic' preachers. A minister should be able to say the word 'Grace' in his sleep."

"I believe they have abandoned me as an old hulk. I have been told that it would require a surgical operation to get a new idea into my head. Anyhow, I know that it would require a good many surgical operations to get the old ideas out."

"The greatest difficulty I have ever had to accommodate myself to the requirements of the Church of England, was on one occasion when I tried to get into a hansom cab with my neighbour, Mr. Burman Cassin, the Rector of Old St. George's, Southwark. He was several inches stouter than I am."

"Follow the example of the cook, who, when she sends up a well-cooked dinner, does not send up the cooking utensils with it. You do the same, leave your cooking utensils in the study, and give the people the result of their use, and see that you prepare something worthy to set before them."

"The Lord walked in the garden in the cool of the day. Walked, lest it should be thought He was in haste to punish. Not in the early morning, lest He seem to be fresh with anger. Not at midday, as though burning with wrath. But in the cool of the day, when the earth was silent, that man might meditate, and the dews began to weep for man's misery, and evening began to light her lamps, that man might have hope in darkness. Then, and not till then, came forth the offended Father."

"God seems to talk to me in every primrose and daisy, and smile at me from every star, and whisper to me in every breath of morning air, and to call aloud to me in every storm."

Occasionally the Friday afternoon was given up to extempore preaching, and Mr. Spurgeon has quoted as the best thing of its kind the response of a student to whom fell the word "Zacchæus." He rose immediately and said, "Mr. President and brethren, my subject is Zacchæus, and it is therefore most appropriate to me; for first, Zacchæus was little of stature, as am I; secondly, Zacchæus was up a tree; so am I; thirdly, Zacchæus made haste to come down; and so will I," and thereupon the speaker resumed his seat. The students called to him to go on, but the President said, "No, he could not add anything to such a perfect little speech without spoiling it."

Of course all sorts of cranks applied for admission to the College, and they were dealt with very abruptly. "I have more than once felt myself in the position of the Delphic oracle," Mr. Spurgeon records, "not wishing to give wrong advice, and therefore not able to give any. I had an inquiry from a brother whose minister told him he ought not to preach, and yet he felt that he must do so. I thought I would be safe in the reply I gave him, so I simply said, 'My brother, if God has opened your mouth, the devil cannot shut it; but if the devil has opened your mouth, I pray the Lord to shut it directly.' Some time afterwards, I was preaching in the country, and after the sermon a young man came up to me and thanked me for encouraging him in preaching. For the moment I did not recall the circumstances, so he reminded me of the first part of my reply to his inquiry. 'But,' I said, ' I also told you that if the devil had opened your mouth I prayed the Lord to shut it.' 'Ah,' he exclaimed, 'but that part of the message did not apply to me.'"

Deacons seeking ministers for their churches often applied to Mr. Spurgeon. One asked him to send a student who could "fill the chapel," and got an answer saying that Mr. Spurgeon had not one big enough, but he thought he could send one who might fill the pulpit. A reply came saying that that was really what they wanted, and a minister was accordingly sent. I believe it was Mr. Whale. Times innumerable the choice of a minister was left to Mr. Spurgeon's discretion, and he took the responsibility of sending men to Australia, New Zealand, Canada, Haiti, the Falkland Islands, South America, South Africa and Amsterdam.

The Tabernacle Church was for many years the largest supporter of the College; it became a point of honour to contribute as many pounds as were represented by the year, £1870 in 1870, and £1890 in 1890. The Church also entertained the men who yearly met for Conference. These Conferences, usually held the week before the Baptist Union week in the spring, began in 1865, and have been continued ever since, frequently attended by some five hundred ministers. The President's address, which Mr. Spurgeon gave twenty-seven years in succession, was the great event of the gathering. The last of these, entitled "The Greatest Fight in the World," was separately published, and had an immense circulation. One gentleman posted a copy to every minister and clergyman in Great Britain, and it was translated into several other languages.

The closing day of the Conferences called forth a sermon by the President, and this was followed by memorable Communion Services, which always ended by the brotherhood singing with linked hands some verses from the metrical version of Psalm cxxii, "Pray that Jerusalem may have peace and felicity." This is now known as The College Psalm, and "Hallelujah for the Cross" is known as The College Anthem.

Two organisations have for many years supplemented the work of preparation for the ministry. The Pastor's College Society of Evangelists, now extinct, furthered mission work in our own country, and sent forth six or eight men in the service, amongst them my colleague of fifteen years, Manton Smith, whose Gospel witness, singing, and cornet-playing were renowned all over the kingdom and beyond. "The Pastor's College Missionary Association," still existent, has helped to support missionaries in

North Africa, France and South America, but has never attained wide dimensions, men generally preferring to go forth in connection with recognised Missionary Societies.

The College itself is still being maintained with vigour. There is room for such a School of the Prophets, and it is to be earnestly hoped that means for its support may be forthcoming for many years.

CHAPTER XII

"SPURGEON'S ORPHANAGE "

PARAPHRASING Elijah's challenge, Mr. Spurgeon once exclaimed, "The God that answers by Orphanages, let Him be Lord." None need fear to uphold the challenge, for by that test Christ is victor. It was He who taught the world the worth of children—"of such is the Kingdom of Heaven."

For many years the Church which now has its home in the Tabernacle has maintained almshouses: in previous chapters it has been noted how Mr. Spurgeon devoted large sums of money to their enlargement. But at one of the Monday evening prayer meetings, which in his day were phenomenal, the Pastor said: "We are a large Church, and should be doing more for the Lord in this great city. I want us to ask Him to send us some new work; and if we need money to carry it on, let us pray that the means may also be sent." So the Stockwell Orphanage was really born in a prayer meeting.

Soon afterwards Mrs. Hillyard, a clergyman's widow, at that time in fellowship with "Brethren," afterwards associated with the Tabernacle Church, determined to devote her money to the service of God, but was doubtful as to the right purpose, and the best means. She was advised to place it in Mr. Spurgeon's hands, as he was a man of affairs, as well as a man of God. Soon afterwards she saw an article in *The Sword and Trowel* for August 1866 advocating the establishment of schools where "all that we believe and hold dear shall be taught to the children of our poorer adherents." Upon this she wrote to Mr. Spurgeon telling him of her desire to establish an Orphanage, and asking his assistance.

He looked upon it as a direct answer to the prayers of the people, and asked for further particulars. In reply Mrs. Hillyard said that there was need of an orphan home requiring neither votes nor patronage, where boys would be trained in simple Gospel principles. Mr. Spurgeon and Mr. William Higgs made an appointment, and when they called at her modest home they feared that there had been some mistake. So they began the interview by saying that they had called about the £200 she had mentioned in her letter. "Did I write £200?" exclaimed the lady; "I meant £20,000." "Oh yes," said Mr. Spurgeon, "you did put down £20,000, but I thought perhaps there was a nought or two too many."

In the subsequent discussion Spurgeon was first of all careful to inquire whether there was not some relative to whom the money ought to be given, and that point settled in the negative, he then made the suggestion that the money should be sent to George Muller at Bristol, for whom he had always a great admiration. But nothing would do but that Mr. Spurgeon himself should inaugurate the work, and as this found a response in his own heart, the matter was settled then and there. In the Board Room of the Orphanage there is a stained glass window representing the interview. Mrs. Hillyard lived for some years to rejoice in the good work which she had so successfully initiated, and her last words as she died on January 13, 1880, were, "My boys! My boys!"

Some astute business brains (including his own) were at once set to work to secure a site and to project plans for the Orphan Homes. The first condition was that they should be within easy reach of the Tabernacle, and though this greatly increased the difficulty, a plot of ground sufficient for the purpose was found behind some houses in the Clapham Road. The negotiations almost broke down when the vendor, presuming on Mr. Spurgeon's anxiety to establish the Orphanage, tried to impose higher terms on him than those at first indicated. The Committee was inclined to seek another site, but Spurgeon himself went to see the owner, pointed out to him the unsuitability of his property for any other purpose, and at length told him that he was inclined to fine him a thousand pounds because of his obstinacy. Upon this the original terms were confirmed, and though there was some delay in realising the securities that Mrs. Hillyard meant to put at Mr. Spurgeon's disposal, the buildings were at length completed, and a festival of praise was held in the grounds on September 9, 1869.

So much interest had by this time been aroused, that several friends were ready each to bear the cost of one of the houses—an illustration of the wisdom of the word that "he that believeth shall not make haste." The Silver Wedding House was raised by a gift which a lady had received from her husband on her silver wedding day. She afterwards willed £25,000 to the Orphanage. The Merchant's House was the gift of a business man. The Workmen's House was the combined gift of the contractors and the artisans at work on the building, the former giving the materials, the latter the work. Unity House commemorated a saintly lady. The Testimonial Houses were the gift of the Baptists of Great Britain. The Sunday School House came from the efforts of the Tabernacle Sunday School and the College House from men educated in the College.

Help poured in, and if at times the stream appeared as if it would cease, the unfailing method was that the Trustees themselves gave what they could and then betook themselves to prayer. Not once or twice, but dozens of times the answer came. At one time £10,000 was given. At another an unknown helper sent £1000 for the College and £1000 for the Orphanage, saying "the latter led me to contribute to the former," a specially grateful evidence that the new venture of faith was not likely to interfere with the older ones.

The coming as Head Master of the Orphanage of the Rev. Vernon J. Charlesworth, who up to then had been assistant to Newman Hall at Surrey Chapel, was an event of first importance. His influence on the boys, his advocacy of the Orphanage, and his guidance of affairs, were a great asset for many years, until in 1914 he finished his course. Mr. Thomas Spurgeon was then appointed Director, and, on his resignation, Mr. Charles Spurgeon took up the work as President-Director, which he is carrying forward with such conspicuous success today.

In 1879 the girls' wing of the Orphanage was inaugurated, Mrs. Hillyard giving the first £50 and Mr. Spurgeon the second £50. Though the extension was undertaken with some hesitancy, similar experiences of God's goodness attended this enterprise, the necessary funds were forthcoming, the quadrangle was completed, with Infirmary, Gymnasium and Dining Hall, and there it stands today, a monument of philanthropy and faith.

In the Main Hall there is a memorial of the Founder executed in terra-cotta by Mr. George Tinworth, and the fine collection of engravings of the Reformation collected by Mr. Spurgeon is exhibited on the walls of the same Hall, where also are the two stained glass windows, one in memory of Mr. Charlesworth, one in memory of Thomas Spurgeon. Mr. F. G. Ladds, once himself a sharer in the benefits of the Orphanage, has been for years Secretary of the Institution.

The President was always received with uproarious joy when he visited the Orphanage. "As to the happiness of the orphans, there is no doubt about it. When Mr. Spurgeon opened the door there was a shout of delight at the appearance of their friend. It was like a welcome to an old schoolfellow, and was repeated in every house we entered; not the kind of cheer which requires a lead, but one that sprang up on the instant when it was known that Mr. Spurgeon was at the Orphanage."[1]

"Some time ago," he said, "a friend who often aids the Orphanage gave us six dozen bunches of turnips, and he merrily added, 'I hope some one will send you the mutton,' and sure enough about an hour afterwards a farmer sent a whole sheep."

Three things are to be noted. The Orphan Homes are open to all denominations—indeed, amongst those who have been received, children of Anglican parents predominate over those of any other denomination. In the second place, need is the supreme plea, there are no votes necessary, and no canvassing is allowed. And in the third place, there is no distinctive dress either for the girls or boys. They are clothed like other young people, with corresponding gain to their individuality and happiness. In its early days a woman with eight children, belonging to the Anglican Church, applied, when the Orphanage was full, to have one of her boys accepted. There was no room, they said. "Never mind," said Spurgeon, "squeeze in the little boy. Squeeze him in," and they did.

---

[1] *Daily Telegraph*, May 6, 1880.

In fact, as I ventured to say at one of its June Festival meetings, the Orphanage is the greatest sermon Mr. Spurgeon ever preached. It has five hundred heads, two hundred and fifty of them girls' heads, two hundred and fifty of them boys' heads, all the heads contributing to the appeal and the application at the end of the sermon—praise to the Great Lover of Children, who taught His people this divine way, and help to those who care for them in His Name.

To end, Spurgeon himself may be quoted: "Somebody has written to me that he will put the Orphanage in the corner of his will. I said, 'Do not do that on any account, because if you put it in the corner you will tear it off some day. Kindly put it in the centre and see that it is done in the right way.'"

CHAPTER XIII

A CHAPTER OF INCIDENTS

A LIFE like Spurgeon's, that touched so many people in so many ways, could not fail of incidents. Many stories about him gained currency which were untrue. Some of them had been told of preachers of previous generations, and some were the inventions of nimble wits, but there are enough remarkable experiences, coincidences, and excitements in his history to warrant at least a chapter to themselves. The difficulty is to know what to choose.

Let us begin with his power of recognising folks. He could tell at a glance whether the regular members of his congregation were present, and his recollection of those whom he had only casually met was phenomenal. Dr, William Wright tells how as a young man he spoke to Mr. Spurgeon on his visit to Belfast, and on his first furlough from Damascus he visited the Tabernacle one Sunday morning. Mr. Spurgeon, to his astonishment, immediately recognised him.

Of course sometimes he failed. "How are you, Mr. Partridge?" he said to one gentleman who came into his vestry to greet him. "I am well, sir," he answered, "but my name is Patridge, not Partridge." To which Mr. Spurgeon instantly retorted, "Ah, well, I promise you that I will make game of you no more." But he was not always even so fortunate as that. After a crowded meeting a man pressed through the throng and made frantic efforts to grasp the preacher's hand. At length he succeeded, and asked whether Mr. Spurgeon did not remember him. Spurgeon was nonplussed for once, but he answered, "My dear fellow, I have forgotten your name, but your face is quite familiar to me." Whereupon the excited individual cried out, "Well, that is singular, seeing that you rendered me the greatest service one man could render another—you buried my wife." "Hullo, Dr. Way-land! I am glad to see you. Are you the author of Wayland's *Moral Science?*" was his greeting to an American visitor. "No," replied the newcomer, "but the author of Wayland's *Moral Science* was the author of me."

Once in New Park Street, at an evening service, Mr. Spurgeon had announced the hymn preceding the sermon, and then he opened the Bible to find his text, which he had carefully studied. But a text on the opposite page caught his eye and he felt impressed to preach upon it. It came upon him like a lion from a thicket. As the people were singing, he was sighing, and wondering what to do. He could not get away from it, so he announced the new text and got through firstly and secondly, but could not think of anything beyond. He was inwardly chiding himself for his rashness, when—the light went out. There was, of course, some excitement, but he quieted the people, told them the gas would soon be lighted again, and went on talking about saints in the darkness and sinners in the light. If he had announced his first text he could scarcely have continued an ordered discourse under the circumstances, but it was quite easy to make the transition when his mind was free. When the lamps were again lighted, the congregation was "as rapt and subdued as ever a man had in his life." And at an early Church meeting two persons came to seek Church membership who had been converted that night, one during the first part of the sermon, the other during the second part.

Many times the preacher has been guided to say things that seemed almost uncanny in their applicability. He once said that there was a man in the gallery listening to him with a gin bottle in his pocket. It so happened that there was such a man, and he was startled into conversion. A woman of the city who had determined on suicide came in with the crowd to hear a last message that might prepare her to die. The text arrested her—"Seest thou this woman." The discourse changed her heart, and she confessed Christ as her Saviour.

There was a man who regularly attended the Tabernacle, but his wife consistently refused to accompany him. But one evening, when her husband had gone to the service, her curiosity overcame her obstinacy. That she might not be recognised she put on some very plain things, and quite sure that she would be unknown, she pushed her way in with the crowd. The text that evening was, "Come in, thou wife of Jeroboam, why feignest thou thyself to be another?" The result was that her prejudices were overcome and she began to attend with her husband. He told Mr. Spurgeon about it, his only complaint being that the preacher should compare him to Jeroboam.

A man was won for Christ because the preacher pointed to him and said: "There is a man sitting there who is a shoemaker; he keeps his shop open on Sundays; it was open last Sabbath morning. He took ninepence and there was fourpence profit on it: his soul is sold to Satan for fourpence." The man was afraid to go and hear Spurgeon again for fear he might tell the people more about him, for what he said at first was all true; but at last he came and the Lord met with him.

One Sunday evening Mr. Spurgeon, pointing to the gallery, said: "Young man, the gloves you have in your pocket are not paid for." After the service a young fellow came beseeching him not to say anything more about it, and the circumstances led to his conversion.

In the Surrey Gardens Music Hall one morning several young men continued to wear their hats even after the service began. In the middle of the opening hymn Spurgeon told the congregation that he had lately visited a Jewish synagogue, and in accordance with the custom of the place he had worn his hat during the service. "But," he added, "it is the Christian practice to uncover in a place of worship. I will therefore ask these young Jewish gentlemen kindly to remove their hats." Of course they did.

A similar flank attack discomfited a party of undergraduates who came to the Guildhall in Cambridge when Mr. Spurgeon was speaking there. They stood up in front of the people, intercepting their view of the preacher. But when the preacher quietly remarked; "If the bodies of those young gentlemen were as transparent as their intentions they might continue to stand. As it is, I hope they will resume their seats." They hastily sat down.

Once, when he was preaching in a country place, he noticed a change come over a woman who sat near the front of the congregation. There was no mistaking it. "I think our sister is dead," he said. His description of the circumstance was that she was "washed into heaven on a wave of joy."

When visiting Tring in his early days he said that God had answered his prayers before he was converted. Some ultra-Calvinists found fault with his teaching, and took him to task for it, quoting a text which they thought was in the Bible, but may be searched for there in vain—"The prayer of a sinner is abomination to the Lord." "How can a dead man pray?" "they asked. There was quite a little ring formed round him, and he maintained his position. But, "after all," he says, "the victory was won not by Barak, but by Deborah." A very old woman in a red cloak managed to squeeze herself into the aisle, and turning to his accusers she said: "What are you battling about with this young man? You say that God does not hear the prayers of unconverted people, that he hears no cry but that of His own children. What do you know about the Scriptures? Your precious passage is not in the Bible at all, but the Psalmist did say, 'He giveth to the beast his food, and the young ravens which cry.' Is there any grace in them? If God hears the cry of the ravens, don't you think He will hear the prayer of those who ate made in His own image? You don't know anything at all about the matter, so leave the man alone, and let him go on with his Master's work."

One evening he advised his people when they went home to get a sheet of paper and write on it either the word "Saved" or the word "Condemned." A man, whose wife and children were members of the Church, who had only gone to the Tabernacle to please them, took a sheet of paper when he went home and began to write the latter word. One of his daughters went up to him, put her arms round his neck and said, "No, father, you shan't write that." Her tears fell on the paper; the mother came up and pleaded with him; they all knelt in prayer together; and when he rose he put another curve to the letter "C" which he had written, turning it into an "S," and then finished the word "Saved."

At a session of the Congregational Union where Mr. Spurgeon was to speak, he entered when some one else was on his feet. There was a little hubbub, and the speaker soon sat down. The Chairman hurriedly chose a hymn, and it happened to be one for an infant baptism. Mr. Spurgeon was sitting beside Mr. Samuel Morley, and leaning over to him, he asked how Mrs. Morley was getting on. "Getting on," said Mr. Morley, "she is quite well." "How is the baby? Alive and well, I trust," continued Mr. Spurgeon, and about this juncture the people began to discover what a blunder had been made. The baptismal hymn was concluded hurriedly, and the people were very much amused when Mr. Spurgeon, on rising to speak, repeated what he had whispered to Mr. Morley, and added that he was very disappointed at not having to witness the very interesting ceremony the hymn had led him to expect.

When he was the guest of Canon Wilberforce at Southampton, in company with a number of High Church clergymen, Lord Radstock and others, the discussion turned on the question of baptismal regeneration. Lord Radstock intervened by saying: "What sort of persons do these become whom you regenerate in baptism?" "I will tell you, 'Eyes have they, but they see not; ears have they, but they hear not; noses have they, but they smell not, neither speak they through their throats. And,'" added Mr. Spurgeon in a whisper that everybody heard, "'they that make them are like unto them.'" Canon Wilberforce afterwards spoke at the Tabernacle on the occasion of Mr, Spurgeon's Jubilee, and applied to Spurgeon some of Augustine's words, "He whose life is lightning, his words are thunders for God."

One year at Mentone Mr. Edward Jenkins, the author of *Ginx's Baby,* was present, and he persistently and somewhat rudely ridiculed believers' baptism. There were quite a number of persons present, and they all looked to Mr. Spurgeon to take up the cudgels. But he was silent. Before they separated, however, he suggested that they should all go on an excursion to Ventimiglia, in Italy, the next day, and the matter was so arranged. On reaching the Cathedral there, Spurgeon, as one familiar with the place, led the way into the crypt. When the company had gathered round the baptistery, he turned to Mr. Jenkins, saying: "You understand Italian better than we do. Will you kindly interpret to us what the guide is saying?" Willingly and unsuspectingly, he consented. "This is an ancient baptistery," he began; "he says that in the early Christian Church baptism was always by immersion." The crypt rang with laughter, and the objector confessed that the answer he had received was no less crushing because it had been given after a day's delay.

Another Mentone experience was of a different character. An organ-grinder had been trying to attract attention for some time in the garden of the hotel, when Mr. Spurgeon, noticing his forlorn look, asked if he might have the instrument. So he began to grind the music: the attention of the people in the hotel, as well as the passers-by, was attracted, and he soon had a pile of coins, amounting to sixteen francs, thrown to him. Then he insisted on some of the others taking their turn, but naturally none of them were so successful.

Even when he was ill he could extract merriment from his surroundings. Quite good-humouredly he told of a curate who felt it his duty to call upon him one year on his arrival at Mentone. He was shown up into the sitting-room, and after introducing himself he said, "And I hope you are bettah." He was assured on the point. Then his visitor went to the stove and said, "I do like a fiah. Something so English about a fiah." Back to the invalid, "And you really are bettah." Again the assurance was given; again preference for an open fire rather than a stove was expressed, and the good man bowed himself out, having really done a great deal of good in another way than he intended. No matter how depressed Spurgeon was afterwards, it always roused him if one asked him if he was not bettah, and if he did not like a fiah.

Another year, depressed and ill, he had reached his hotel in Marseilles, and asked for a fire to help him to bear his pain, about which he once wrote: "Lucian says, 'I thought a cobra had bitten me and filled my veins with poison; but it was worse, it was gout.' That was written from experience, I know." When the porter came to light the fire he brought vine branches to kindle it, and Spurgeon simply called out in agony, as he thought of the destiny of fruitless branches of the Vine, good for no work, only fit to be burned.

Yet another Mentone story. A simple lunch of biscuits and milk, taken in the hotel garden, often formed Mr. Spurgeon's midday meal. He was, as all the residents in the hotel were aware, a total abstainer from intoxicants. Amongst the residents was a lady, anything but well-disposed towards him, and one day she thought her chance of doing him an ill turn had come. He was evidently a humbug, and she was at no pains to conceal the fact. She had heard his secretary come downstairs and ask for whisky and milk, and it was therefore clear that drinking was being done on the sly. One of the ladies to whom she imparted the information happened to be a friend of Mr. Spurgeon, and she frankly said she did not believe a word of it. Then the mystery was explained by the defective hearing of the suspicious person. Mr. Harrald had simply asked for "biscuits and milk" for the accustomed lunch.

On December 30, 1888, after conducting a service at Mentone, Mr. Spurgeon went to a villa to have tea. Resting his stick on the marble outside the carpet, it suddenly gave way and he fell down the marble steps. He turned over twice, two of his front teeth were shaken out, and the money in his pocket was thrown into his Wellington boots. On being picked up he remarked, "Painless dentistry," but in writing to his friend Newman Hall, he said, "Yet I pity the dog that has felt as much pain in his four legs as I have in one."

In the summer of 1890 the clock on the Tabernacle rostrum was stolen by a humorous burglar under the plea that "the reverend gentleman was less concerned with Time than with Eternity."

When Mr. Spurgeon went, years ago, to preach for Dr. Clifford, whose church was then at Praed Street, he said in the vestry before the service, "I cannot imagine, Clifford, why you do not come to my way of thinking," referring to his Calvinistic views. "Well," answered John Clifford, "you see, Mr. Spurgeon, I only see you about once a month, but I read my Bible every day." Dr. Clifford is one of Mr. Spurgeon's most ardent admirers: he has treasured some Spurgeon relics, amongst them the notes of one of his sermons, written on the back of an envelope; another a copy of the printed sermon No. 95, on "The Day of Atonement," which he heard Spurgeon deliver in New Park Street on April 10, 1856, coming to London on purpose. On his copy of the sermon he has written, "The atmosphere of expectation and of admiration; the ease and energy of the preacher, made the occasion memorable.—J. Clifford."

Mr. Spurgeon generally arrived at the Tabernacle early enough to choose the hymns for the service, and often he chose the tunes too. One day he said to the precentor, "What tune shall we have to this hymn?" He answered that "Redhead" would be suitable. At this juncture one of the deacons, whose hair was decidedly bright, entered. "Why," said Spurgeon, mentioning his name, "here is your tune—Redhead." "My hair is not red, but golden," he answered. "Yes," said Spurgeon in a flash, "eighteen carat."

On three occasions Mr. Spurgeon had an interview with a madman under dangerous conditions, but his coolness triumphed in each case. One came into the vestry at the Tabernacle, shut the door, and declared that he had come to cut Mr. Spurgeon's throat. "I would not do that," he replied, "see what a mess it would make on the carpet." "Oh, I never thought of that!" he said, and was quietly led out of the room.

The second occasion was when he was lying ill at the Hotel des Anglais at Mentone. He had persuaded all his friends to go for a walk, and scarcely had they left when a man, evidently mad, rushed in and said, "I want you to save my soul." With presence of mind, Spurgeon told him to kneel down by the bed, and he prayed as best he could. Then he told him to go away and return in half an hour. It turned out that he had eluded the vigilance of his keepers. As soon as he was gone, the doctor and servants were summoned, but he had stabbed some one in the street before he could be overtaken, and in a few days he met with a tragic end.

The third was in his own house. Spurgeon happened to be in the entrance hall when some one knocked loudly at the door, and to save trouble he opened it himself. A man with a huge stick sprang in, slammed the door, and stood with his back against it, declaring that he had come to kill Mr.

Spurgeon. The great thing was to get rid of him, so Mr. Spurgeon said, "You must mean my brother: his name is Spurgeon." He thought he could give his brother at Croydon warning in good time. "Ah!! said the maniac, "it is the man that makes jokes I mean to kill." "Then you must mean my brother, he makes jokes," Mr. Spurgeon said, and the unwelcome visitor was evidently shaken in his intention. But he drew himself up and said, "No, I believe you are the man," and then he asked Spurgeon whether he knew a certain asylum. "That's where I live, and it takes two men to hold me. Are you strong?" "Yes, terrific," said Spurgeon. "Stronger than ten men?" "Ten men!" thundered Spurgeon in his loudest voice, "that's nothing: you don't know how strong I am. Give me that stick." Thoroughly cowed, the man handed it over, and Spurgeon, opening the door, told him that if he was not out of the house that minute he could break every bone in his body. The man fled, and information was given to the police that soon resulted in his being again under restraint.

Impostors often tried to see him. One, who represented himself as the son of Beecher, obtained an interview and walked round the garden with Spurgeon, When he asked that a cheque might be cashed, suspicion was aroused, and he was shown off the premises as soon as possible. A few days afterwards a gentleman was murdered in a tunnel on the Brighton Railway. The murderer was caught, and when his portrait appeared in the newspapers, Spurgeon at once recognised his visitor.

One afternoon he visited the home of one of his deacons at Orpington. His hostess took him out for a drive in a dog-cart with a very spirited horse. Passing under a railway bridge just as a train was crossing, the horse began to rear, and Mr. Spurgeon in alarm said, "Oh! what shall I do?" "Do," said his hostess, a strong, self-reliant woman, perfectly familiar with horses, as she pushed him back into his seat, "Do what I do in the Tabernacle when you are preaching, and I want to shout—sit still."

One day, when dining with a friend, a foreign Rabbi was also a guest. Hot ducks were part of the fare, of which the Rabbi was not allowed to partake. He gave two or three significant sniffs, and got in that way as much of the ducks as he dare. Then, turning to Mr. Spurgeon, he said, "Moses very hard, Moses very hard." "Yes," Spurgeon answered, "there is a yoke upon the neck which neither your fathers nor you have been able to bear."

"I remember spending a very pleasant evening with Dean Stanley," he once said. "The Dean was in excellent spirits and spoke of disestablishment. 'When we are all disestablished and disendowed,' he said, 'what do you propose to do with the Abbey and St. Paul's? Which do you propose to buy for your own use? But really, you must not buy St. Paul's, that you must leave for the Cardinal, it will remind him of St. Peter's.' And so he went on, laughing heartily at his fancy sketch of the future of the disestablished Church. He was always very cordial."

Mr. Charles Spurgeon tells two stories of occasions when he preached with his father. In the East of London the father was announced to preach on behalf of a small Baptist Chapel, and the Congregationalists lent their building opposite for the service. There was such a crowd that the son preached in the Baptist Chapel to the overflow. In the evening he was announced to preach in the Baptist Chapel, but again there was an overflow, and his father came at his call and preached in the schoolroom opposite. The second occasion was at Pollockshaws, when the father preached in a church to a congregation of about a thousand, and the son took the overflow of three thousand or more; an incident that greatly amused the father.

At one of the College Conferences Dr. Usher prayed very earnestly for the children of the assembled ministers. This suggested to Spurgeon that he might write to the sons and daughters; so he had two letters lithographed, one suitable for the younger children, and the other adapted for those older, and these were sent to those whose names were furnished by members of the Conference. Many were led by these letters to decide for Christ. Years after, this suggested to me the idea of addressing the senior scholars of our schools in Leicester in this way; so I had two letters prepared in facsimile, one for boys and one for girls, and scores of them responded. Mr. Thomas Spurgeon once did the same thing in the Tabernacle School.

A clergyman and his wife gained seats in the first gallery near the preacher. The sermon over, they rose to go, and in trying to get out of the pew knocked down some hymn-books and made a noise. The husband pulled the wife's dress to try and detain her. Mr. Spurgeon, who had been quietly looking on, said in a confidential whisper, "You had better go, sir, or you will hear more of it."

Spurgeon had a rooted objection to instrumental music in the worship of God. But he came at length to tolerate an American organ in mission services, and he made Manton Smith a present of a silver cornet, on which was inscribed the text from the ninety-eighth Psalm, "With trumpets and sound of cornet, make a joyful noise before the Lord the King." Once when asked his opinion of a grand organ, he answered, "Yes, it praises its maker very well." He also disliked choirs and he detested anthems. After a special musical performance he was told that one of the pieces was supposed to have been sung by David. "Then I know why Saul threw his javelin at him," he replied, much to the chagrin of the choirmaster.

When he went to Kingston-on-Thames to preach for his first student, Mr. Medhurst, an old woman, in answer to the question how she liked him, said that she would have liked him much better "if he had not imitated our dear pastor so much." That almost equals the story of the person who did not appreciate Shakespeare, because he was so full of quotations.

During the Irish Revival of '59, Mr. Spurgeon crossed to Ireland. He was greeted in the steamer as "Brother," and discovered that of the crew, all but three had been converted. Coming back, one man came up to him and showed him a leather-covered book in Welsh, asking, "Do you know the likeness of that man in front?" He answered that he knew and asked if they read the sermons the book contained. "Yes, sir," came the answer, "I read them aloud as often as I can. If we have a fine passage coming over, I get a few round me and read them a sermon." Another man told him of a gentleman who stood laughing while a hymn was being sung, so one of the sailors proposed that they should pray for him. They did so, and the man was suddenly smitten down, and on the quay began to cry for mercy, and plead with God for pardon.

At one of the Annual College Conferences, the first meeting on the Monday evening was to be at Kingsgate Street Chapel. A number of the ministers were passing through Lincoln's Inn Fields on their way to the meeting, when somebody asked, "Is this the Royal College of Surgeons?" (The Royal College is there.) "No," one of the men answered, "it is the Royal College of Spurgeons." Alongside this retort may be put the answer of a boy at an examination in one of our Secondary Schools. "What is caviare?" he was asked. He answered, "Spurgeon's roe."

On his way to the poll on one occasion, Spurgeon met his friend Mr. Offord, and told him where he was going. His friend reminded him of his heavenly citizenship, and chided him for taking part in political matters. "You should mortify your old man," he said. "That is what I am going to do," said Spurgeon. "My old man is a Tory, and I am going to vote Liberal."

There is a pretty story of an old lady whom he visited in her illness. She began to tell him how much she owed to him spiritually, and he told her not to talk any more about it. "But I will," she answered, "for my former pastor, Joseph Irons, once preached a sermon on the words, 'Thou, O Solomon, must have a thousand, and those that keep the fruit thereof two hundred.' And he said, 'Give Solomon his thousand, but let his ministers have their two hundred.' So I must tell you how I have been blessed through your ministry. You shall have your two hundred."

Spurgeon began preaching as a boy, and even to the end there was much of the boy in him. Once he longed so much for the coming of his holiday that he persuaded Mrs. Spurgeon to mark a piece of tape with the dates and hang it on the chandelier over the table. Each day a bit was solemnly cut off after dinner, and at length only about an inch was left. Preparations were then made for the journey, but at the last moment he was taken ill, and never more was a tape hung up to mark the passing days.

In visiting a friend he saw a rosemary bush in the garden, and playfully remarked, "Oh, rosemary! you know what people say about it, I suppose?

'Where the rosemary grows, the missus is the master.'" Next time he was in his friend's garden the rosemary bush was gone.

When he visited Mr. Tinworth, the artist complained to him of a criticism that had been passed on his panel, "The enemy sowing tares." "You see I have depicted him sowing with his left hand, and this person said that was not correct. I did not know what to say to him." "Why," said Spurgeon, "you should have told him that he never saw Satan sowing tares with his right hand."

A minister once put a case to him. There was a hearer who objected so much to the Gospel he preached, that though for the look of the thing he attended the church, when the sermon began he put a finger in each ear so that he could not hear. The question was, what would Spurgeon do in a case like that. "Why," he said, without hesitation, "I would pray that a fly might light on his nose."

Some of his critics even to the end pursued him with their pin-pricks. He was really troubled once at Mentone when a person, without sense of the fitness of things, sent a letter through the post to him, after addressing it "To the Unprofitable Servant, C. H. Spurgeon."

On one of the occasions when the Regent's Park students met with those of the Pastor's College, Mr. Spurgeon left the choice of subjects to Dr. Angus. He suggested the two titles "Culture "and "Go," evidently thinking that the second would be appropriate to Spurgeon, and with courtesy asked him which he would select. Spurgeon mischievously chose "Culture "! Both speakers acquitted themselves well.

Mr. George Moore, the London merchant, was a generous supporter of Mr. Spurgeon. Once when visiting him at his home in the North, Mr. Spurgeon complimented Mrs. Moore on her husband's influence. "You are a Queen," he said, "for your husband is 'King of Cumberland'"—referring to his power amongst the farmers and people around. "Oh no, he is not that," the wife replied. "No," was the quick reply, "he is Mo(o)re." Samuel Smiles tells the story.

Sir Evan Spicer tells how his father once asked Spurgeon to speak at a meeting on Saturday, and the answer was, "I wouldn't go to heaven on a Saturday—if I had to come back again."

Once he was asked where the devil is in this age. "Time enough to ask the question," he answered, "when we miss him."

One of his friends, whose business chiefly consisted in the sale of a celebrated brand of ox tongues, sent him a number of packets as a present. In return Spurgeon sent him two or three of his books of sermons, with the inscription, "Samples of my own preserved tongue."

Dr. Jowett recounts a conversation he had with Lord Rosebery, who once, when visiting the Tabernacle when the service was somewhat disturbed by a fainting woman, was very much struck with the calmness with which Spurgeon regarded the incident. Looking round he said, "Oh, it's only Mary So-and-so," and she was soon removed. Contrasting this with an experience he had when a little while after he went to hear a great preacher in Brooklyn, who was quite upset when a similar incident happened in his congregation, Lord Rosebery praised Spurgeon for his absolute self-control, and his genial, all-inclusive humanity.

A baby cried during one of the services at the Tabernacle, and instead of being irritated, the preacher prayed that the little life might early be claimed for God. As the boy grew up he was, of course, told that Mr. Spurgeon had prayed for him, and at length he became a minister of the Gospel. To one who was also present on the occasion he lately wrote, "As we were both there that day, early in the 'eighties, just after I had made my decision for Christ, my father took me in to see C. H. S., and recalled the incident. 'Yes,' he said, 'it was about 1872. I have prayed like that twice. The Lord has found you, do you go and find the other one.'" The following week he used the incident on Exeter Hall platform as an illustration of prayer answered after many days.

At breakfast one morning in his own home, when he and I were alone, and talked about intimate things, he said, "Fullerton, there is one prayer I have lately been praying—that the Lord would give me a short memory for grudges." Never man, I think, needed to pray such a prayer less, but he knew his own heart best, and ever illustrated the pregnant saying of Agassiz, that "heavy heads always bow."

During Mr. Spurgeon's short convalescence in his last illness, his neighbour, Robert Taylor, the Presbyterian minister of Upper Norwood, who often visited him, asked him one day if he could put into few words his Christian faith. "It is all in four words," he answered, and the answer is memorable— "Jesus died for me."

CHAPTER XIV

A BUNDLE OF OPINIONS

THERE have been so many and diverse opinions expressed about Mr. Spurgeon and his work that it seems desirable that some of them should have permanent place in the record of his life. They will form a sort of composite picture of the man that may perhaps be nearer the reality than any description or estimate issuing from one pen. This chapter will therefore consist of extracts selected with some discrimination from material that has not been absorbed by previous chapters.

"Among these names, as lustrous as the brightest, and yet shining with a radiance all its own, gleams that of Charles Haddon Spurgeon, the greatest of modern Puritan preachers, who approached nearer to Bunyan than any other in the quality of his imagination, and to Wesley in the thoroughness of his practical endeavours, who rivalled Hooker in the mastery of Saxon speech, and Henry Ward Beecher in his poetic temperament and Shakespearean acquaintance with the varying moods of the human microcosm."[1]

"It has been said that none of his sermons are masterpieces of eloquence, like some of Bossuet's, Saurin's or Lacordaire's, and that they even fail as models, being excelled by those of Frederick Robertson and Alexander Maclaren. All this may be so; but unless I misjudge humanity, his discourses will long continue after his life to be an unfailing source of comfort to simple and troubled souls. Estimated by their attractiveness and their immediate spiritual force, they undoubtedly surpass all contemporaneous preaching."[2]

"The voice was that of Chrysostom, the ardour was that of Wesley, the unction was that of Savonarola, the doctrine was that of Bunyan, the wit was that of Thomas Adams, the originality was that of Christmas Evans, the fervour was that of John Howe, the boldness was that of Calvin, the simplicity was that of Whitefield, the pathos was that of Toplady. Yes, it was the composite character of Spurgeon's preaching which really accounted for its infinite charm. Herein he differed from every other preacher, and herein is to be found the reason of the almost amusing perplexity of innumerable critics. Again and again he used to say, with a gleam in his eyes, that American hearers had accosted him in his vestry with refreshing candour, assuring him that they really wondered what it could be that made him so famous, as they had many more remarkable preachers than himself. They

---

[1] George C. Lorimer's *Biography*, p. 11.
[2] George C. Lorimer's *Biography*, p. 60.

might as well have wondered why a kaleidoscope elicits delight, with its endless varieties of beautiful forms flung out by the simplest materials."[1]

"Though he was not equal to Liddon for subtlety of thought and refinement of expression, or to Beecher for philosophic presentation of Bible truth, or to Parker for striking and suggestive sayings, or to Maclaren for deep and connected exposition of Scripture, yet he towered above them all, and occupied a unique place as a herald of the Gospel, a preacher to the common people. Men have discussed the secret of his power, and have given different explanations of it, but all have been agreed about the fact of power.

"To hear him preach, especially in his own Tabernacle, was to feel his marvellous power, even though it was difficult to understand or explain it. There was the perfect ease of manner, the voice of such remarkable clearness, compass, flexibility and volume; the directness of the address, the tremendous force of conviction that throbbed in each sentence, the purpose that from the beginning to the end of the service was kept well in view, the pure, homely, Saxon style and apt illustration, the earnest and pathetic appeal. And withal there was a strong magnetic force which riveted the attention of his audience and kept them spellbound. 'We are never great,' says Schiller, 'but when we play,' and listening to the orator in the Tabernacle, carried away on the full flowing tide of his own thought and emotion, speaking so easily, simply, naturally and effectively, we have found in him the truest greatness."[2]

"In the intensity and purity of his inner life Spurgeon had more in common with old-fashioned saints of the type of John Woolman and George Muller than with the Laodicean type of religion which is prevalent in the churches of today. Mr. Spurgeon was a humourist and an orator. The saint pure and simple is not always a genial person. Readers of the lives of Woolman and Muller may have their hearts touched to finer issues, but inasmuch as their mental outlook is narrow, and their prevailing temperament sombre and serious, they have little or no influence over people given to humorous and innocent hilarity."[3]

"He has been, not unjustly, compared to the friar preachers of the Middle Ages, and, of course, the parallel has been drawn between him on the one hand and Wesley and Whitefield on the other. He was like any mediaeval mission preacher: he accepted the system in which he found himself and upon its basis preached a repentance of heart. On the other hand, he resembles the Wesleys, and still more Whitefield, in the style of his preaching, in the quality and character of his theology, and in the personal

---

[1] *Christian Commonwealth*, Feb. 4, 1892.

[2] *Christian World*, Feb. 4, 1892.

[3] *Edinburgh Evening News*, Feb. 1, 1892.

effect of his preaching. He, too, had a personal following, as had the Wesleys and Whitefield. He knew that definiteness and sincerity are the qualities of a great preacher. Thus well-educated men could be moved by the reality of his preaching as well as charmed with its literary merits. A greater mistake cannot be made than that which thinks or speaks of Mr. Spurgeon as an uneducated man. He was the master of an English style which many a scholar might envy, and which was admirably fitted for his purposes. This style could only have been acquired by great pains, and by the constant study of the best literary models, which it recalls. Mr. Spurgeon's knowledge of the Bible was, of course, thorough; he knew it in its subject matter, and he knew it in its old-fashioned English dress, and with that he was content."[1]

"The truth is, that instead of limiting himself to commonplace illustrations, Spurgeon turned round his gaze on nature, on society at large, and gathered from each and all whatever he saw available for the illustration of the subject he had before him. He cared little for authority, or the formulas of creeds and articles, and instead of confining himself to the language of the schools, and of previous divines and theologians, he would ransack the stores of modern literature, profane as well as sacred, not objecting to a phrase or a sentiment because it came from Shakespeare or Scott, Dr. Johnson or Robert Bums."[2]

"He could not help talking sense, and the sense of a master of strong English often assumes a more or less comic form. You see precisely the same thing in *John Ploughman's Talk,* where many of his strings of sentences, in their crisp and energetic form, rouse just the sense of unexpectedness and enlightening incongruity which is the foundation of all true humour."

"Mr. Spurgeon knew his audience, and spent his life in trying to warm respectability into virtue, and acquiescence in Christianity into energetic obedience to its commands; and if that is not good work, there is none. Whether he succeeded or not, is for a higher knowledge than ours to decide; but he turned a vast chapel into a sort of college for making good ministers, and made of a huge middle-class congregation, drawn together mainly by delight in his preaching, an effective centre of all good work. *That looks, at all events, like Christian success.*"[3]

"For directness and felicity of homely illustrations he was Cobden's sole rival. His discourses were full of shrewd sayings—pithy Saxon utterances such as Franklin loved. Their style was, however, exquisitely simple, and

---

[1] *Church Times*, Feb. 5, 1892.

[2] *Morning Post*, Feb. 1, 1892.

[3] *Spectator*, Feb. 6, 1892.

everything was put with a touch of pathos, a homely humour, which gave even to his platitudes the semblance of vivid and vigorous originality."[1]

"His intellectual qualities were of the supremest kind. I have met many great men, but never one so swift in perception, so rapid in seizing on the prime element in every cause, so prompt in discussion. To listen to his talk on books one would think that he had done nothing but read in the library all his life, and to mark his publications would fancy that he had done nothing but write. His heart had twelve gates that were not shut at all by day. There were few such men of business. He had resource, ingenuity and judgment that gave him infinite self-reliance. He worked swiftly, while such was his humour, his fertile mind, his ready thought, his affluent speech, that no speaker had ever equalled him in our generation—perhaps few in any generation, in power of swaying masses of his fellow-men."[2]

"There is a passage in Carlyle's article on Burns in *The Edinburgh Review* which might have been written of Charles Haddon Spurgeon: 'To every poet, preacher, or orator, we might say: Be true, be sincere if you would be believed. Let a man but speak with genuine earnestness of the thoughts, the emotions, the actual condition of his own heart, and other men, so strangely are we all knit together by sympathy, must and will give heed to him. In culture, in extent of view, we may stand above the preacher or below him; but in either case, his words, if earnest and faithful, will awaken an echo within us; for in spite of all casual varieties in outward or inward rank, as face answers to face, so does the heart of man to man.'"[3]

"He was utterly free from cant. He hated it and denounced it, and no trace of it was found in his own language. He was what we call racy. There was a fine, honest brusqueness about him. He never feared the face of man. In vituperation in its best sense he had no rival. His irony was not a keen rapier, but a terrible bludgeon, with which he dealt blows that never needed repetition. He introduced a note of new realism into the pulpit. He spoke out of the depths of himself, and followed the traditions of no man's eloquence. If he soared into the heights of poetic imagination it was by accident, it was a natural flight; it was too spontaneous to be despised."[4]

"Mr. Spurgeon displayed his innate strength of character whilst he was still young; and we think of him as old, not because of his years, but rather because of the marvellous opulence of his activities, and the irresistible energy with which he seized the sceptre of pulpit pre-eminence, and the indisputable ability with which he held it to the close of his career. In short,

---

[1] *Black and White*, Feb. 6, 1892.

[2] Dr. Richard Glover of Bristol.

[3] *Daily Telegraph*.

[4] Rev. W. J. Dawson in *The Young Man*.

it is a chief element in the problem of the prophet-preacher's unannounced but indisputable fame, that he took a foremost place amongst the leaders of the religious life of the world in his dawning manhood; took it easily and with full assurance of conviction, and kept it with unbroken steadfastness for more than thirty-five years out of his fifty-seven.

"He substituted naturalness for a false and stilted dignity, passion for precision, plain, homely Saxon for highly-Latinised English, humour and mother-wit for apathy and sleepiness, glow and life for machinery and death. It is difficult to say what rank coming generations will assign to Mr. Spurgeon amongst the world's preachers; but it is certain that his work as a leader of our religious life introduced a new era, and filled it with seeds of energy that will be reproductive for ever."[1]

"There never was a man more spontaneous in all he did, and less ambitious. He studied day and night, and filled his unerring memory with pious thoughts and suggestive histories, but it was never as men read for examinations, or even as men investigate for research and discovery; it was solely with the object of winning souls to Christ. Whatever could be done for this end, with might and main he would do. Whatever could be spoken to reach the intricacies of the human heart, that he longed to speak. He was a consummate dramatist, and might have earned a reputation either as an actor or a novelist, had he chosen, but his heart was in one sacred direction, and, like St. Paul, he emphatically knew nothing save Jesus Christ and Him crucified. He was the finest possible elocutionist, and yet he never formally studied elocution. He was the most consummate mimic, and yet had never trained himself artistically. Constant devotion to one aim and end drew out all his faculties to their most definite expression, so that he was throughout the orator born, and not in the least item artificially moulded. That, however, which infused vitality into his speaking, and relieved it from an otherwise inevitable monotony when always addressed to one topic was a native mother-wit. Spurgeon was essentially a humourist. This lent buoyancy to his spirits, brightness to his imagination, and perpetual freshness to his discourses. He was an often unconscious but always close observer of men and morals. The kaleidoscope of humanity invariably yielded to his inspection its most charming colours."[2]

"Very solid and even commanding qualities were requisite in Mr. Spurgeon's youth to gain the suffrages of the vast tract of the middle classes which formed his constituency—a mass which was in its way a fastidious one. Eccentricity, if carried far enough, was always effective, but *then* it required a considerable amount of moral courage for its practice, and moral

[1] Dr. John Clifford in *The Review of the Churches*.
[2] *The Rock*, Feb. 5, 1892.

courage implies a good deal more than mere eccentricity. It has seldom been the chosen mission of the reformer, or the revivalist, or in general of the awakener of souls to preach to the *bourgeoisie*. The class is by no means so easily moved as the miner and the peasant; it seems trenched in an armour of respectability, which, for that matter, appears to put it outside the need for collective conversion. It will remain among Mr. Spurgeon's titles to honour that he reached the most difficult class by legitimate and honourable means."[1]

"To come into contact with Mr. Spurgeon was to feel in his personality a potent charm which can scarcely be described. It was instinctively realised that the man was richer, nobler, than his words and works. To spend a day with him was to observe a wonderful play of faculty. Now there is an outburst of tenderness and sympathy which reveals the wealth of a gentle, loving heart; anon there are flashes of wit and humour which light up the topic of conversation; then there is some telling epigram, or racy anecdote, or kindly sarcasm; and again some scathing denunciation descends upon that which he regards as evil. And all is so natural and unconstrained as to suggest vast reserves within, as yet untouched, and that the nuggets thus brought to the surface are only a faint indication of the untold wealth of the mine."[2]

"Charles Spurgeon passed through the greatest peril that can beset a man's character, and he came out of it not only unscathed, but with an ever-increasing reputation. A preacher who attains unbounded popularity at twenty is exposed to temptations which few can successfully withstand. He was for a year or two the sensation of the town. The cleverest satirical writers of the period made him the butt of their almost constant attacks. Exaggerated praise on the one hand, and ignorant and ill-tempered vituperation on the other, would have effectually spoiled any but a man of genuine sincerity. But fame was by no means Mr. Spurgeon's only snare. From an early period in his career he has been trusted with the dispensing of enormous sums of money. Others, also, have been similarly trusted, have doubtless been equally honest, but it has happened to few to escape, as he has done, even the breath of suspicion."[3] "Taking all things into account, Mr. Spurgeon seems to be the greatest preacher of the century—above Chalmers, Robertson, Newman, Liddon. He was learned in certain departments of theology that lent themselves to spiritual preaching, and he had an inexhaustible store of noble words which waited upon him like nimble servers. He was as

---

[1] *The Globe.*
[2] *Christian World*, Feb. 4, 1892.
[3] *Morning Advertiser*, Feb. 11, 1892.

characteristic an Englishman as our generation has seen, and possibly, after Mr. Gladstone, the ablest."[1]

"Mr. Spurgeon has been to a large extent no unfair representative of English life and thought, capable of putting before men in words, an adequate expression of their half-unconscious thought. To condemn Mr. Spurgeon is thus to pass sentence on no small part of his countrymen."[2]

"Nobody ever heard Mr. Spurgeon preach without remembering something that he had said.

"What is more, there is not one in the whole of that great mass of human beings (in the Tabernacle) who does not feel that Mr. Spurgeon's discourse is absolutely addressed to him as much as if it were given to him alone."[3]

"A young man after hearing Spurgeon wrote to his mother, 'They say there were six thousand present in the Tabernacle, but to me it was as though I were alone, and he was speaking to me.'"

"The Church of England owes him a deep debt of gratitude, and if he would stoop to the office would profit more largely by making him Bishop of Southwark and St. Giles, and having an exchange between St. Martin's Church and the Tabernacle."[4]

"It might be said of his style what Macaulay said of Bunyan's: 'The vocabulary is the vocabulary of the common people.' Yet no writer has said more exactly what he meant to say. For magnificence, for pathos, for vehement exhortation, for subtle disquisition, for every purpose, the poet, the orator, the divine, this homely dialect, the dialect of the plain working-man, was perfectly sufficient."[5]

"Spurgeon is not to be classed with types like Erasmus or Fenelon or Leighton, but with men like Knox and Luther, and Cromwell and Baxter. He was a man of infinite capacity, with a sense of ready wit, and felt it more seemly that he should even make his congregation smile than allow them to slumber. God, death, judgment and the life to come, were intense realities with him."[6]

"He was as far above Liddon as Liddon was above Farrar."[7]

"I confess that when I had the privilege of a little talk with Mr. Spurgeon I have looked at him, and listened to him, and said to myself, 'What is there in this man that has made him the most popular preacher that ever spoke the English tongue?' I have always believed that the chief secret of his

[1] Dr. John Watson.

[2] *The Times*, Feb. 1, 1892.

[3] *Daily Telegraph*, Dec. 24, 1880.

[4] *Vanity Pair*, Dec. 10, 1870.

[5] Resolution of the Baptist Union Council, Feb. 10. 1892.

[6] Bishop Boyd Carpenter in Ripon Cathedral, Feb. 14, 18:12,

[7] *British Weekly*, Feb. 4, 1892.

attractiveness was the fact that, in every sermon, no matter what the text or the occasion, he explained the way of salvation in simple terms. There are thousands of people everywhere who, beneath their superficial indifference or apparent opposition, long in their hearts to know what they must do to be saved.

"Once when I happened to be in Mr. Spurgeon's study, he showed me a book which he had just received. It was a Russian translation of a select number of his sermons, published with the imprimatur of the Archimandrite of Moscow for the use of the Greek Church. If the Archbishop of Canterbury would follow the example of the exalted Russian dignitary it would prove a great blessing to many of his parochial clergy. An acquaintance of mine, crossing the Atlantic, met a Jesuit Father from South America, and that priest told him that he regularly read every sermon of Mr. Spurgeon's that he could lay his hands on, and that he owed more to Mr. Spurgeon than to any other living man. The Day of Judgment alone will reveal the extent to which millions of all faiths in all lands have been converted and edified by Mr. Spurgeon's sermons, and all because he was not too clever and too learned to explain the way to Christ intelligibly."[1]

"As we have said, he was positive from the very nature of his work. Once when he was sailing past the coast of Ayrshire, the land of Burns, and some one remarked, 'Surely He who gathers up the fragments that nothing be lost, will find something worth saving, something good in poor Burns '; he replied quickly, 'O, that is no use to me.' Doubtless he meant that to his six thousand he must sharply draw the line black or white, no tints—he must say, 'You are saved or lost, for ever saved, for ever lost.'"[2]

"Charles Haddon Spurgeon is not one of a class, but an individual chosen for the accomplishment of a special work; and mentally, morally and physically, he is in every way adapted to his mission. His seeming defects, in the eye of some, are special excellences. He is not to be judged by the petty rules that poor mortals have derived from the creeping experience of the past. Nothing were easier than to prove that he is often wild and erratic, and transgresses the canons of the schools. He is above the schools. He is a law to himself, and wholly unamenable to the tribunals of criticism. He simply exerts the powers, peculiar and wonderful, with which God has endowed him. He reads, he expounds, he prays, he preaches, as nobody else ever did, or probably ever will do. He is an original and rebel in everything. But his insurgency notwithstanding, he is the impersonation of the profoundest

---

[1] Rev. Hugh Price Hughes in *The Methodist Times*, Feb. 4, 1892.
[2] Rev. J. H. Shakespeare in *The East Anglian Daily News*, Feb. 10, 1892.

loyalty to a higher law. Comets are not less amenable to law than suns. Through his disobedience he achieves his triumphs and rules his millions."[1]

"England's greatest contribution to the spread of the Gospel in the nineteenth century was Charles Haddon Spurgeon. Through him God wrought signs and wonders, adding another chapter to the Acts of the Apostles. There is no class or type in which Spurgeon can be included. He stands alone, a new species among the varieties of ministers, a sun that outshines the stars in splendour.

"No great preacher retains his supremacy except by becoming universal. Spurgeon, the sturdy Protestant Baptist, was a true Catholic. No modern preacher has touched and held so large and varied a constituency. I recognise that the surest way to the dethronement of kings in the realm of thought is to claim for them despotic sovereignty. Each teacher elected to permanent influence must die to live. The local and the sectional fall away. The dross is taken away that the gold may go into the currency of the Kingdom.

"In 1854, *The Baptist Magazine,* at the end of its pages, recorded that C. H. Spurgeon had removed from Waterbeach to New Park Street, that the chapel was filled and several candidates awaited baptism. This was told in a brief paragraph. The cautious editor made no comment. He did not know he was chronicling the most noteworthy event in the history of British Baptists, and the advent of a preacher without a compeer in the story of the Christian pulpit.

"The poor pedants of the pulpit who made merry over young Spurgeon's homely Saxon speech, did not observe that almost all the words he used came from the Authorised Version of the English Bible, which, as Mark Rutherford declares, 'is sufficient for nearly everything, including science, that a human being can know or feel.'"[2]

"Mr. Spurgeon reckoned as the highest compliment ever paid to him the words of an open enemy who said: 'Here is a man who has not moved an inch forward in all his ministry, and at the close of the nineteenth century is teaching the theology of the first century, and in Newington Butts is proclaiming the doctrine of Nazareth and Jerusalem current eighteen hundred years ago.'"[3]

Dr. J. H. Jowett, at the welcome meeting of the present pastor of the Tabernacle, Rev. H. Tydeman Chilvers, declared that Spurgeon's greatness had four qualities: The tremendous Gospel he preached, which was not only that man could be saved, but that he could be saved to the uttermost. The fact that he was so joyous—he always brought a song-bird into his sermon.

---

[1] Dr. Campbell in 1861.

[2] Dr. J. C. Carlile at the Berlin Congress of Baptist Churches.

[3] *Life and Work of C. H. Spurgeon,* by G. Holden Pike, Vol. V. p. 108.

Ruskin had declared that the first sign of renaissance of art was the introduction of a bird into a certain picture. Then there was his human touch, and finally his humour. "As far as I can read Spurgeon, and I am always reading him, whenever he brought in humour, it was not a drawing-room lamp, lighting up a single room; it was always a street lamp, to show people the way home."

CHAPTER XV

BOOK TALK

THE title of this chapter has been chosen so that we can wander among books, and browse where we will.

The largest book that Spurgeon produced was *The Interpreter*. It consists of selected Scriptures for each morning and evening in the year, with a homily and hymns. But as the author did not approve of printing prayers, it lacks the very thing which would commend it to many families. It is as big as a family Bible, and in past years was often to be met with in Christian households.

The smallest book he wrote was *The Clue of the Maze,* one of those waistcoat-pocket volumes which at one time were so popular. It was written during a holiday at Mentone, and is designed to lead doubters back to faith.

The greatest of Mr. Spurgeon's works is undoubtedly *The Treasury of David.* I have the original edition of seven volumes, in calf, a wedding present from the early publishers, and the new edition of six volumes, in cloth, with a frontispiece to each volume, sent to me by the later publishers. It is a monumental work, containing not only comments on all the Psalms by Mr. Spurgeon, but extracts from authors of all ages and conditions. There is nothing like it in literature. Years ago, when crossing the Rocky Mountains, and lost in wonder as I gazed, a friend came to my side, and said, "There is only one word for it." I waited breathlessly to have my own feelings interpreted. "It is immense," he whispered. Well, the research evidenced in this work is just that. Dr. Jowett says about it: "I have for many years sought and found nutriment for my own pulpit in this marvellous exposition. He is not eclipsed even when set in the radiant succession of Calvin and Luther and Paul." The first volume was issued in 1869, the last in 1885, so that about twenty years were spent in its production. The author tells us that only those who have meditated profoundly on the Psalms can have any adequate conception of the wealth they contain, that sometimes, as he pondered over them, holy fear fell upon him, and he shrank from the attempt to explain themes so sublime. The work seems to have grown more difficult as he advanced, the material available on the later Psalms being much more meagre than on the early ones. The hundred and fourth Psalm demanded forty pages; the hundred and ninth Psalm was interpreted with the news of the Bulgarian atrocities then ringing throughout the world; the hundred and nineteenth Psalm almost occupies a whole volume, having nearly four hundred pages given to it, and Mr. Spurgeon's own comments on it were afterwards published separately under the title, *The Golden Alphabet of the Praises of Holy Scripture.* At the end of all the author speaks of his joy in the

184

whole work: "Happier hours than those which have been spent on these meditations on the Songs of Zion he never expects to see in this world."

The Gospel of the Kingdom, a Commentary on the Gospel according to Matthew, one of the last of Mr. Spurgeon's works, is issued in similar style to *The Treasury.*

There are three volumes of daily readings: *Morning by Morning; Evening by Evening;* and *The Chequebook of the Bank of Faith,* the latter written during the troubles of the Down-Grade Controversy, greatly sustaining the author as he wrote them. These have permanent value.

In addition to the sixty-three volumes of the regular issue of the *Sermons,* there are three volumes of "The Pulpit Library," now almost unobtainable, and five other volumes selected at different times: *Types and Emblems, Trumpet Calls to Christian Energy, The Present Truth, Storm Signals,* and *Farm Sermons,* containing about twenty sermons each. *Messages for the Multitudes,* and *Sermons: a Selection,* have been issued by separate publishers. Another volume, entitled *Till He Come,* contains some Communion addresses, while *Facsimile Pulpit Notes* gives views of the Tabernacle, as well as the sermons preached from the notes, and there are seven volumes of reprints on various topics—The Song of Solomon, the Parables, the Miracles, the Messiah, etc. In addition to these, over thirty different selections have been issued in the "Twelve Sermon Series." *The Saint and the Saviour* and *Grace Triumphant,* published by other firms, also contain original material, so that there are at least seventy-five distinct sermon volumes.

There is a collection of proverbs in two volumes, entitled *The Salt Cellars.* About these a friendly reviewer said: "We are more interested in Mr. Spurgeon's applications than in many of the proverbs. The reader asks himself as he lights on some familiar or unfamiliar proverb, 'Come, now, I wonder what Mr. Spurgeon will make of that.' For one never knows what he will make of it. The old-fashioned application of Æsop's Fable every child could anticipate, but there is no such commonplace and prosaic certainty about Mr. Spurgeon's applications, and therefore they have to be read." And in response to another criticism he wrote to George Augustus Sala: "I like the parts in which you pitch into me quite as well as those in which you praise." These volumes contain many of the proverbs published year by year in *John Ploughman's Almanack,* with shrewd comments thereon.

That brings us to *John Ploughman's Talk,* and its scarcely less successful second, *John Ploughman's Pictures.* Dr. Stalker thinks that the first "is certain of immortality among the popular classics of England." It has had a great vogue, and is just packed with wit and wisdom. *Sermons in Candles,* the famous lecture, is issued in the same style, and, since Mr. Spurgeon's death, Mr. J. L. Keys, his amanuensis, has issued, through another publisher, another of Mr. Spurgeon's lectures, *What the Stones Say,* an illustrated volume.

Of illustrations and extracts there are ten volumes, including one from Thomas Brooks, to which reference has been made in an earlier chapter, and another from Thomas Manton, described as *Flowers from a Puritan's Garden, Distilled and Dispensed.* There is also the *Spurgeon Birthday Book.* Nine popular volumes are addressed to various classes, and a series of seven little books form the shilling series, *The Bible and the Newspaper* leading the way.

Two of the most valuable books to put into the hands of those who are seeking Christ are *All of Grace,* which is crystal clear, and has been the means of leading scores of persons to the Saviour, and *According to Promise,* which seeks to entice people to Christ. Spurgeon used often to say that the best way to get a hungry man to eat a dinner is to put a dinner on the table before him. *Around the Wicket Gate* is another volume with the same intent.

Already in the "College" chapter the nine volumes for students have been mentioned, and another, issued against Mr. Spurgeon's will by another house, entitled *The Pastor in Prayer,* is very choice. Mr. Spurgeon's prayers were in later years always reported for his own use, but he steadfastly refused to publish them. Here are twenty-six that have escaped from their prison.

Prayers suggest hymns. Dr. Theodore Cuyler mentioned among his virtues this—that he had never compiled a hymn-book. But the compilation of *Our Own Hymn-Book* is to Mr. Spurgeon's credit, and the section of it entitled "The Golden Book of Communion with Jesus" is not to be equalled in any other collection of hymns of similar character. He himself has written some hymns that have already an assured place; amongst them, "Sweetly the holy hymn," "Amidst us our Beloved stands," "The Holy Ghost is here." There are others, less well known, that yet attain a high standard of excellence. Take, for instance, his version of the fifteenth Psalm—

> "Lord, I would dwell with Thee
> On Thy most holy hill;
> Oh, shed Thy grace abroad in me,
> To mould me to Thy will.

> "Thy gate of pearl stands wide
> For those who walk upright;
> But those who basely turn aside
> Thou chasest from Thy sight.

> "Oh, tame my tongue to peace,
> And tune my heart to love;
> From all reproaches may I cease,
> Made harmless as a dove.

"The vile, though proudly great,
No flatterer find in me;
I count Thy saints of poor estate
Far nobler company.

"Faithful, but meekly kind,
Gentle, yet boldly true,
I would possess the perfect mind
Which in my Lord I view.

"But, Lord, these graces all
Thy Spirit's work must be;
To Thee, through Jesus' blood I call—
Create them all in me."

A number of booklets by Spurgeon have also been issued. Perhaps *The Greatest Fight in the World,* his last Conference address, published in the form made familiar to us by Henry Drummond, has had the largest circulation. *Spurgeon's Almanack* was also published year by year.

At intervals pictorial albums have been issued describing the Tabernacle, the Orphanage, and Mr. Spurgeon's home, and the last work that engaged him was a memorial of his early days, *Memories of Stambourne.*

There yet remain the annual volumes of *The Sword and the Trowel,* which began in 1865, and was continued until the end—twenty-eight years. Buried in these volumes is some of the best work the Editor ever did, and they will repay working over.

The whole Spurgeon Library, therefore, taking no count of tractates, consists of no less than 135 volumes, of which he was the author, and twenty-eight which he edited, 163 volumes in all, or, including the reprints, 176! If we add the albums and the pamphlets, we get an output of 200 books!

At the time of his death there were 12,000 volumes in Mr. Spurgeon's library, in addition to those that he had sent to furnish the well-filled shelves of the library in the College. The Westwood collection was scattered, some souvenir volumes going to friends in this country, and the remainder to America.

The story is interesting. When the Baptist World Congress was being held in London in 1905, a friend of the William Jewell College in Missouri viewed the collection, and after he returned home, the trustees of the College, whom he had interested, determined to purchase it, and cabled over an offer of £500, asking Dr. Thirtle to carry through the negotiations. Two days later the evening papers of St. Louis announced that the William Jewell College had become possessors of Spurgeon's library. The books, varying in size from folios to duodecimos, and numbering some 7000, many of them rare volumes, were on their arrival welcomed as the sign of a new era in the College life. It was argued that the College must have a new library building to hold them, and that expansion must proceed everywhere else in the Institution. The appeal for enlargement was made, and the "Spurgeon Library" formed the chief factor in bringing a response of a million dollars for the College treasury. Americans are disposed to boast that the most eloquent memorial of the great preacher is with them, rather than with his British kinsfolk and friends.

If it is asked what did Mr. Spurgeon himself read, the answer is that he read everything. His daily newspaper was *The Times.* The Bible was his constant study, perhaps next came John Bunyan— "prick him anywhere," he says, "and you will find that his blood is Bibline." Carlyle's *French Revolution* was read again and again. Boswell's *Johnson,* Lockhart's *Life of Scott,* and Mrs. Oliphant's *Life of Irving* were favourites. Scott and Dickens had their turn, and of course the Puritans. Then he read the books he reviewed in his magazine, and he was always on the look-out for rare volumes that he desired, as they might be catalogued by secondhand booksellers. Dr. Maclaren once had a race with him for an old volume. Dr. Angus on another occasion was also just too late.

In many of Mr. Spurgeon's books the autograph of the author was preserved, and Spurgeon's own comments lent value to some of the volumes. As an example, on the fly-leaf of *Things New and Old,* by John Spenser, MDCLVIII—

"The richest book in my library,
"C. H. SPURGEON.

"I had an old, dilapidated copy given to me by that great offender W. L. Oliver. When he was condemned I found that it was not his book, and therefore he had no right to give it to me. I returned the copy to its rightful owner, mourning because my treasure was gone. But my generous God instantly sent me this complete copy, and the dear brother who sent it knew nothing of my thoughts and wishes. Praise be to my generous God!"

He delighted in scattering books. Of Mrs. Spurgeon's Book Fund we have already spoken in the "Intimate" chapter. At every Conference she presented a volume to the ministers attending, and those who took special part were sure to have a book, autographed by Mr. Spurgeon, in acknowledgment.

The Metropolitan Tabernacle Colportage Association, founded in 1866, was always Mr. Spurgeon's special care. At the close of 1891 some ninety-six colporteurs were employed, and from the beginning up to that time the total value of the sales was no less than £153,784, while nearly twelve million visits had been paid to the homes of the people. The Association still continues its good work, having its office and packing-room in the College buildings.

So Mr. Spurgeon, the preacher, was in a very real sense a Bookman. He knew books, he wrote books, he read books, he distributed books, he reviewed books; his opinions on current literature were greatly valued, and his own books eagerly bought. By them he still speaks today to many who never heard, and never could have heard, his voice. So the seed is multiplied, some thirtyfold, some sixtyfold, some a hundredfold, and the harvest is at length gathered into the barn.

CHAPTER XVI

SOME MINOR DISCUSSIONS

FOR years Mr. Spurgeon was probably the most discussed man in the kingdom, and it was inevitable, when the tongues and pens of other people were so busy, that he himself should be drawn into the fray.

The first discussion began soon after his advent in London. It arose amongst the high Calvinists, and began by the publication in *The Earthen Vessel* of an article by Mr. Charles Waters Banks, who afterwards became his loyal friend. The article just raised the question as to Mr. Spurgeon's standing in the Christian Church. After recording the success of his ministry it proceeds: "But, then, very solemn questions arise. 'What is he doing?' 'Whose servant is he?' 'What proof does he give that, instrumentally, his is a heart-searching, a Christ-exalting, a truth-unfolding, a sinner-converting, a church-feeding, a soul-saving ministry?'"

In the following month, January 1855, "Job," who was doubtless the Rev. James Wells of Surrey Tabernacle, a preacher then at the zenith of his power, wrote, expressing doubts as to the young man's conversion, and declaring that though he spoke some truth, and had a partial moral influence, yet his hearers were likely to be fatally deluded. In later numbers of the magazine the Editor could go no further than to ask prayer "for this young man, whom we earnestly hope the Lord has sent among us."

It makes quaint reading, and in view of the future most foolish. Probably some of the things discussed by others today will seem as quaint and foolish in the days to come. Mr. Wells and Mr. Spurgeon, after the building of the Metropolitan Tabernacle, were neighbours. It is said that they once met in the street, and Mr. Wells asked Mr. Spurgeon whether he had ever seen the inside of Surrey Tabernacle. He replied that he had not, but would very much like to see it, upon which Mr. Wells said that if he would come some Monday morning he would show him round, and there would then be time enough to thoroughly ventilate the place before the next Lord's Day. Upon that, Mr. Spurgeon asked Mr. Wells if he had ever seen round his Tabernacle, and Mr. Wells answered that he had looked in one Saturday, giving the date. "Ah," said Spurgeon, "that accounts for the delightful fragrance of the services the following Sabbath!"

Though Mr. Spurgeon did not belong to them, he had ever a great admiration for the Strict Baptists. One of the permanent influences of his career was, indeed, the early training he received amongst the Calvinists of the Eastern Counties. The wonder is that he broke away from the sterner school. Baptists in those days were a puzzle to outsiders, they were divided into "Particular," those that believed in particular redemption; and

"General," those who affirmed that Christ died for all men. There was another division, "Strict Baptists"—those who admitted to the Lord's Table only such as had been baptised; and "Open Baptists those who welcomed all believers to the Communion Service. Then, again, amongst the Open Baptists were, and are, those who grant Church membership apart from baptism, and those who, though they have an open table, demand baptism before entrance to the Church. The General and the Particular Baptists have long since united, but there are still those who, being high Calvinists, hold aloof, and indeed these again are divided into two sections. But the doctrinal and ecclesiastical lines do not necessarily agree.

Mr. Spurgeon's position was Calvinistic, accompanied by Open Communion. He once told me with appreciation how he was worsted in argument by an American divine. During a drive, the visitor made a number of inquiries, and discovered the practice of the Church at the Tabernacle, how it admitted people to the Lord's Table who were not baptised, and refused them membership unless baptised. "Which means, that they are good enough for the Lord, and yet not good enough for you!" said his guest. And Spurgeon had to admit that the logic was not on his side. But, then, neither the world nor the Church can live on logic alone.

What is known as "The Rivulet" controversy rose over a little book of verse published by Rev. T. T. Lynch under that title. Here, again, in retrospect it seems much hubbub about very little. Some of the poetry has found its way into our hymn-books, some is forgotten. In *The Christian Cabinet* of May 28, 1856, Mr. Spurgeon wrote a lengthy article, good-humouredly pointing out the weaknesses of the book. "If I should ever be on amicable terms with the chief of the Ojibewas, I might suggest several verses from Mr. Lynch as a portion of a liturgy to be used on the next occasion when he bows before the Great Spirit of the West Wind. Hark! O ye Delawares, Mohawks, Choctaws, Chickasaws, Blackfeet, Pawnees, Shawnees, and Cherokees, here is your primitive faith most sweetly rehearsed—not in your own wild notes, but in the white man's language," and then he quoted the verse, "My God in nature I confess." The controversy was so fierce at the time that the autumn meeting of the Congregational Union was postponed because of it.

But in spite of this, perhaps because of it, in a speech at Exeter Hall, while the feeling was still bitter, Mr. Spurgeon said, "I am about to quote the words of a good man, who I think is very much misunderstood." Then he gave the verse—

> "Let us with a wind-like song
> Freshen all the air of life:
> Singing makes the heart grow strong;

Now to win seems worth the strife."

And only a little while before his death he reviewed a volume of Lynch's sermons, and said that they contained "a great deal of the Gospel in solution."

Four years afterwards the storm raged around the head of Baldwin Brown, who had just published his volume *The Divine Life in Man*. Two articles by Howard Hinton in *The Freeman* condemning the book were so unfavourably reviewed by that journal, that seven ministers, amongst them Mr. Spurgeon, wrote a protest, which, with gaucherie characteristic of the time, was itself criticised.[1] This led to further discussion and a final letter from Mr. Spurgeon to two other papers, and a retort by Baldwin Brown. Even one of the papers that published Mr. Brown's letter expressed surprise that the doctrines of Maurice, which he championed, could be counted compatible with the evangelic faith.

The next discussion was with Dr. Cumming, who, in the midst of his prophetic studies, was also known as *The Times* Bee Master. In a book on "Bees" in 1864 he made some strictures on the Baptismal Regeneration Controversy, to which reference will be made in the next chapter, and said: "I wish somebody would send Mr. Spurgeon a super of good honey. Three months' diet on this celestial food would induce him to give up those shockingly bitter and unchristian tirades he has lately been making against the clergy of the Church of England." In answer Spurgeon in *The Times* advised his brother of Crown Court to give less honey and more salt in his public ministrations, reminded him that honey was prohibited in the ancient sacrifices, because it so speedily became acid, whereas salt was good. In the end Dr. Cumming was offered a brick of the best salt, carriage paid, if only he would follow this reasonable advice.[2]

On Monday, June 29, 1868, the Bishop of Oxford, speaking on the Irish Church in the House of Lords, amidst much responsive laughter, referred to a letter Mr. Spurgeon had written in April to John Bright, who had presided at a meeting of the Liberation Society in the Tabernacle, Mr. Spurgeon being too ill to be present. Bishop Wilberforce poked fun at Spurgeon's rheumatic gout, and said that he had sent a written communication in which he said that the Irish clergy were the very best of the clergy of the Establishment, and that for that reason he thought that they should be the first to be favoured with the great blessing of disendowment. Their lordships would remember how Isaac Walton said they were to treat the frog, put it on the hook "tenderly, as if they loved it." The Bishop then, amid further laughter and cheers, quoted another letter of Spurgeon's, addressed to the Baptist Churches, complaining of their niggardly support of their ministers.

---

[1] *Autobiography*, Vol. II. p.. 270.
[2] *Life and Work of C. H. Spurgeon*, by G. Holden Pike, Vol. III. p. 113.

To this Mr. Spurgeon made a spirited reply in *The Daily Telegraph,* which, in a leading article, sums up the situation and vindicates Spurgeon. Some sentences will bear quotation—

"There are gleeful sounds of merriment in many a country rectory over the discomfiture of Spurgeon by Wilberforce; there is a grim smile of delight on the face of many a Dissenting Minister at the discomfiture of Wilberforce by Spurgeon.

"Whether it was altogether decorous for a spiritual peer of the realm to caricature in his place in Parliament the voice and manner of a Dissenting Minister, we do not care to discuss. All we mean to say is that if Mr. Spurgeon mimicked the Bishop of Oxford in the Tabernacle, or on the platform of Exeter Hall, every Churchman in the Bishop's School would have considered the act as a proof of 'the vulgarity of Dissent.' We know, however, that it is impossible for a Bishop to be vulgar: he can't manage it; the nature of his office prevents him; and accordingly we are convinced that the Bishop of Oxford was really very gentlemanly after a new fashion.

"Mr. Spurgeon has displayed a creditable amount of good taste and good temper in his reply. Compared with the ordinary line of religious polemics his rejoinder is mildness itself. There is, however, an undercurrent of drollery in it which may make the Bishop tremble for his laurels. The sting of his adversary's letter lies in the 'Dr. Samuel Wilberforce' at the end of it, and in the date 'Clapham.' As it happens, the world already associates those two names very intimately together; but a new and grotesque juxtaposition is suggested when we remember that the son of William Wilberforce, sitting in the House of Lords, does not miss an opportunity of sneering at the school with which his father used to work."[1]

Six years afterwards Spurgeon became the centre of a controversy on Tobacco Smoking. Dr. George F. Pentecost, who had been a guest at Mr. Spurgeon's home, and had expressed in glowing terms his admiration of the preacher and his work, on his return from his continental tour again visited the Tabernacle. Mr. Spurgeon asked him to divide the sermon with him, one taking the doctrine and the other the enforcing and illustration of it. All unwittingly, as Dr. Pentecost afterwards declared, he spoke of his struggles in renouncing his cigar, and Mr. Spurgeon afterwards felt that he could not allow the matter to go by default. So he rose and declared that he hoped that very evening to smoke a cigar to the glory of God.

The utterance was very widely discussed: many were grieved; many applauded; before long Spurgeon's photograph appeared on tobacco packets. In a letter to *The Daily Telegraph* he gave his view of the situation, the irony

---

[1] *Daily Telegraph*, June 6, 1868.

of which is not lessened by the fact that Dr. Pentecost afterwards himself became a smoker. Mr. Spurgeon wrote—

"I demur altogether and most positively to the statement that to smoke tobacco is in itself a sin. It may become so, as any other indifferent action may, but as an action it is no sin. Together with hundreds of thousands of my fellow-Christians I have smoked, and, with them, I am under the condemnation of living in habitual sin, if certain accusers are to be believed. As I would not knowingly live in the smallest violation of the law of God, and sin is the transgression of the law, I will not own to sin when I am not conscious of it. There is growing up in society a Pharisaic system which adds to the commands of God the precepts of men; to that system I will not yield for an hour. The preservation of my liberty may bring upon me the upbraidings of many good men, and the sneers of the self-righteous; but I shall endure both with serenity, so long as I feel clear in my conscience before God. The expression 'smoking to the glory of God' standing alone has an ill sound, and I do not justify it; but in the sense in which I employed it I still stand to it. No Christian should do anything in which he cannot glorify God, and this may be done, according to Scripture, in eating and drinking and the common actions of life. When I have found intense pain relieved, a weary brain soothed, and calm, refreshing sleep obtained by a cigar, I have felt grateful to God and have blessed His Name: this is what I meant, and by no means did I use sacred words triflingly. If through smoking I had wasted an hour of my time—if I had rendered my mind less vigorous— I trust I should see my fault and turn from it; but he who charges me with these things shall have no answer but my forgiveness. I am told that my open avowal will lessen my influence, and my reply is that if I have gained any influence through being thought different from what I am, I have no wish to retain it. I will do nothing upon the sly, and nothing about which I have a doubt."[1]

On April 25, 1890, there appeared in *The British Weekly* "An Open Letter—Parker to Spurgeon." It was the week the Pastor's College Conference was in session, and the letter aroused strong feeling amongst "Spurgeon's men," as well as amongst the general evangelical public. Mr. Spurgeon gave the word that no notice was to be taken of it, did not speak of it himself, and getting a hint that Mr. Hugh D. Brown of Dublin, who was to be one of the speakers at the College meeting that evening in the Tabernacle, intended to speak of the open letter of Sanballat to Nehemiah, he deftly managed to crowd him out.

---

[1] *Ibid.*, Sept. 28, 1874.

The letter was all the more astonishing because hitherto Dr. Parker had shown great friendliness to Mr. Spurgeon. In November 1865, on two successive Fridays he had lectured in the Metropolitan Tabernacle on "Nonconformity in Relation to the Book of Common Prayer," and on "Reasons for a Nonconformist Aggressive Policy," to crowded audiences. On February 15, 1883, Parker and Spurgeon had exchanged pulpits, Spurgeon preaching in "The City Temple" on behalf of a Colportage Society for the City of London which Dr. Parker was founding. At the Orphanage Festival of June in the same year Parker offered to preach for the Orphanage in his church, and afterwards did so.

Spurgeon was scarcely as much surprised as some of his friends, for something had happened in between. The something was that on February 23, 1887, Dr. Parker wrote to him—

"MY DEAR FRIEND,

"There is nothing worth preaching but the old Evangelical faith. The longer I live and work the more I see this to be the case. Upon this subject I want a public conference between ministers of all denominations—gathered from all parts of the country, and beginning, say, on October 25th. I want you to preach the opening sermon in your pulpit—or in my own. That is all. The occasion should be devoted to clear and simple testimony as to our faithfulness to Evangelical doctrine. I earnestly entreat you to co-operate— make your own suggestions, fix your own time and place, lay down your own conditions, only let us unite in the holy and needful work. The God of heaven be your daily comfort and eternal hope!

"Ever yours,

"JOSEPH PARKER."

To this Spurgeon replied the next day, February 24, 1887—

"DEAR SIR,

"I agree with you that there is nothing worth preaching but the old Evangelical faith, and I would gladly co-operate with all believers in the spread of it, but—

"I feel I have no right whatever to question you about your course of procedure. You are a distinguished man with a line of your own, but your conduct puzzles me. I can only understand a consistent course of action, either for the faith or against it, and yours does not seem to exhibit that quality. I am sorry that frankness requires me to say this, and having said it, I desire to say no more.

"I think that we had better each go his own way in brotherly friendliness, each hopeful of the other. To discuss your procedure would not be wise. In your letter just received I greatly rejoice, and if this line of things is to be followed up, you will find me the heartiest of friends, but at this present I had better say no more.

"Yours with the kindest wishes, and great admiration of your genius,

"C. H. SPURGEON."

Dr. Parker answered on March 1, 1887—

"MY DEAR FRIEND,

"I have no idea as to your meaning. If thou hast aught against thy brother, go and tell him his fault between thee and thy brother. But as your health is uncertain, I will so far modify the terms as to go to you at your house at any mutually convenient time. This strikes me as the Christian way—the Lord's own way—why should we invent another?

"You have no warmer friend on earth than

"JOSEPH PARKER."

The next day, March 2, 1887, Mr. Spurgeon responded—

"DEAR DR. PARKER,

"If I had aught against you I would see you gladly; but I have no personal offence, nor shadow of it. Your course to me has been one of uniform kindness, for which I am most grateful.

"The question is very different. You ask me to co-operate with you in a Conference for the vindication of the old Evangelical faith. I do not see my way to do this. First, I do not believe in the Conference; and secondly, I do not see how I could act with you in it, because I do not think your past course of action entitles you to be considered a champion of the faith.

"There is nothing in this which amounts to having aught against you. You have, no doubt, weighed your actions and are of age. These are not private but public matters, and I do not intend to go into them either in my house or yours.

"The Evangelical faith in which you and Mr. Beecher agree is not the faith which I hold; and the view of religion which takes you to the theatre is so far off from mine that I cannot commune with you therein.

"I do not feel that these are matters in which I have the slightest right to call you to account. You wrote to me, and I tried to let the matter go by. You write me again and compel me to be more explicit, altogether against my will. I do not now write; for any eye but your own, and I most of all desire that you will now let the matter drop. To go further will only make you angry and it will not alter me. I do not think the co-operation sought would be a wise one, and I had rather decline it without further questioning.

"To make this public would serve no useful end. I have told you of the matter alone, and now I must decline any further correspondence.

"Yours with every good wish,

"C. H. SPURGEON."

To which the same evening a post-card reply was written—

"Best thanks, and best regards.—J. P."

Then came the Open Letter. The first wonder is, why it was written. The second, why it was published. The references to Mr. Spurgeon's doctrine may be omitted.

"My dear Spurgeon,

"I know I may speak frankly, because I am speaking to a man whose heart is big and warm, a heart that has an immense advantage over his head. When people ask me what I think of Spurgeon, I always ask, which Spurgeon—the head or the heart—the Spurgeon of the Tabernacle or the Spurgeon of the Orphanage.

"I will speak frankly as to a brother beloved. Let me advise you to widen the circle of which you are the centre. You are surrounded by offerers of incense. They flatter your weakness, they laugh at your jokes, they feed you with compliments. My dear Spurgeon, you are too big a man for this. Take in more fresh air. Open your windows, even when the wind is in the East. Scatter your ecclesiastical harem. I do not say destroy your circle: I simply say enlarge it. As with your circle, so with your reading.

"Other men will write you in a vein of condolent flattery, and will hold up their riddled gingham to save you from the refreshing shower, but you know as well as I do that their good offices are meant for themselves and not for you.

"Good-bye, you sturdy, honest old soul. You have been wondrously useful, and wondrously honoured. I would double all your honours if I could. Am I become your enemy because I tell you the truth? In your inmost soul you know I am not your enemy, but your friend."

During Mr. Spurgeon's illness Dr. Parker wrote another letter to him in *The British Weekly* of October 8, 1891, which somewhat atoned for the first.

"I tell you," he said, "that your way of taking what seems to me a hard lot quite breaks me down into a new experience of love. I know how sadly I should have failed. What if, after all, you should prove to be the broadest-minded man among us?"

And after Mr. Spurgeon's death Dr. Parker paid a generous tribute to him in *The Times,* in which occur the following sentences: "The only pulpit name of the nineteenth century that will be remembered is no longer the name of a living man. His simplicity, his constancy, his stand-stillness, won for him, through many difficulties, a unique and invincible position in Christian England. Mr. Spurgeon had but one sermon, and it was ever new. Other young preachers are naturally great in the treatment of Biblical narrative and anecdotes. They can handle drama better than doctrine. Mr. Spurgeon boldly went at once to the deepest and greatest themes. At nineteen he preached to countless thousands from such texts: 'Accepted in the Beloved'; 'No man cometh unto Me except the Father draw him'; 'And of His fulness have all we received, and grace for grace.' Some men have never ventured to take those texts even after a lifetime of service. Mr. Spurgeon took them at once, as the very seven notes that made all God's music, and he did so by Divine right and impulse. As he began, so he continued: he never changed; he never went in quest of the fourth dimension or of the eighth note; his first and his last were one."

"That great voice has ceased. It was the mightiest voice I ever heard: a voice that could give orders in a tempest, and find its way across a torrent as through a silent aisle. Very gentle, too, it could be, sweet and tender and full of healing pity."

And on December 8, 1902, Thomas Spurgeon wrote: "Dr. Parker has gone. I was at the funeral service. One forgets even 'The Open Letter' at the open grave."

And now neither Spurgeon nor Parker has any need of controversy. They both know.

CHAPTER XVII

TWO GREAT CONTROVERSIES

MR. SPURGEON was too earnest, too intent on the eternal meaning of things, too sure of his own standing, to be a good controversialist. His instinct led him to conclusions that others approached only by logic, and he was therefore not apt to be too patient with those who debated every step of the way, or lost themselves in details, failing, as he judged, to see the wood because of the trees, and the city because of the houses.

He was a witness, not a debater. He could plead nobly, but he had such faith in the Truth that he preferred to trust it to do its own work. "The best way to defend a lion," he frequently said, "is to let it out of its cage." "I am no enemy, no disputant, no caviller," he wrote to Charles Williams. "I only want to do the right thing, and if it should seem harsh, I want to do it in love and tenderness." And at an earlier time: "A little anger costs me so much, and is so apt to blaze into a battle royal, that it is a calamity to be aroused, and an event memorably mournful." But, speaking for the Baptist Missionary Society in Exeter Hall on April 28, 1864, he said: "When the gage of battle is thrown down, I am not the man to refuse to take it up."

If we look at his life steadily, and endeavour to see it whole, we shall note that its two great unrelated controversies were, from his central evangelical standpoint, the complement of each other. Whatever heat they engendered at the time, together they complete his testimony. In the first he contended against superstition, and in the second against modernism, aiming one blow at Anglicanism, and another at Nonconformity; opposing first those who had a creed they did not believe, and then those who would not put their belief into a creed. He stood in the centre, and it was his jealousy for God which made him warn first the left wing and then the right wing of the army, that they were in danger of being captured by the enemy. He went out to the fray in both cases assured of result, but in neither did he foresee what the result would be. In the first he was prepared to suffer, and things turned out to his advantage; in the second he expected sympathy, and he suffered. In both cases it was, at the time, a drawn battle, stalemate, in fact; but the witness remains, and the scars of the conflict are to the combatant but signs of honour.

During the second controversy a suggestive comparison was made: "When Newman went abroad in 1832 with his consumptive friend, Hurrell Froude, his thought by day and his dream by night seems to have been the quickening of a Church which would fight against the spirit of the day and fix the minds of its children upon the eternal realities, which the modern spirit of our own time is so anxious to soften, blanch and water down. There was a passion at this time in all Newman said and did. He harps upon the lukewarmness of the age and the indifference to eternal truth which it displays. He felt to the bottom of his heart that he was doing a work of which he himself knew neither the scope nor the goal, and that so far as he was acquitted by his own conscience, he did not much care what man said of him."[1]

The Baptismal Regeneration Controversy was inaugurated by a sermon in the Metropolitan Tabernacle on June 5, 1864. Before he preached it, Mr. Spurgeon warned his publishers that he was about to destroy at a blow the circulation of his printed sermons, but the blow must be struck. Instead of destroying the sale of them, there has never been such a demand for any sermon as for that. In these days, when newspapers circulate a million copies a day, it may seem a small thing to say that a sermon had at once a circulation of a quarter of a million, but in those days, and for a sermon in any day, such a sale is phenomenal.

The text was: "Go ye into all the world and preach the Gospel to every creature. He that believeth and is baptised shall be saved, and he that believeth not shall be damned." The preacher plunged at once into his protest: "If I should, through speaking what I believe to be the truth, lose the friendship of some and stir up the wrath of more, I cannot help it. The burden of the Lord is upon me, and I must deliver my soul. I have been loath enough to undertake the work, but I am forced to it by an awful and overwhelming sense of solemn duty.

"I know of nothing more calculated to debauch the public mind than a want of straightforwardness in ministers. If baptism does regenerate people, let the fact be preached with a trumpet tongue, and let no man be ashamed of his belief in it. God forbid that we should censure those who believe that baptism saves the soul, because they adhere to a Church which teaches the same doctrine. So far they are honest men; and in England, wherever else, let them never lack full toleration. I hate their doctrine, but I love their honesty."

"Never," said Dr. Campbell, "has the error been exhibited to the public eye with colouring so vivid, and never was it pressed home on the clerical conscience with a force so thrilling, resistless, and terrible."

"Oh, for a truly reformed Church of England and a godly race to maintain it!" the preacher cried. "The world's future depends on it, under God, for in proportion as truth is marred at home, truth is maimed abroad."

The sermon is sixteen pages long, so it must have occupied more than an hour in delivery. It is well worth reading today. On the day following, the

---

[1] *British Weekly,* Feb. 17, 1888.

students of the College united with Mr. Spurgeon in spending the whole afternoon in prayer for a blessing on the sermon when it should be printed.

Upon its appearance the whole religious world joined in the fray. Mr. Spurgeon's part in the controversy was to preach other sermons; one three weeks later: "Let us go forth unto Him without the camp, bearing His reproach;" a month after that a sermon on "Children brought to Christ, not to the Font," and two months after that a sermon on "The Book of Common Prayer weighed in the Balances of the Sanctuary."

In these discourses he answered directly and indirectly the blizzard of pamphlets and sermons which his original sermon had called forth—there must have been a hundred and fifty of them. At my side as I write are nine volumes of pamphlets, leather-bound, and five of them contain those that were issued on this subject. In the corner of my room is another pile of them. Spurgeon himself looks down on me from his portrait on the wall in front of me, framed in the palm branches that came from France on his coffin, and as I think of the furore which his words aroused more than fifty years ago, of the friendship which afterwards grew up between him and the leaders of that very Church against which he then bore his witness, of the self-same Church today still continuing in the self-same way, I wonder at the seeming futility of it all. But then I remember that though the waves break, the tide comes surely in, that even half a century is but a hand-breadth in the cycles of God, and that no witness for Christ and the truth of Christ can be lost.

It must not be supposed that Mr. Spurgeon was much troubled in the midst of the conflict. "I hear you are in hot water," said a friend to him at the time. "Oh no," he answered, "it is the other fellows who are in the hot water. I am the stoker, the man who makes the water boil."

A quarter of a century afterwards, the second controversy began, with result strangely similar to the first. Then it became necessary for Mr. Spurgeon to resign from the Evangelical Alliance, now he resigned from the Baptist Union. But as he afterwards returned to the Alliance, it might have been hoped, had his life been spared, that he would again enjoy the fellowship of his Baptist brethren. We do not forget that he wrote: "Garibaldi complained that by the cession of Nice to France he had been made a foreigner in his native land, and our heart is burdened with a like sorrow; but those who banish us may yet be of another mind, and enable us to return."[1]

When Thomas Spurgeon and Archibald G. Brown were co-pastors of the Church at the Metropolitan Tabernacle, some question was raised as to whether the Baptist Union might meet in the building. Said Thomas Spurgeon: "The Baptist Union almost killed my father." "Yes," said Mr. Brown, "and your father almost killed the Baptist Union."

---

[1] *Sword and Trowel*, 1887, p. 515.

Yet until this severance Mr. Spurgeon had been most cordial towards the Baptist organisation. In the autumn of 1865, the Baptist journal, *The Freeman,* had lamented that "there are voices in our midst which would ring through the land, but which are silent except to their own congregation. There are men whom we should all gladly follow, but they carry no standard, and utter no call. Almost the only exception to this statement is Mr. Spurgeon. But through the peculiarity of his position Mr. Spurgeon has hitherto stood very much alone. He is the head of a denomination *within* a denomination. He takes little part in the concerns of the Baptist body *as such.* We believe this is not Mr. Spurgeon's own desire. If we are not mistaken, he has expressed, again and again, the desire to unite more heartily with his brethren. Why should he not do so? Is there anything that keeps him apart from the Baptist body in spite of himself? No man would be welcomed more cordially by the denomination generally, as a counsellor and a brother beloved."

In the metropolis there is another union of Baptists—"The London Baptist Association." Mr. Spurgeon had preached for it, and his discourse was often referred to as its "Funeral Sermon," for although crowds came to hear the preacher, the Association itself languished for years. At length, in this same year, 1865, the new Association which still flourishes was formed. The invitation asking for co-operation in its foundation was sent out by Mr. Spurgeon and a few other ministers. The first meeting was for ministers only, the second included deacons. Eighty were present at the first gathering, when Mr. Spurgeon presided. "The brethren assembled represented well-nigh every shade of opinion amongst us, although, if any party predominated, we should say it was that of our Strict Communion brethren. Still, it was most apparent that the ruling wish of all present was to give as little place as possible to differences of opinion, and rather to find the common basis on which they could practically agree. We are thankful, too, that the basis of this new Association is so broad," wrote *The Freeman.* "It does not rest in a creed, but simply with wide basis of evangelical sentiment."[1]

It may be of interest to record that one of the first acts of the new Association was to appoint a day of fasting and prayer. November 5 was chosen, and the brethren were reminded that intercession would be more profitable than bonfires and fireworks. Mr. Spurgeon was its President in 1869.

For many years Mr. Spurgeon preached at the Autumn Assembly of the Baptist Union in the provinces, and occasionally he took part in the spring meetings, especially in 1878, when he proposed Rev. George Gould for the office of Vice-President.

[1] *Life and Work of C. II. Spurgeon,* by G. Holden Pike, Vol. III. p. 140.

In 1881 he wrote to *The Baptist* newspaper a letter which appeared on May 27, in which occurs the sentence: "No one more heartily desires the prosperity of the Union than I do; no one is more satisfied with its designs and plans. If there be any mutterings of tempest, they certainly do not arise from me or from any of those who gathered with me at the Conference."

His last appearance at the Union meetings was at Liverpool in 1882, when he yielded to the twice-repeated invitation of Hugh Stowell Brown, protesting at the same time that it was unfair always to ask him to be the preacher, when so many others could fulfil the service. On this occasion, after the sermon, a spontaneous collection of some £131 was given to the Orphanage.

During the Assembly Mr. Spurgeon listened to the paper read by Rev. T. Vincent Tymns on "Evangelistic Work in Large Towns." In one passage he declared that the spirit of the Cross was often manifested outside recognised Christian circles, and he illustrated his point by referring to the brawny English soldiers on the Egyptian battlefield, of whom they had read a few days before. "The terror-stricken army exclaimed, 'The Nazarenes are coming,' and expected immediate slaughter; but lo! the hated Nazarenes bound up their wounds, gave the sick their own day's allowance of water in that dry and scorching land, and left the harvest of their fields to be gathered in unharmed. Truly, a little of the Nazarene was there in many a rude soldier who confessed Him not, and amidst those scenes of carnage, I read a prophecy of victory for Him who first said: 'If thine enemy hunger, feed him; if he thirst, give him drink.'" As Mr. Spurgeon listened the tears rolled down his cheeks, and he afterwards commended the paper by describing it as "All good."[1] That was his farewell to gatherings of the Baptist Union.

In March and April 1887 there appeared in *The Sword and Trowel* two unsigned articles entitled "The Down-Grade," dealing largely with the history of the past, and drawing attention to the insidious ways in which heresy creeps into the churches. A footnote was appended to the first: "Earnest attention is requested for this paper. There is need of such a warning as history affords. We are going downhill at break-neck speed." That was the first shot in the campaign which is now known as "The Down-Grade Controversy." In August an article by Mr. Spurgeon himself appeared in his magazine under the title "Another Word concerning the Down- Grade"; "A Reply to Sundry Critics and Inquirers" in the September magazine; "The Case Proved" in October; "A Fragment upon the Down-Grade Controversy" in November; "Restoration of Truth and Revival" in December. In the Preface to the 1887 volume occur the words: "Something will come of the struggle over The Down-Grade. The Lord has designs in connection

---

[1] Rev. W. J. Avery in *The Baptist Union Magazine,* 1892, p. 61.

therewith which His adversaries little dream of. Meanwhile, it behoves all who love the Lord Jesus and His Gospel to keep close together, and make common cause against deadly error. There are thousands who are of one mind in the Lord; let them break through all the separating lines of sect, and show their unity in Christ, both by prayer and action."

At first Mr. Spurgeon wrote in general terms as to the growing declension in faith, but gradually details were given and the Baptist Union was named. On October 8, he wrote withdrawing from it, and at a specially summoned meeting on December 13, the Council of the Union deputed four of its members to visit him at Mentone (whither he had gone for his winter's rest), "that they may deliberate with him as to how the unity of our denomination in truth, and love, and good works may best be maintained." Mr. Spurgeon telegraphed that he would prefer to see them when he returned to England, so on January 13, 1888, Dr. Clifford, Dr. Culross and Dr. Booth, the Secretary, had an interview with him at Westwood.

At the meeting of the Council on January 18, what has been termed "The Vote of Censure" was passed. "As Mr. Spurgeon declines to give the names of those to whom he intended them to apply, and the evidence supporting them, those charges, in the judgment of the Council, ought not to have been made." An answer which was more worthy of a pettifogging lawyer, a peevish woman, or a petulant child, than of a body of high-minded men. What the resolution said was the thing that Mr. Spurgeon himself ought to have been allowed to say. There was no principle involved: it was only a question of good manners; and if one clear, strong voice had said as much that day, I think the resolution would not have been passed. This is the vote which some of Mr. Spurgeon's friends have since then sought to have erased from the Minutes of the Council. But Mr. Spurgeon himself wrote: "All questions about the vote of censure, as far as I am concerned, may be set aside, and let the one question be discussed in all good temper, and let the truth be contended for in the name of our Lord Jesus Christ. Shall the Baptist Union be a resort for men of every school of thought, or shall it be declared to be an evangelical institution?"

The issue at last was narrowed down to that, and though at the time I was unconnected with the Union, not being a pastor of a Church, he wrote to me to the same effect. Had he lived, that was the point at which he would have aimed, and today we may rejoice that there is the Declaratory Statement published with the Annual Report—

"1. That the Lord Jesus Christ, our God and Saviour, is the sole and absolute authority in all matters pertaining to faith and practice, as revealed in the Holy Scriptures, and that each Church has liberty to interpret and administer His Laws.

"3. That Christian Baptism is the immersion in water, into the Name of the Father, the Son, and the Holy Ghost, of those who have professed repentance toward God, and faith in our Lord Jesus Christ, who 'died for our sins according to the Scriptures, was buried, and rose again the third day.'

"3. That it is the duty of every disciple to bear personal witness to the Gospel of Jesus Christ, and to take part in the evangelisation of the world."

At the Council Meeting of February 21 a Declaratory Statement was suggested; on April 23 it was altered as to the question of the interpretation of Matt. xxv. 46, which was cited, with a footnote saying that some brethren "have not held the common interpretation of those words of our Lord."

At the Assembly in the City Temple on April 23, Charles Williams of Accrington moved the resolution accepting the Declaration with the footnote, and made a speech dealing more with the footnote than with the resolution. Dr. James A. Spurgeon seconded the resolution, but not the speech, and so it was hoped that the difficulty had been solved.

In the February 1888 *Sword and Trowel* there was an article on "The Baptist Union Censure," and as a supplement to the May *Sword and Trowel* there was a statement modifying somewhat the "Notes" that had been written and printed before the City Temple meeting. Mr. Spurgeon says: "In the Declaration I rejoice, and still more in the kindly spirit which found joy in conciliating opponents; but the speech of Mr. Williams launches us upon a shoreless sea."

That was written on April 27. On April 26, in a personal letter to a friend, he says: "My brother thinks he has gained a great victory, but I believe we are hopelessly sold. I feel heart-broken. Certainly he has done the very opposite of what I should have done. Yet he is not to be blamed, for he followed his best judgment. Pray for me, that my faith fail not."

The Pastor's College Conference this year was reorganised as The Pastor's College Evangelical Conference. Some eighty of the old students held aloof, and a threat from one of them that he would force his way into the Conference, of which he rightly said he was a member, led to the dissolution of the old body, and the inauguration of the new, on a basis which the minority were not willing to accept.

There was a wrong turning taken somewhere, when men whose hearts drew them together found themselves sundered. At the end, Mr. Spurgeon had no other honourable course than to withdraw, but a little prescience on the part of the Union might have avoided that dilemma. I venture to say that if, say, Dr. Shakespeare had then been Secretary, the Down-Grade Controversy would have taken a different direction. The protest would have been uttered, and rightly uttered, but the personal equation would have been different. The leading members of the Council felt that they could not submit to what they thought to be the tyranny of Mr. Spurgeon, while he would not trust what he thought to be the "trimming" of the Council. The Assembly voted for what they thought to be the settlement of the Controversy; had they known the inwardness of the case the Union would have been rent in twain. The whole question was taken in hand too late. The Autumn Assembly at Sheffield was allowed to pass without any action; what was done the following Spring might then have been anticipated. Mr. Spurgeon asserted that he had spoken and written to the leaders again and again; the officials declared that he had never made any representations to them on the subject— they probably meant that particular aspect of the subject; and he probably meant the whole case, and not the case only as it concerned the Baptist Union.

Could the lamentable result have been avoided? I cannot but believe that if Spurgeon himself could have come to the Assembly and spoken face to face with the delegates, an atmosphere would have been created in which clearer vision would have been possible. But he had already resigned. Had there even been a telephone, things might have been different. Might. Who can say?

William Carey was separated for some years from the Baptist Missionary Society that he had, in effect, founded. The Committee and he could not see eye to eye. If he had only met the Committee it would have been different. But, then, he never took a furlough. Happily it all came right in his case at last.

To Dr. Culross, Spurgeon wrote: "I am in fellowship with you—Union or no Union." To Dr. Clifford, Spurgeon said: "You are a General Baptist, and you hold your own views: you and I understand one another." Dr. Maclaren never took any part in the controversy, though he was one of the four appointed to interview Spurgeon. Dr. Booth, singularly enough, had consulted Spurgeon on "Down-Grade "matters even before Spurgeon had made any protest at all.

The outcome of the controversy has been both good and bad. In the fog of the moment the blows meant for one man fell on another, the protest against one thing branched out into something quite different; useless remedies were proposed; energy that might have been better directed was spent in pursuing shadows. But many a man wavering in the faith was recalled to his old allegiance, many a simple believer was encouraged, and the Greatheart who dared the hazard for the sake of his Lord, and for the faith that was dear to him, though he suffered for it, did not suffer in vain. The last words he said to one of his dearest friends, on the platform of Herne Hill Station, before he went to Mentone for the last time, were: "The fight is killing me." But he never for a moment thought of turning back; the man who had lived for Christ was also willing to die for Him, and he had so greatly won the love of his friends, that if it only might have been possible, many of them would have been willing to die instead.

The very Baptist Union from which he differed, when it built its Church House, counted it its chiefest honour to put a commanding statue of Spurgeon in its Entrance Hall, and there the noble figure stands today, evidence to all that his memory is cherished and his name revered.

CHAPTER XVIII

TWO IMPORTUNATE QUESTIONS

IN review of this influential life two questions arise and insist on an answer. The first: What was the secret of Mr. Spurgeon's success? the second: Things being as they were, why did he not found a new denomination?

Let us take the second question first. If Spurgeon has not left behind him a body of Spurgeonites, it is not because the idea never occurred to him, nor because he lacked the opportunity of founding a sect; not because occasion did not arise when such a coterie seemed inevitable, nor that he was without prompting to establish it. In view of the peculiar position he occupied in relation to the ecclesiastical organisation of his day, and the extent of his following, it is surprising that he resisted the pressure, both from within and from without, towards the embodiment of his spirit in a Church order all his own.

Considering that up to the outbreak of the Great War 1226 students had been trained in the College, and that many of these were pioneers, often organising Churches in new districts, it would have been a comparatively easy thing to have formed them into a distinct regiment in the Church of Christ, especially as, at the beginning, Spurgeon's men were looked upon with some coldness, not to say suspicion, even among the Baptists to whom they were attached. That some thought of organising his men into a body was in his mind, even in the early years, is evident by a reference in a letter to his first student, written probably in 1866: "I hope to see all our Churches in one host. The time approaches for the formation of a distinct body or confederation. We will fill the nation with the Gospel, and then send our armies out the world over. Big words, but written in faith in a great God."[1]

When Spurgeon in later years withdrew from the Baptist Union, it seemed almost inevitable that, he would attempt to realise his early dream. The thought and hope of many people at the time were voiced in the following paragraph—

"Dr. Dale may be more intellectual, Dr. Maclaren more eloquent, and Dr. Parker more eccentric, but, for a variety of reasons, Mr. Spurgeon's personality looms bigger on the horizon than any of his contemporaries. Now that he has ceased to belong to the Baptist Union, he will feel that it is more than ever his duty to use plain words about solemn truths. His secession is condemned by those who differ from him, but has he lost a single member of his congregation? Spurgeon may not endeavour to bring into existence a

---

[1] *Life and Work of C. H. Spurgeon*, by G. Holden Pike, Vol. II. p. 868.

new sect: he cannot help his followers calling themselves by his name. Spurgeonism will have no infancy and no childhood, it starts in the vigour of manhood; and bearing in mind its origin, it would not be rash to predict that it will supplant the creed it repudiates, for there is no room in the constitution of Nonconformist organisation for Catholic theologians."[1]

"I have often been suspected of sinister designs," he said on June 1, 1868, at the Stockwell Orphanage, where there was so great a gathering that a ton of bread was cut up for the visitors. "A little time ago I was talking to a brother who himself told me the reasons why he used to dislike me. He said he was afraid, for one reason, that I was going to start a new denomination. 'Well,' I said, 'I could have done it had I liked, could I not?' 'Undoubtedly,' was the answer, 'and many would have followed you.' 'Well, but I did not do it.' The thought of doing such a thing might have been pleasing to human flesh, but I consider that there are sects enough without making another."[2]

There can be no doubt that if after his Down-Grade protest he had had inclination and vigour enough to come out into the open, and call people to his own standard, there would have been a large response, not only from the Baptists, but from all evangelical denominations, including Anglicans, and many of those called Brethren would probably have joined too. He must have been strongly tempted to make the venture. But he maintained his charity and sanity on the subject.

Here are some words of his, uttered in the very thick of the conflict: "Why not found a new denomination? It is a question for which I have no liking. There are denominations enough, in my opinion, and if there is a new denomination formed, the thieves and robbers who have entered other gardens walled around would climb into it also, and nothing would be gained. Besides, the expedient is not needed among Churches which are each self-governing and self-determining: such Churches can find their own affinities without difficulty, and can keep their own coasts clear of invaders. Oh, that the day would come when, in a larger communion than any sect can offer, all those who are one in Christ may be able to blend in perfect unity! This can only be by way of growing spiritual life, clearer light upon the more eternal truth, and a closer cleaving to Him who is the Head, even Jesus Christ."[3]

All the time, even when he withdrew from some of his brethren, his heart was crying out for fellowship with all the saints. He never was a sectarian, scarcely even a denominationalist. The great increase in the body of Baptists during his lifetime was chiefly owing to his influence, but always his sympathies reached far beyond that Church. It was a singular irony that he

[1] *Figaro*, Nov. 7, 1887.
[2] *George Moore: Merchant and Philanthropist*, by Samuel Smiles, p. 450.
[3] *Sword and Trowel*, 1887, p. 560.

who loved all who loved Christ in sincerity, should find himself at last isolated from those who were nearest to him. That was the iron that entered into his soul.

"There is no word," he wrote long before, "so hateful to our heart as Spurgeonism: no thought further from our soul than attempting to form a new sect. We preach no new Gospel, desire no new objects. We love the truth better than any sect, and are in open unison with the great body of Baptists because not able to endure isolation. 'Let my name perish, but let Christ's name endure for ever,' said George Whitefield, and so has Charles Spurgeon said a hundred times."[1]

The way was open for him to follow John Wesley, and he had the opportunity and ability to take it, but he deliberately chose the way of George Whitefield, his hero from earliest days; and though Whitefield's name is not borne by any Church, his influence, especially amongst the Calvinistic Methodists of Wales and amongst the Presbyterians of America, is probably as lasting as Wesley's; Spurgeon's influence, too, not only amongst the Baptists, but in the evangelical ranks of all the Churches, will endure for ever. He greatens [becomes greater] with the years.

What, then, was the secret of his success? I have asked the question of many, and the most remarkable answer was given by Sir William Robertson Nicoll. He must often have asked it of himself, for without an instant's hesitation he answered: "The Holy Ghost." That is inclusive and all-sufficient . Spurgeon was not alone. "The Lord was with Joseph, and he was a prosperous man," we read, or, as Tyndale puts it, "he was a luckie fellow." That, too, is the solution of Spurgeon's achievements. And if he was the fit and chosen instrument for God, we must believe that he was raised up at the right moment, and trained in the best way for the work he had to do; that God, who was with him from his infancy, chose also his heredity, and endowed him with the powers and grace that fitted him for his task.

Spurgeon himself ascribed his success not so much to his preaching of the Gospel, as to the Gospel he had to preach. To him it was the truth that prevailed, but, then, others preached the same truth without the same success, so there must be added reasons for the result in Spurgeon's case. Often he said that the reason of the blessing was "My people pray for me," but, then, other Churches pray for their pastors too.

The silvery voice has again and again been credited with the drawing power of the preacher. It suited him perfectly, it was a trumpet, clear, startling, arresting—not a violin. But opinion was not unanimous even on this subject. "In point of compass and richness, the voice of Mr. Spurgeon is not to be mentioned," says an early writer, "in comparison with that of Mr.

---

[1] *Christian Commonwealth*, Feb. 4, 1892.

James of Birmingham, or with that of Dr. Raffles; and to compare his power in this way with that of the late agitator, O'Connell, would indeed be to compare small things with great. It is a comparatively level voice. So that, while Mr. Spurgeon has made the pulpit more attractive than any living man, he has done so by means of a voice which can scarcely be called oratorical."[1]

Another early critic who set himself to fathom the problem said: "If I cannot discover the secret of your popularity in *what* you preach, can I find it in any peculiarity in your mode of preaching? Here is, in my judgment, the explanation of the secret. You have strong faith, and, as a result, intense earnestness. In this lies, as in the hair of Samson, the secret of your power."[2]

Years afterwards another observer stumbled on the same explanation: "Mr. Spurgeon's most striking characteristic was in his extraordinary earnestness. It is not for nothing nowadays that one meets a man so desperately in earnest as he is."[3] While still another wrote: "One who is as great a teacher with his pen as Mr. Spurgeon is with his tongue has told us 'that there is no substitute for thoroughgoing, ardent, and sincere earnestness.' Spurgeon's earnestness was indeed Zeal, and there were many in those early days who called him Zealot, and questioned the sincerity of such apparently consuming ardour."

"Were we asked to give in half a dozen words the secret of Mr. Spurgeon's commanding influence over the hearts of men," says another, "we should attribute it first to his courage and earnestness. and secondly to his practical common sense."[4]

"Mr. Spurgeon's art," said the leading English newspaper, "was to put old truths into a new dress, or to present them in a new form, in which they were more likely to come home to the apprehension and to the hearts of his hearers. In all this his want of learning was in one way a distinct advantage to him. His range of view was narrowed by it, but his standing ground was more secure."[5]

With equal confidence another verdict is given: "Undoubtedly the great secret of Mr. Spurgeon's success has been his utter indifference to popularity, combined with manly sincerity, and the genius for commanding an audience."[6]

An interviewer has added another quality to the list: "He might be a great orator—one could almost detect that by the music in his voice and the play of his mouth, even if we had not known it before—but I judged that it was

---

[1] *Review of the Churches*, Vol. I. p. 349.
[2] *Life and Work of C. H. Spurgeon,* by G. Holden Pike, Vol. II. p. 200.
[3] *Pictorial World*, Feb. 6, 1892.
[4] *Daily Telegraph*, Feb. 1, 1892.
[5] *The Times*, Feb. 1,1892.
[6] *Daily Chronicle*, Jan. 1,1879.

his inestimable quality of good-fellowship, as well as his greatness as a preacher and philanthropist, that had won him such widespread affection and regard."[1]

"What was the secret of this great man's success in life?" asks *The Speaker.* "Unquestionably the foundation of Mr. Spurgeon's success was his wonderful gift as a preacher. Some are inclined to belittle his oratorical powers. It can only be because they have not themselves been 'under the wand of the magician'—of its own kind there was nothing to equal it in the pulpit of any church in the land.

"But other churches have had preachers of an eloquence hardly inferior to that of Mr. Spurgeon. How comes it that they never won the hearts of the people of Great Britain as he did? Canon Liddon's name occurs so naturally when we speak of pulpit eloquence; Bishop Alexander, Archbishop Magee, and many others might fairly have competed, so far as mere gifts of speech were concerned, with the pastor of the Tabernacle. Yet not one of them held his place in English life, or anything approaching to it. We mean no disrespect to these eminent men when we say that Mr. Spurgeon's triumph, his unrivalled success in holding the hearts of so large a body of his fellow-countrymen, was distinctly a triumph of character. The British public had arrived at the conviction that he was absolutely sincere, simple, unpretending and straightforward.

"In this triumph of personal character, and in one other feature of his life's work we may read the secret of his astonishing success. That other feature was the stern fidelity he showed, from first to last, to the Puritan creed of his forefathers. Never for a moment did he waver in the conviction that the truth he learned as a boy was everything. Is it wonderful that when the old Puritanism was preached, not merely with eloquence, but with such genuine fervour of conviction, the preacher should have rallied round himself thousands, and scores of thousands, who found in him the very champion and leader for whom they had long been hoping and praying? Narrow-minded, bigoted, crude, ignorant, all these terms of reproach were flung in turn at Mr. Spurgeon, and they hurt him no more than did the passing breeze.

"Nor can those who know him, and who knew his preaching, forget that, despite the stern fidelity which he showed to a creed that was no longer that of the world, he had a heart filled with love for his fellow-creatures, with compassion for the sinner, with the burning desire that when the end of all things had come, and the Great Account was closed, no human soul which had found itself moved by the Divine Spirit might fail of salvation. And with it all he was no priest. Never once were the sympathies of a priest-hating

[1] *Christian World*, Feb. 4, 1892.

people ruffled by the slightest assumption of spiritual authority on the part of their teacher."[1]

In all these estimates it is taken for granted that there was a secret to be discovered in Spurgeon's life. The thing was so inexplicable along ordinary lines, so different from that of ordinary people, and yet the product was so simple and inevitable, that it is natural to ask if there is not behind something occult and unusual.

I asked his son the secret, and he was inclined to ascribe it to the fact that he was always working, never off duty, putting all his powers under tribute to one end. That indeed is true. Here, for instance, is the record of a day: "Leaving home early in the morning, I went to the chapel, and sat there all day long, seeing those who had been brought to Christ by the preaching of the Word. Their stories were so interesting to me that the hours flew by without my noticing how fast they were going. I may have seen some thirty or more persons during the day, one after the other, and I was so delighted with the tales of mercy they had to tell me, and the wonders of grace God had wrought in them, that I did not know anything about how the time passed. At seven o'clock we had our prayer meeting. I went in and prayed with the brethren. After that came the Church Meeting. A little before ten I felt faint, and I began to think at what hour I had my dinner, and I then for the first time remembered that I had not had any! I never thought of it. I never even felt hungry, because God had made me so glad."[2]

His friend, W. P. Lockhart of Liverpool, tells how he introduced him on one occasion to Mr. Alexander Balfour of the city. Mr. Balfour, sitting down beside him, said with that intensity of manner which always characterised him: "Mr. Spurgeon, I want to know how you get through the work you do. Tell me how you manage it." Mr. Spurgeon, looking up with a smile, said: "I suppose you think that a man who works twelve hours a day can get through a good deal of work?" "Yes," said Mr. Balfour. "Well," said Spurgeon, "I work eighteen!"

"We can no more tell why Mr. Spurgeon was a great preacher than why Turner was so great a painter, Napoleon so great a general, or Pitt so great a statesman."[3] "If you come to analyse the success of most men you cannot do it, for success defies analysis. It depends, primarily, of course, on a man's integrity and ability, but it is the little touches—what M. Thiers called the negligences—which make a picture complete."[4]

A sporting paper praised Mr. Spurgeon's voice, but added: "Of course it is not enough to have a fine organ to discourse excellent music. You must

---

[1] *The Speaker*, Feb. 6,1892.
[2] *Autobiography*, Vol. II. p. 187.
[3] *Baptist*, Feb. 12,1892.
[4] *Daily News*, Feb. 2, 1892.

have the music too, and this was supplied in Spurgeon's case by his bluff common sense, his humour, and his fluency of speech, combined with a faith that was almost childlike in its simplicity and freedom from guile. In Spurgeon's case one of the first circumstances prepossessing the auditor in his favour was that he had no Sunday voice."[1]

There is considerable divergence in these estimates of the man. On the human side the reasons assigned for his greatness are his voice, his faith, his earnestness, his courage, the novelty of his presentation, his indifference to popularity, his sincerity, his good-fellowship, his character, his fidelity to Puritan doctrine, combined with love to the people and the absence of priestism, his powers of work and devotion to the task in hand, his common sense, his fluency of speech, his freedom from guile.

Which of them is right? None. Nor if we single out other qualities not named in the list shall we be any nearer the solution. It was not the possession of one outstanding characteristic which worked the miracle, but the combination of all—and one other thing beside.

How often some brilliant endowment in a man is neutralised or weakened by the absence of some balancing characteristic. And how frequently a man of mediocre talents who holds them in poise succeeds where the man of outstanding genius fails. Once in a century there is given to us the balanced man of genius, the brilliant man who is a whole man, and then the world wonders. We may say it is this or that which accounts for his career: as a fact it is this, and that, and a dozen other things in combination, in proper proportion, in living unity, that creates the wonderful result.

"We shall not again see the singular combination of qualities that made Mr. Spurgeon such a pioneer," writes a newspaper which none of the readers of this biography ever sees. "His distinguishing traits were leonine courage, perfect sincerity, thorough conviction, and a manly determination to do the work that he specially felt himself called to."[2]

I quote again his friend W. P. Lockhart, a man of lesser gifts but similar character: "It was not his voice nor his fertility of illustration; the richness of his Bible knowledge nor the abundance of his Puritanic lore; his seer-like faculty nor his power to express in lusty Saxon exactly what was passing before his mind's eye; his mother-wit (used as a servant, and never allowed to become a master), his lion-hearted boldness, nor his tearful tenderness. Not one of these, nor all of them put together, made him what he was."

"Nor all of them put together!" His neighbour, Dr. W. Wright of the Bible Society, says: "Mr. Spurgeon had a marvellous combination of gifts which contributed to his greatness, a voice that you heard with pleasure and could

---

[1] *Referee*, Feb. 7, 1892.
[2] *Reynolds' Sunday Newspaper*, Feb. 7, 1892.

not help hearing, a mind that absorbed all knowledge, whether from books or nature, that came within his range, an eye that took a wide angle and saw everything within view, a memory that he treated with confidence which never disappointed him, a great, large heart on fire with the love of God and the love of souls. And then he showed a practical common sense in doing things, both sacred and secular, and a singleness of aim, joined with transparent honesty, that ensured the confidence of all who knew him. You could not help loving him if you came within his spell. But the chief secret of Mr. Spurgeon's power was his faith in the living God, and in the power of His Gospel. He had as real a belief in the Gospel as a merchant has in his money."[1]

But he might have had all these and yet missed the mark. "It is possible, say the men of science, to produce separately by chemical means every constituent of a glass of vintage port. The one thing science cannot do is to mix them so as to make a glass of port: put them together and only a nauseous mess results. Some gifted human beings are as mysteriously deficient. There is a type of man who possesses most of the qualities of greatness, but lacks the one quality of all—the mysterious force that fuses them into a living whole. The Italian Eclectic school of painting illustrated this imperfect synthesis. It aimed at perfection by the apparently rational plan of combining all possible perfections. It strove at once for the fire of Michel Angelo, for the design of the Roman school, for the glowing colour of Lombardy, the action and light and shade of the Venetians, for Correggio's grace and the symmetry of Raphael. It failed. The Caracci were, no doubt, great painters, but leagues behind the greatest."[2]

The great man is not an aggregation of qualities, however luminous or beautiful. He is, as we have seen, a living unity, and his great qualities are but the expression of something greater within.

> "His life was gentle, and the elements
> So mixed in him, that nature might stand up
> And say to all the world, This was a man."

It is the living mixture that produces the result, and when, as in Spurgeon's case, there is added to the great gifts of nature, the power of the Spirit of God dwelling within the man, as in a holy temple, who can be surprised at the result, at once so natural, so singular and creative? It has been well said that "Spurgeon was born with the key to the heart of humanity in his hand."[3]

---

[1] *British Weekly*, Feb. 4, 1892.

[2] *All and Sundry*, by E. T. Raymond, p. 27.

[3] *British Standard*, March 4, 1864.

CHAPTER XIX

THE TRIUMPHANT END

In the last hour of the last day of January 1892, the spirit of Spurgeon sped home from his loved Mentone. After forty years of unexampled ministry, he entered into rest. Two or three days before the end he said to his secretary, "My work is done," and after that he had nothing to do but to await the summons. There were no raptures, no heroics, nor were there any fears or hesitations. Shortly after ten o'clock Harrald was sure he saw a company of angels hovering over the Berceau; at five minutes past eleven only the body was left on the bed; before twelve Mrs. Spurgeon led the little group in praise and prayer. It was so quiet, yet it was so triumphant. All the bugles were blown as he departed, and the trumpeters sounded for him on the other side. It was a right enough instinct which made the mourners choose as his text, "I have fought a good light; I have finished my course; I have kept the faith." When it was quoted at the funeral people asked when he said it. He never said it, he did it all the time.

Like John Calvin, Jonathan Edwards, Jeremy Taylor, George Whitefield and William Tyndale, Spurgeon was fifty-seven when he died, but he was not young, for he began early and he had laboured long, and departed full of days and of grace.

The earliest premonition of the end was on April 26 1891, when, for the first time for forty years, he was compelled by a fit of nervousness to leave the pulpit after entering it. The next Lord's Day he was able to preach, on the following Sunday too, and also on the morning of May 17. Then illness overtook him, and only once more, on Sunday morning, June 7, did he stand in his pulpit commending Christ to the people. In spite of his weakness he insisted on going that week to Haverhill, that he might revisit Stambourne in preparation for the book of boyhood's memories which he was writing. There on the Friday his illness reappeared, and he returned to London. For more than a month he lay, most of the time unconscious, sometimes imagining that he was in a strange house and asking to be taken home, only now and then free from the delirium that was such a grief to those who waited round his bed.

During one of these times a letter arrived from Mr. Gladstone for Mrs. Spurgeon, which read—

"Dear Madam,

"In my own house, darkened at the present time, I have read with sad interest the daily accounts of Mr. Spurgeon's illness; and I cannot help conveying to you the earnest assurance of my sympathy with you and with him, and of my cordial admiration, not only of his splendid powers, but still more of his devoted and unfailing character. May I humbly commend you and him, in all contingencies, to the infinite stores of the Divine love and mercy, and subscribe myself,

"My dear Madam,
"Faithfully yours,
"W. E. GLADSTONE."

To this Mrs. Spurgeon sent a suitable reply, but the invalid insisted on adding a postscript. This is it—

"P.S.—Yours is a word of love such as those only write who have been into the King's Country, and seen much of His Face. My heart's love to you.— C. H. SPURGEON."

Many other distinguished persons also wrote.

How well I remember the suspense of that anxious month. I was at the Manor House, Newton Harcourt, near my home in Leicester, and every morning a porter from Great Glen Station would come along the canal towpath with the telegram from Westwood giving the doctors' bulletin. The tide ebbed and flowed. At the Tabernacle prayer meetings were held continually, and it seemed as if every promise of the Scripture, and every argument of faith, were used in pleading with God for the patient's recovery.

"Rarely, if ever," wrote Dr. Clifford, "has a warmer regard, or a more widespread interest in an invalid been excited. Love is victorious. Convictions are like bands of iron that cannot be broken; but opinions are as the weakest twine snapped in a moment, or burnt in the first outleap of the flame of affection."[1]

On August 9, the first letter in the Pastor's own hand was read to the congregation at the Tabernacle—

"The Lord's Name be praised for first *giving* and then hearing the loving prayers of His people ! Through these prayers my life is prolonged. I feel greatly humbled, and very grateful, at being the subject of so great a love and so wonderful an outburst of prayer.

"I have not strength to say more. Let the Name of the Lord be glorified.

"Yours most heartily,
"C. H. SPURGEON."

It soon became evident that though he was better there could yet be no thought of resuming work, so in October a fortnight's change was arranged

---

[1] *Review of the Churches*, Vol. I. p. 41.

at Eastbourne. As day after day Mr. Spurgeon went for a drive, respectful crowds would be outside his hotel waiting to see him start. He bore the change so well that, arrangements having meanwhile been made for Dr. A. T. Pierson to occupy the Tabernacle pulpit, he started for the South of France on Monday, October 26, accompanied by Mrs. Spurgeon, who after years of illness felt able to undertake the journey, by Dr. and Mrs. James Spurgeon, and the devoted "armour-bearer," Rev. J. W. Harrald.

They reached the Hotel Beau-Rivage, Mentone, without incident, and there his wife and he had, in spite of his weakness, three months of earthly paradise. To his son in New Zealand he wrote in triumph, "And your mother is here! "On the last evening of the year, and on the first of January, he gave two addresses, which were afterwards published under the title *Breaking the Long Silence*. On Sunday evenings, January 10 and 17, he conducted a brief service in his room, reading some of his own writings, and at the close of the second service, he announced the hymn "The sands of time are sinking"— and that was the end of all service for him on earth. A fortnight more he waited; people at home were anticipating his return, they were building a "lift" at the rear of the Tabernacle to save him the exertion of walking up the stairs, but they were waiting for him, too, in the unclouded country, and it was thither he went. What a welcome he must have received from the thousands who had already found their way there through his ministry!

In the first of his last two addresses occur the sentences: "During the past year 1 have been made to see that there is more love and unity among God's people than is generally believed. I feel myself a debtor to all God's people upon earth. We mistake our divergencies of judgment for differences of heart; but they are far from being the same thing. In these days of infidel criticism believers of all sorts will be driven into sincere unity."

The news of his home-going flashed round the world. On Monday the newspapers had but one thing on their Contents Bill—"Death of Spurgeon." The only experience at all resembling it was the day during the war when another single announcement sufficed—"Death of Kitchener." It was difficult that day to secure a newspaper, the demand was so great.

In spite of other suggestions it was arranged that Spurgeon must be buried among his own people. So on February 4, at the Presbyterian Church, Mentone, Rev. J. E. Somerville conducted a memorial service there, and then the coffin was conveyed across France, and arrived on Monday, February 9, at Victoria Station, London; it was met by a little group of friends and brought to the Pastor's College, where it remained that afternoon. At night it was carried into the Tabernacle, and there the next day some sixty thousand persons passed through to pay their homage to the dead.

Memorial services, unexampled in their wide expression of sympathy, were held four times on the Wednesday, great interest attaching to Mr.

Harrald's account of Spurgeon's last days, and to the presence of Mr. Sankey, who sang twice. The culminating moment of the day was when Berber Evans, with almost Welsh "hwyl," said: "But there is one Charles Haddon Spurgeon whom we cannot bury; there is not earth enough in Norwood to bury him—the Spurgeon of history. The good works that he has done will live. You cannot bury them." None who were there will ever realise more concentrated emotion than then.

Dr. Pierson rose with combined wisdom and grace to the occasion, preaching no less than five sermons during the eight days. The funeral was on the Thursday. One newspaper said that you might have searched London and not have found three women who did not wear black on the street on that day. Along the route to Norwood Cemetery there were crowds fronting the closed shops. At the Stockwell Orphanage the children sat on a raised platform, in deep mourning. At the grave, Archibald G. Brown, the most distinguished of Mr. Spurgeon's men, and his close friend, pronounced a eulogy by which he will be remembered for ever. Here it is in cold type.

"Beloved President, Faithful Pastor, Prince of Preachers, Brother Beloved, Dear Spurgeon—we bid thee not ' Farewell,' but only for a little while ' Goodnight.' Thou shalt rise soon at the first dawn of the Resurrection-day of the redeemed. Yet is the goodnight not ours to bid, but thine; it is we who linger in the darkness; thou art in God's holy light. Our night shall soon be passed, and with it all our weeping. Then, with thine, our songs shall greet the morning of a day that knows no cloud nor close; for there is no night there.

"Hard worker in the field! thy toil is ended. Straight has been the furrow thou hast ploughed. No looking back has marred thy course. Harvests have followed thy patient sowing, and heaven is already rich with thine ingathered sheaves, and shall still be enriched through the years yet lying in eternity.

"Champion of God! thy battle, long and nobly fought, is over; thy sword, which clave to thy hand, has dropped at last: a palm branch takes its place. No longer does the helmet press thy brow, oft weary with its surging thoughts of battle; a victor's wreath from the great Commander's hand has already proved thy full reward.

"Here, for a little while, shall rest thy precious dust. Then shall thy Well-Beloved come; and at His voice thou shall spring from thy couch of earth, fashioned like unto His body, into glory. Then spirit, soul, and body shall magnify the Lord's redemption. Until then, beloved, sleep. We praise God for thee, and by the blood of the everlasting covenant, hope and expect to praise God with thee. Amen."

As the casket was lowered into the grave there was nothing to be seen but the text at the foot of it about the good fight, and the Bible that lay on the top of it., open at the text that led Spurgeon into the light "Look unto Me and be ye saved, all the ends of the earth, for I am God and there is none else."

All the services are described in the volume which I edited, entitled, *From the Pulpit to the Palm Branch,* and I may be permitted to quote from the Preface my own words.

"Since this good gift, which the Giver of all good bestowed upon the Church, and upon the world, was to be taken from us, we are constrained to say that he could have gone from our midst in no better way. This is not only a matter of faith, but, having tried to imagine other methods of departure, we are compelled to fall back on God's way us the wisest and the best.

"Had Mr. Spurgeon been called suddenly, we should have been so stunned by the blow as to have been scarcely able to stand upright beneath it; a waiting time was, therefore, in mercy, granted to us, during which the forces at command were organised in such a way that, with the exactness of a machine, all worked smoothly when the terrible tidings at last came.

"Had Mr. Spurgeon been taken before such marvellous solicitude was shown around his sick bed, the enemies of the truth would have blasphemed; now they are fain to be silent, seeing that, even in this life, fidelity to the truth and faithfulness to conviction have been so greatly honoured.

"Had Mr. Spurgeon passed away amid the fogs of London, we should have imagined that, had he only been permitted to live beneath bluer skies, his life would have been prolonged; now we thank God that those three bright months were added to it, and that he was able, with his beloved wife, to have such uninterrupted joy on earth, ere he passed to his reward in heaven.

"Had Mr. Spurgeon ended his course in England, for a few days only would people have paused to have asked the secret of his marvellous influence; whereas, under the actual circumstances, *for twelve days* the attention of the civilised world was centred in the testimony borne, not only to the servant of God, but to the Gospel he preached, in column after column of almost every newspaper. Truly, the Lord hath done all things well!

"Many years ago, in one of his sermons, published at the time, he attempted to picture the scene at his own funeral, and expressed his own desire concerning it.

'In a little while,' he said, 'there will be a concourse of persons in the streets. Methinks I hear some one inquiring—

'What are all these people waiting for?'

'Do you not know? He is to be buried today.'

'And who is that?'

'It is Spurgeon.'

'What! the man that preached at the Tabernacle?'

'Yes; he is to be buried today.'

'That will happen very soon. And when you see my coffin carried to the silent grave, I should like every one of you, whether converted or not, to be constrained to say, 'He did earnestly urge us, in plain and simple language, not to put off the consideration of eternal things; he did entreat us to look to Christ. Now he is gone, our blood is not at his door if we perish.'''

"Far more abundantly than he dared to hope have his wishes been fulfilled, and only in the day when all things shall be revealed, shall it be known how many have been turned to the Lord by the death of the man who was so greatly honoured to lead people to the feet of Jesus during his life."

In *John Ploughman's Talk* there is a sentence[1] which runs, "Let the wind blow fresh and free over my grave, and if there must be a line about me, lift it be—

> Here lies the body of
> JOHN PLOUGHMAN,
> waiting for the appearing of his
> Lord and Saviour
> Jesus Christ."

A few days before the end, at Mentone, he said, "Remember—a plain slab, with C. H. S. upon it: nothing more." But love denied the last request, and reverence substituted the name "Charles Haddon Spurgeon" for that of John Ploughman. Then on one side of the tomb is the verse of the hymn he was accustomed to write in albums, and the verse that follows it.

> "E'er since by faith I saw the stream
> Thy flowing wounds supply,
> Redeeming love has been my theme,
> And shall be till I die."

There is little more to add. Mrs. Spurgeon lived for some years afterwards at Westwood, and her body now lies in the same grave as her husband. The tomb of Thomas Spurgeon is near by. The Tabernacle Church still continues; the College is still training men to preach the Gospel; the Orphanage still shelters and educates five hundred girls and boys. But a now era has dawned, and it may be that the Lord who called and equipped Spurgeon has another prophet somewhere preparing to utter His message to this generation, or it may be that there may dawn on the earth that great day of Epiphany which shall usher in the golden years.

---

[1] *John Ploughman's Talk*, p. 157.

For the rest, Spurgeon's own last words to the little Mentone group shall also be his last words to the readers of his biography: "The vista of a praiseful life will never close, but continue throughout eternity. From psalm to psalm, from hallelujah to hallelujah, we will ascend the hill of the Lord, until we come into the Holiest of all, where, with veiled faces, we will bow before the Divine Majesty in the bliss of endless adoration. Throughout this year may the Lord be with you! Amen."[1]

---

[1] *Sword and Trowel*, 1892, p. 55.

SPURGEON JUST BEFORE HIS LAST ILLNESS

CHAPTER XX

SPURGEON IN HISTORY

GREATNESS needs distance. Close at hand little things sometimes appear great—"the black fly on the window-pane looks like the black ox on the distant plain." And great things are often dwarfed by nearness. Mont Blanc cannot be properly appreciated from the village of Chamonix; to crown it the monarch of the mountains you must either climb it, or get further away. Jerusalem cannot be seen in its glory by the easy approach from the west; you must get across the Valley of the Kedron and stand on the Mount of Olives before the majestic picture bursts on your view.

The estimates of their own generation generally exaggerate or depreciate heroes, the calm judgment of history, though not infallible, is fairer. Some of earth's great ones have, no doubt, sunk into oblivion, but amongst those whom history remembers only those are great whom history greatens. Spurgeon is amongst the number.

It will be conceded without argument that he was greater than any of his pulpit contemporaries. In an earlier chapter the comparison has been made, and the fact is so evident that it needs no insistence. There is perhaps no detail in which he was not excelled by others of his time, but none approached him in the sum of his gifts. He himself was much impressed by the oratory of MORLEY PUNSHON, and once after hearing him declared, "If I could speak like that, I would turn the world upside down." At the same time, he was quite aware that such excessive rhetoric was apt to pall. Rhetoric, too, was the chief characteristic of CANON LIDDON in the pulpit. "When he closed his manuscript, the congregation, after an hour's rapture and breathless attention, appear as if a weight had been lifted off their spirits." It has been well said that Liddon was the Jeremiah of that age, and Spurgeon its Isaiah. The present verdict as to these three pulpit orators is clear. Equally clear when comparison is made with HENRY WARD BEECHER, who in his time was judged by many to be a greater preacher than Spurgeon—"a man who always comes out of the front door when he wishes to give his opinions an airing;" or with THOMAS GUTHRIE, that other polished orator, who has himself, in speaking of Spurgeon, unconsciously described the difference between them—"one man is a Boanerges and another a Barnabas."

It would be tedious to attempt to characterise all the eminent preachers of the Spurgeon era. ALEXANDER MACLAREN, more intense but less human; R. W. DALE, a deeper thinker with a much smaller orbit; DEAN STANLEY, more influential but with less abiding influence; CANON FARRAR, more florid and fugitive; PHILLIPS BROOKS, as pictorial but not as popular; JOSEPH PARKER, with a more modern accent, but with less of the eternal speech;

BOYD CARPENTER, beyond compare the great preacher of his own Church in his own time, but not as incessant nor as far-reaching as Spurgeon; ALEXANDER WHYTE, a greater spiritual surgeon, but a less skilful physician. The fact that CARDINAL MANNING died a fortnight before Spurgeon suggested a comparison of their respective places in the life of their epoch. It was freely said that Manning was as great a loss to the Catholic work! as Spurgeon to the Protestant. Today Manning has less influence than Newman, but the savour of Spurgeon's life and ministry abides.

As for the leaders of the Church in other ages, Spurgeon's saying has been already quoted: "You may take a step from Paul to AUGUSTINE, then from Augustine to Calvin, and then—well, you may keep your foot up a good while before you find such another." When he visited the Simplon Hospice, he said, "I was delighted to find that they are Augustine monks, because, next to Calvin, I love Augustine. I feel that Augustine was the great mine out of which Calvin digged his mental wealth; and the Augustine monks, in practising their holy charity, seemed to say: 'Our Master was a teacher of grace, and we will practise it, and give without money and without price to all comers whatsoever they need.'"[1]

This seems to suggest that he himself would have stepped from Augustine to JOHN CALVIN, and the references in Chapter VI strengthen that conviction. But he would first have stopped, perhaps, at MARTIN LUTHER, and Gustav Kaweran has told us that "his knowledge of Luther was much more accurate than that of many of Luther's fellow-countrymen." The same author believes that, as in the case of Luther, one of the secrets of his influence was "the violence of his preaching, the rock-like conviction of the power of the Word to save souls. He was unmatched in the history of preaching, the most original of modern preachers, his style a bold departure from traditional usage, unconscious unstudied oratory, not the rhetoric of the schools; his art concrete, not abstract, it is given content and body; the men of whom he speaks are men of flesh and blood, not shades whom no man has ever seen evolved from the preacher's inner consciousness. His attraction consists in the force with which he witnesses to the power of the Gospel to renew personality and to create cheerful and courageous human beings, and that witness is borne with all the spontaneity of one who has himself lived and experienced that power, and daily realises it afresh."[2] Words from the land of Luther, equally true of Luther and of Spurgeon.

Another great stride brings us to JOHN WESLEY. We pause over JOHN KNOX, who was, as we have seen in Chapter IV, one of Spurgeon's heroes, but glorious as he was, we find him scarcely big enough to find a place

[1] *The Times,* August 22, 1860.
[2] *C. H. Spurgeon ein Prediger von Gottes Gnaden,* pp. 28, 42-48.

224

amongst the worthiest. The name of JOHN BUNYAN is amongst those of the immortals, but his influence depends altogether on his books. Spurgeon was strongly attracted to GEORGE WHITEFIELD, as is evident in Chapter V, but Wesley was undoubtedly the greater man. He stands in the apostolic succession, and influences people to the ends of the earth today. But though Spurgeon steadfastly refused to found a new denomination, and so far fails to perpetuate his name, it can scarcely be doubted that he made as great a mark on his own age as Wesley, and began a movement which will influence all future time. Both appealed to the common people.

Our steps are next arrested at the name of WILLIAM CAREY, the greatness of whose contribution to the Kingdom of God is not yet appreciated by the Church of Christ. Carey and Spurgeon had both learned of God, both appealed to the whole world, both were indefatigable workers, and both were perfected by suffering.

While Carey in India gave a new impulse to the Christian faith, THOMAS CHALMERS, the greatest man that Scotland has ever produced, fought at the same time for the freedom of faith in his own land. "If ever a halo surrounded a saint it encompassed Chalmers," declared Lord Rosebery. As a pulpit orator he was unrivalled in his own day, and between his life and Spurgeon's there are other points of contact—their personal experience of grace, their unceasing contest for the Crown Rights of Christ, their chivalrous care for the poor, and their realised desire for the training of men for the ministry of the Gospel.

Other men of the same period arrest us only for the moment: ROBERT HALL, the greatest preacher in England of his day, of whom it is recorded that, sometimes the business men of Leicester who heard him on Sunday were unable to attend to their business on Monday; Spurgeon no doubt being greatly influenced by him when he joined the church at Cambridge of which he had been the pastor: EDWARD IRVING, whose meteoric career blazed with such brilliance, compared with whom Spurgeon shone as a fixed star: F. W. ROBERTSON, one of the great pulpit names of the Victorian age, as Mr. Asquith has reminded us in his Romanes Lecture, "Some Aspects of the Victorian Age," but in an altogether different category from Spurgeon, more nervous and less telling: J. B. H. LACORDAIRE, who invented a new form of religious service, the "Conference," and attracted crowds at Notre Dame, Paris, and at Toulouse, and, speaking of his own unexpected call to preach, says: "Moreover, it is with the orator as with Mount Horeb: before God strikes him he is but a barren rock, but as soon as the divine hand has touched him, as it were with a finger, there burst forth streams that water the desert but his sermons were only occasional as contrasted with Spurgeon's sustained ministry: THOMAS BINNEY, who before Spurgeon's appearance in the metropolis was its most popular preacher, and from a critic of the new minister was soon transformed into his ardent defender.

D. L. MOODY belongs to another order, is to be remembered as one of the great spiritual forces of the world, and is, I suppose, to be classed with CHRYSOSTOM, SAVONAROLA, and TAULER, who in a previous chapter have been ruled out of comparison with Spurgeon. PATRICK, BERNARD, FRANCIS, XAVIER, and WILLIAM BOOTH are of the same noble company, and yet do not rise to the highest in the mountain range of Church history.

It may be difficult to determine the heights of the eight majestic peaks our dim eyes discern above the rest, as, white and glistening, they pierce the blue, but there they stand, a series of mighty summits, still catching earliest the morning light, and still at eventide with the rosy glow upon them when others are in the shadow—PAUL, AUGUSTINE, LUTHER, CALVIN, WESLEY, CAREY, CHALMERS, SPURGEON— and the last is not the least.

It is not for us to apportion greatness to them: the primacy must, of course, be given to the Apostle, but it may be affirmed with some assurance that as many troubled souls looked to Spurgeon for comfort as to any man that ever lived; and since his departure countless others have been influenced by his words, and blessed through the agencies he set in motion. What service is permitted to those who have passed, we may not know, whether the spirits of just men made perfect are allowed to help the saints on earth or not; but if that is possible, his ardent desire would be to minister to the heirs of salvation. In a recent biography, indeed, it is recorded that one of the leaders of this generation, who has recently gone to his reward, was on his dying bed persuaded that Spurgeon had actually visited him.[1] Whether that is true to fact, it is certainly true to nature: in any event it is an indication of the place he holds in the hearts of others, and we may be sure that in some sphere he is still actively witnessing to the grace of his Lord, that was ever his theme while he was here.

To me he is master and friend. I have neither known nor heard of any other, in my time, so many-sided, so commanding, so simple, so humble, so selfless, so entirely Christ's man. Proudly I stand at the salute!

---

[1] *Evan H. Hopkins*, by Alexander Smellie, D.D., p. 219.

WILLIAM YOUNG FULLERTON was a prominent Baptist evangelist, writer, and administrator whose influence spanned both the 19th and early 20th centuries. Born in Belfast, Ireland on March 8th, 1857, during the Victorian era, he would go on to become one of the most respected figures in British Baptist history.

As a young man growing up in Belfast, Fullerton was deeply immersed in the rich Protestant tradition of Northern Ireland. However, the defining moment in his spiritual journey came when he encountered the preaching of Charles Haddon Spurgeon, the renowned "Prince of Preachers." This encounter profoundly shaped his future ministry, and Spurgeon not only became his mentor but also a close personal friend, a relationship that would influence Fullerton's own preaching style and theological perspective.

His administrative abilities were recognized when he was elected to serve as President of the Baptist Union, a position of significant responsibility within the British Baptist community. In his role as Home Secretary of the Baptist Missionary Society, he demonstrated his commitment to both domestic ministry and global missions, helping to coordinate missionary efforts across multiple continents.

The Keswick Conventions, known for their emphasis on practical holiness and deeper Christian life, frequently featured Fullerton as a speaker. His messages at these gatherings were noted for their combination of doctrinal depth and practical application, drawing attendees from various denominational backgrounds.

Fullerton was also a prolific author whose written works demonstrated his broad range of interests and deep historical knowledge. His biographical works included carefully researched accounts of several significant Christian figures including: *John Bunyan: A Biography*, a comprehensive account of the life and works of John Bunyan, (the author of *Pilgrim's Progress*), *The Prince of Preachers*, the personal and insightful biography of his mentor C. H. Spurgeon, and *J. W. C. Fegan: A Tribute*, a biography of James William Condell Fegan, known for his work with orphans. and *F.B. Meyer: A Biography*, the story of Frederick Brotherton Meyer, the Baptist minister and evangelist.

Beyond biographies, he contributed significantly to Christian literature through his missionary histories and devotional writings, which were widely read and appreciated throughout the English-speaking world. His work as a hymnal compiler helped shape the worship life of Baptist congregations across Britain.

Perhaps his most enduring legacy in church music is his hymn "I Cannot Tell Why He, Whom Angels Worship." In a stroke of cultural genius, he set these deeply theological lyrics to the melody of "Londonderry Air" (also known as the tune to "Danny Boy"), creating a bridge between his Irish heritage and his Christian faith. This hymn continues to be sung in churches today, particularly in the United Kingdom and Ireland.

Fullerton always remained faithful to evangelical Christianity while maintaining a winsome approach that earned him respect across denominational lines. He continued his active ministry until near the end of his life, finally passing away at Bedford Park, Middlesex, on August 17, 1932, at the age of 75, leaving behind a legacy of faithful service, scholarly work, and spiritual influence that is a value to the church of Christ until the present day.

If you enjoyed
The Prince of Preachers
you'll love

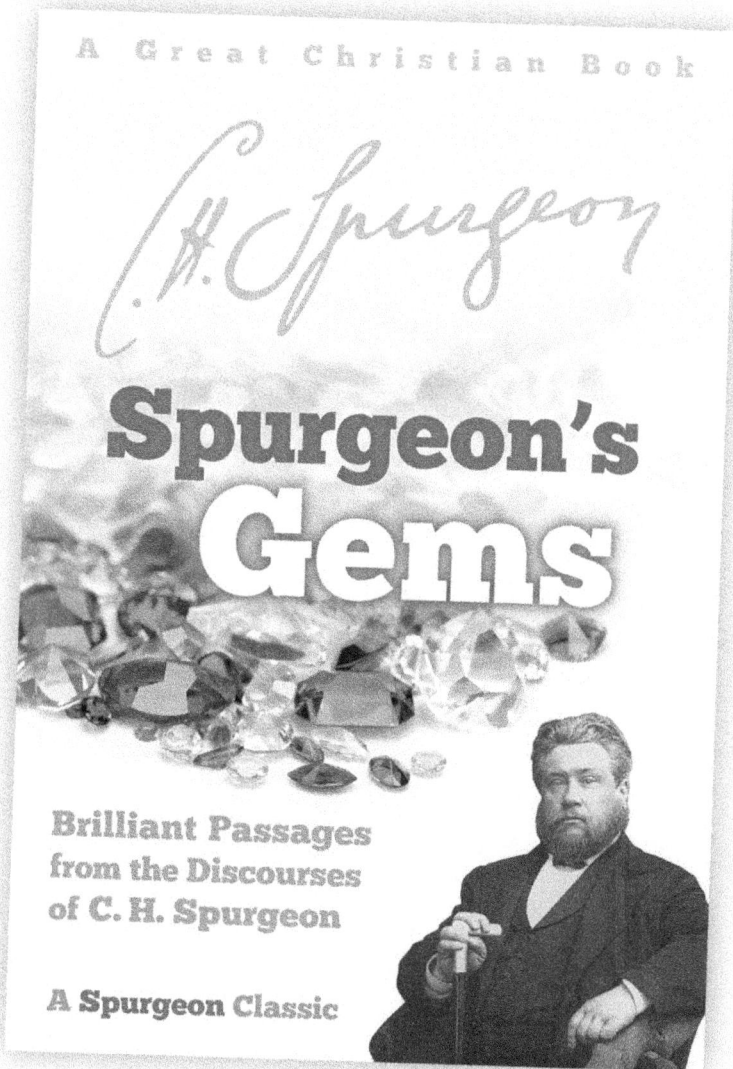

In this volume, collected under one cover, are the very best gems of knowledge, wisdom and insight into Christ and the Christian life—culled for your convenience and blessing from the hundreds of literary works and transcribed sermons that Spurgeon produced.

ISBN: 978-1610100281

THE MISSION OF GREAT CHRISTIAN BOOKS

The ministry of Great Christian Books was established to glorify The Lord Jesus Christ and to be used by Him to expand and edify the kingdom of God while we occupy and anticipate Christ's glorious return. Great Christian Books will seek to accomplish this mission by publishing Gospel literature which is biblically faithful, relevant, and practically applicable to many of the serious spiritual needs of mankind upon the beginning of this new millennium. To do so we will always seek to boldly incorporate the truths of Scripture, especially those which were largely articulated as a body of theology during the Protestant Reformation of the sixteenth century and ensuing years. We gladly join our voice in the proclamations of— Scripture Alone, Faith Alone, Grace Alone, Christ Alone, and God's Glory Alone!

Our ministry seeks the blessing of our God as we seek His face to both confirm and support our labors for Him. Our prayers for this work can be summarized by two verses from the Book of Psalms:

"...let the beauty of the LORD our God be upon us, And establish the work of our hands for us; Yes, establish the work of our hands." —Psalm 90:17

"Not unto us, O LORD, not unto us, but to your name give glory."
—Psalm 115:1

Great Christian Books appreciates the financial support of anyone who shares our burden and vision for publishing literature which combines sound Bible doctrine and practical exhortation in an age when too few so-called "Christian" publications do the same. We thank you in advance for any assistance you can give us in our labors to fulfill this important mission. May God bless you.

Visit us for other

GREAT CHRISTIAN BOOKS

including additional titles

by C. H. Spurgeon

www.greatchristianbooks.com

Join our email list and

receive free ebooks.

www.ingramcontent.com/pod-product-compliance
Lightning Source LLC
Chambersburg PA
CBHW020152090426
42734CB00008B/792